9

Challenges of
Multicultural Education

Challenges of
Multicultural Education
Teaching and Taking
Diversity Courses

Edited by
Norah Peters-Davis and **Jeffrey Shultz**
Arcadia University

Paradigm Publishers
Boulder • London

Copyright © 2005 Paradigm Publishers

Published in the United States by Paradigm Publishers, 3360 Mitchell Lane, Suite E, Boulder, CO 80305 USA.

Paradigm Publishers is the trade name of Birkenkamp & Company, LLC, Dean Birkenkamp, President and Publisher.

Library of Congress Cataloging-in-Publication Data
Peters-Davis, Norah.
  Challenges of multicultural education : teaching and taking diversity courses / Norah Peters-Davis and Jeffrey Shultz.
        p. cm.
  Includes bibliographical references and index.
  ISBN 1-59451-106-3 (hc : alk. paper)—ISBN 1-59451-107-1 (pbk)
1. Multicultural education—United States. 2. Critical pedagogy—United States.
3. Minorities—Education—United States. I. Shultz, Jeffrey J. II. Title.
  LC1099.3.P58 2005
  370.117'0973—dc22

                                                                    2005008732

Printed and bound in the United States of America on acid free paper that meets the standards of the American National Standard for Permanence of Paper for Printed Library Materials.

10 09 08 07 06   2 3 4 5

CONTENTS

EDITORS' PREFACE

This book was born in the midst of conflict. In the summer of 2000, six Arcadia University faculty members, including us, met for two weeks to plan the curriculum and teaching assignments for "pluralism in the United States, a core requirement for sophomores. The course is team-taught and so the summer workshop is an essential part of the planning process.

Among the group of six, two of us are male, four female; four white, two persons of color; two lesbians, the rest of us straight. As we began our conversations, the two persons of color, Ana María García and Angela R. Gillem (also the authors of Chapter 7 of this collection), brought the other four of us up short and called us to task. Their assertion was that in this course, with its emphasis on issues of race, class, gender, and sexual orientation, we were teaching about the concepts while they were teaching about their lives. Thus began a conversation in which tears were shed, voices were raised, accusations and recriminations flew right and left.

We survived the workshop, still friends, tired and spent but hopefully wiser. In the end, we came to realize that if we, as the faculty of the course, had issues related to denial, anger, and frustration, how must our students feel about dissecting and exploring subject matter that is not generally talked about in our society? This is the challenge we continue to face in teaching this course.

As a result of these exchanges, we (Norah and Jeff) decided to ask colleagues and students, both at Arcadia and elsewhere, to write about their experiences teaching and taking these courses. In the chapters that follow, we present our colleagues' and their students' responses to our questions. Represented among them are small colleges and large state universities; geographically they range from New England to Texas. What is clear when reading the various accounts is that many of the same issues we encountered four years ago are not exclusively ours. But we'll allow you, the reader, to determine this for yourself as you explore these issues with us.

Many people play key roles in putting together a collection of this sort. In our search for a publisher, we had to face the fact that market forces might determine whether or not this book would be published. Somehow, the subject matter didn't fit neatly into any of the publishers' marketing categories. Dean Birkenkamp at Paradigm Publishers saw the possibilities and was willing to take a chance with the manuscript. We are grateful to him for his vision and support. As the focus of the book changed over time, some potential contributors dropped away while others joined up. Those that stuck it out provided us with their work in a timely manner, responding, for the most part, promptly to our nagging e-mails. We are thrilled they continued to work with us to help make this book a reality.

At Arcadia University, Mike Berger, vice president for academic affairs and provost, the person to whom we both report, encourages his staff and faculty to engage in works such as this one and is a role model for us because he does this sort of work himself. His interest and encouragement accompanied us throughout the process. Our colleague, Sharon M. Ravitch, in addition to the two wonderful chapters she contributed to this volume, pulled us out of the doldrums when we most needed it. Her enthusiasm for the project was always a breath of fresh air. We would like to thank Anna Wagner of the Office of Undergraduate Studies for her logistical and emotional support. She is a gem and everyone who works on a project like this would be lucky to work with someone like Anna. In spite of all of the support we received, we alone are responsible for any mistakes that escaped the various reviews of the manuscript.

It is not just our colleagues who have contributed to our understanding of these issues. Four remarkable women have played a significant role, as well. Our mothers, Salle Wolf Peters and Dina Shultz, taught us from a young age the importance of fairness and equity. Our daughters, Reilly Dempsey and Julia Shultz, have exposed us to the perspective of yet another generation, one closer in age to that of our Pluralism students. The four of them have been and continue to be our teachers and guides.

Finally, Jonathan Church, Ana María García, Angela Gillem, and Lisa Holderman shared that fateful workshop in the summer of 2000 with us. We can't begin to enumerate what we learned from them and where we have come as a result of those difficult, painful, yet enlightening discussions. It is to them, with much affection, that we dedicate this book.

CHAPTER ONE

Introduction
Pluralism, Power, and Politics: Discourses of Diverse Pedagogies and Pedagogies of Diversity

Sharon M. Ravitch
Arcadia University

Learning to teach requires a journey into the deepest recesses of one's self-awareness, where failures, fears, and hopes are hidden. (Kagan, 1992)

Across the landscape of higher education in the United States, courses that focus on diversity, race relations, intercultural communication, pluralism, and multicultural education have emerged within several fields and disciplines. These courses, often called diversity, pluralism or multicultural courses, have largely surfaced over the past decade as a response to diversity requirements that have been added to most liberal arts, social science, and teacher education curricula at both the undergraduate and graduate levels. As an outgrowth of the progress made in the areas of multicultural education, diversity awareness, and identity politics during the civil rights movement (Gay, 1990; Laubscher and Powell, 2003), multicultural courses are typically developed within institutions of higher learning that are pushed to become more supportive of diversity by offering courses with multicultural content. While these courses tend to be isolated from, and even marginalized within, their broader institutional contexts, the instructors who teach them have a serious interest in, and passionate concern for, issues of equity and social justice. These educators work from a belief that students from all backgrounds must be provided with structured learning opportunities in which they can develop their knowledge of and perspectives on a diverse range of people, reflect on and challenge their own biases and stereotypes, and hone their skills for communicating, living, and working within an increasingly multicultural and multiracial United States and an ever-developing global community. Instructors involved in multicultural courses and initiatives also work from an understanding that as we begin the twenty-first century, the neo-conservative political climate in the United States and the backlash against "political correctness" in society generally and college campuses particularly bring with them particular opportunities as well as serious challenges with respect to efforts to increase students' cultural awareness and sensitivity to issues of oppression and inequality. All of the authors in this book—instructors, graduate and undergraduate students—share their insights, experiences, and reflections on the opportunities and challenges that they face in

1

their processes of teaching and learning in multicultural classrooms in the academy.

To achieve our goals of broadening and deepening students' awareness of, and ability to critically reflect on and engage in, dialogue about issues of culture, race, class, sexual orientation, gender identity, and inequality in American society, instructors design our courses to create learning environments in which students are guided through a focused and critical analysis of the relationship between society, ideology, and policy, as well as individual and group identity and agency. Further, students are challenged to rigorously explore educational and social inequality and how people's social locations and sociopolitical forces converge to create and sustain the oppression of people of color, women, gay, lesbian, bisexual and transgender people, non-European immigrants, people with disabilities, and people living in under-resourced areas. The overarching goal of multicultural courses is to broaden students' perspectives by exposing them to the experiences and points of view of marginalized groups, as well as to serious interdisciplinary scholarship in the areas of diversity and multiculturalism. Such exposure, it is hoped, will serve to raise their cultural awareness, cultivate their perspective-taking skills, and, ultimately, to help them live in ways that are more inclusive and socially aware as well as less judgmental, deficit-oriented, and territorial. As the future workers, leaders, voters, educators, scholars, parents, and citizens of this country, such learning is essential to the development of a more equitable future.

Critical multicultural courses are expressly designed to facilitate a "critical interrogation" (hooks, 1994) of students' constructions of their own and others' identities and processes of socialization.[1] This means that students are challenged to critically reflect on their views on a wide range of people who are different from them, issues of racism and discrimination, and their perspectives on how aspects of identity and social location relate to social realities. Further, these courses are designed to create a structure in which students are challenged to deconstruct and examine their belief systems and in which students are provided with the conceptual tools necessary for them to practice new ways of thinking, doing, and being. In order to fully understand what happens within these courses, it is first necessary to discuss the broader social and ideological contexts in which multicultural education has been developed and shaped. These broader contexts create the ideological, theoretical, and pedagogical foundations of the multicultural teaching and learning that are at the center of this book.

ON CRITICAL MULTICULTURAL EDUCATION:
A THEORETICAL CONTEXT

The chapters in this book are written by instructors, graduate instructors, and graduate and undergraduate students who teach, learn, and collaborate in expressly multicultural contexts. While there is incredible range and variation in the structure and content of these courses and collaborations, they all work from a critical multicultural framework. Each chapter describes how teaching and learning happen within the ideological, pedagogical, and political framework of critical multicultural education, as well as how such pedagogy is experienced by both the teachers and learners who are involved in it. Understanding the theoretical and ideological underpinnings of critical multicultural education is crucial to understanding the breadth and depth of multicultural pedagogy as well as why it is a type of pedagogy that, as Nieto (1999a) warns us, "encourages dangerous discourses" (p. 209).

Multiculturalism—the ideologically based intellectual movement that created the foundation for multicultural education—first emerged during the era of the civil rights movement, gained momentum in the late 1960s, and has continued to develop as a response to the cultural, social, and political inequality and hegemony in the United States (Gay, 1990; Sleeter, 1996). Multicultural education—the educational outgrowth of multiculturalism—is a response to the ways in which U.S. schools and social institutions reflect and perpetuate a hegemonic social order (Banks, 1996; Erickson, 2004; Giroux, 1994; Goldberg, 1994; McCarthy, 1993; McLaren, 1994; Nieto, 2004). Goldberg (1994) describes multiculturalism as the emergence of "a new standard . . . new set of self-understandings, presuppositions, principles, and practice . . . a new way of thinking about the social and institutional, the intellectual and academic" (p. 9). Building from the ideological framework developed within the broader multiculturalism movement, multicultural education localizes its tenets and goals within the educational realm, placing a primacy on the critical examination and reconstruction of pedagogical practices, educational institutions, and issues of curriculum and resources. This examination is steeped in the systematic critique of the broader social, political, and economic forces that both shape and influence all areas of education. Gorski (2000) provides an overarching framework of multicultural education, describing it as:

> a progressive approach for transforming education that holistically critiques and addresses current shortcomings, failings, and discriminatory practices in education. It is grounded in ideals of social justice, education equity, and a dedication to facilitating educational experiences in which all students reach their full potential as learners and as socially aware and active beings, locally, nationally, and globally. Multicultural education acknowledges that schools are essential to laying the foundation for the transformation of society and the elimination of oppression and injustice. The underlying goal of multicultural education is to affect social change. The pathway towards this goal incorporate . . . 1. the transformation of self; 2. the transformation of schools and schooling; 3. the transformation of society. (p. 2)

As these statements make clear, multiculturalism is an intellectual and political movement that refuses to accept the Eurocentric ideal of American society as natural and, further, that refuses to accept responses to it that do not transform the foundation of American society along cultural, political, social, educational, and institutional lines (Giroux, 1994; Martin, 1995; McCarthy, 1993; McLaren, 1994). Multicultural education is the way that multiculturalism becomes conceptualized and operationalized within and across educational contexts and discourses.

Multicultural education has significantly grown over the past three decades in terms of its definition and the scope of its political and educational articulations (Gay, 1990; Sleeter, 1996; Nieto, 1999a; 2004). Multicultural education has become a discourse that pushes the margins of education and actively works to re-vision American society and to develop pedagogical tools, methods, and theories that operationalize a new social order which reflects the diversity, lifestyles, learning styles, and cultural and economic realities of all Americans. Proponents of multiculturalism and multicultural education view schools, from preschool to graduate school, and the educational policies and discourses surrounding education and schooling, to be essential sites for social transformation (Erickson, 2004; Goldberg, 1994; Levinson and Holland, 1996; Nieto, 2004). From the perspective of multicultural theorists and educators, the modes and philosophies of schooling, which are based in myths of democracy, meritocracy, and equality, are not acceptable given the reality of our nation's population, which is diverse, multiracial, and multicultural. Therefore these mythical and oppressive systems of pedagogy and education must be critically analyzed, challenged, and, ultimately, transformed.

Anthropologists, sociologists, critical theorists, and educators have contributed theoretical models of multicultural education to the growing body of literature in this area. The pedagogical approaches described in this book represent a range of positions on multicultural education. Each approach is based on distinct assumptions and beliefs about society, culture, power, identity, education and schooling, pluralism, communication, and interaction. The theories underlying these approaches differ in a variety of ways and spring from several disciplines. This range of approaches and disciplinary vantage points holds important implications for the dialogue around, and potential points of development and intervention within, classroom-based multicultural education. Debates in multicultural education, and thus the perspectives, approaches and courses of the authors in this book, are shaped by differences in views about: (1) the relationship between power and social oppression; (2) conceptions of race, social class, gender, culture, sexual orientation and ethnicity and their relationship to issues of oppression; (3) the mobilization of the themes of race, diversity, pluralism, and culture (McCarthy, 1993); and (4) the role of education and schooling in the processes and practices of social transformation. Even given the differences in these focal areas and our different standpoint epistemologies (e.g., feminist, hermeneutic), the authors in this book share the understanding that our current educational, social, and political institutions are fraught with racism, discrimination, and oppression, and, therefore, that they must be transformed. We work towards these transformations by constructing pedagogical roadmaps that lead us, along with our students, to a more equitable and inclusive vision and reality of American society.

Because of its focused agenda of social, political, educational, and institutional change and transformation across activists, educators, policymakers, and civil rights proponents, multicultural education is often discussed as a social movement similar to the civil rights movement (Sleeter, 1996; Laubscher and Powell, 2003). Laubscher and Powell (2003) argue that this perspective on multicultural education results in a guiding conceptualization of "the educational space as a mobilizing site of struggle for social justice" (p. 212). In this sense, those who work toward and agitate for social change through engaging in critical pedagogy are doing work that is situated both between and across borders: between intellectual work and activism, the personal and political, critical theory and real-world practice. Additionally, the educational spaces that we create are intended to precipitate intellectual reflection and social and political movement. These spaces are often viewed as being only of nominal importance in their respective institutions and therefore are most often situated on the margins. Thus, this kind of pedagogy, as you will read throughout each chapter of this book, requires instructors to "teach against the grain" (Cochran-Smith, 1991) of our monocultural, traditional, and conservative institutions of higher learning. As each author in this book documents, this kind of teaching is complex, challenging to both teacher and students, exhilarating and enervating, heartening and disheartening in profound ways. What follows is a discussion of the experiences of instructors who teach these courses, the nature of their collaborations with each other, and their insights into the processes involved in teaching and learning with their students.

THE PERSONAL IS POLITICAL, THE PEDAGOGICAL IS PERSONAL: ON THE PUSHES AND PULLS OF TEACHING AND LEARNING MULTICULTURALLY IN THE ACADEMY

Multicultural education, in its critical forms, offers no less than a re-visioning of American society and its institutions, trappings, and citizens. In speaking about multicultural education, Giroux (1994) asserts that one of the main objectives of multicultural education is to "reassert the importance of making the pedagogical more political, to analyze how a broader definition of pedagogy can be used to address how the production of knowledge, social identities, and social relations might challenge the racist assumptions and practices that inform a variety of cultural sites, including but not limited to the public and private spheres of schooling" (p. 325).

What this understanding of multicultural education suggests for higher education is that institutions of higher learning must be conceptualized as crucial sites in which the relationship between diversity, democracy, and pluralism should be acknowledged and incorporated into the curriculum. Further, as Giroux (1994) argues, multiculturalism must be utilized as much more than a "critical referent for interrogating the racist representations and practices of the dominant culture, it [must] provide a space in which the criticism of cultural practices is inextricably linked to the production of cultural spaces marked by the formation of new identities and pedagogical practices that offers a powerful challenge to the racist, patriarchal, and sexist principles embedded in American society and schooling" (p. 337). The goals of multicultural education point directly to the spaces in which such identities and pedagogical practices are developed—multicultural classrooms—and conceptualize every classroom as a unique forum for discussing and confronting issues of diversity, inequality, and social justice. Given the opportunities that college campuses provide, namely, an audience of young learners who are poised to try on new ways of thinking, it becomes the responsibility of multicultural educators to create learning opportunities that help to interrupt students' fears, mistrust, and avoidance of issues of diversity, pluralism, inclusion, power, and privilege. Working within this perspective, instructors become critical pedagogues who teach in ways that have at their core an agenda of social transformation that begins with each individual student and every group of students and works out into the world from there.

So what then, given the ambitious goals for and transformative agenda of multicultural education, and its concomitant critiques of the academy in which such courses are housed, are the experiences of the instructors who teach these courses? Of the students who take them? Of their learning processes together? Given the enormity of the task of teaching against a monocultural and largely conservative grain of higher education and the intense and challenging nature of material that focuses on cultural, social, and institutional discrimination as well as on self-critique and change, how do instructors learn to teach in ways that help them to engage with students in a manner that leads everyone involved on a journey of serious critical reflection, cultural perspective-taking, and systemic critique? How does it feel to continuously teach within these "radical" political contexts? What are the points of connection, disaffiliation, and conflict?

Courses—such as the ones described in this volume—that teach this substantive content within a dialogic style (rather than a dogmatic one) do so by employing alternative, innovative pedagogical practices—practices that rely on the ability to both engage each student where he or she is and to orchestrate a critical and challenging group dialogue that can help move students beyond their typically uncritical and mainstream perspectives on issues of diversity. The instructors of these courses work hard to integrate a variety of curricular materials that invoke the voices of the individual and collective, both those who are in the classroom and who live in the world around it. Throughout this process, these instructors experience a continual push and pull between two forces: on the one hand our courses are intellectually rigorous and teach the kinds of material and critical-thinking skills that are expected at colleges and universities. On the other hand, our courses have at their center content that is politically and ideologically charged and are built upon pedagogical practices that tend to engender anxiety, confusion, fear, resistance, and/or anger on the part of the students (McIntyre, 1997; Tatum, 1992/1996). For the instructors teaching these courses, who are most often, as you will read throughout this book, passionate about and deeply committed to the topics and issues addressed in our courses, our teaching is more than just an intellectual, pedagogical experience, it is deeply personal, moving, emotionally trying, and at times difficult and threatening. Particularly for instructors of color, or instructors who are gay, lesbian, bisexual, and transgender, who are immigrants and/or who have disabilities, teaching provocative material from the margins of the academy brings with it particular challenges and vulnerabilities. This increased vulnerability is caused in part because these instructors are not just teaching the material as their White, heterosexual, nondisabled counterparts do, but, rather, they are living the realities of oppression and marginalization that are the focus of their course material and discussions. Therefore, the ways in which students react, resist, or resent the course content and structure are aimed at them not only as professionally but personally (Laubscher and Powell, 2003). For those of us who teach these kinds of courses, our pedagogy, is on the edge and is provocative in the truest sense of the term, is often confusing and threatening to our students, and departs from the norm in content and style, leaves us open to more careful scrutiny as well as to questions about the legitimacy of our scholarship from our students, colleagues, and superiors. It also pulls us into dangerous dialogues, unknown places, points of rawness as well as personal and professional self-consciousness.

Clearly, critical multicultural courses have as their main goal the shifting and expanding of students' worldviews, even the attempt to facilitate paradigm shifts from monocultural, Eurocentric ways of thinking to more inclusive, culturally aware, and socially responsible perspectives. Such goals require their stewards to teach from a more personal and intimate framework, so that students are able to develop the trust and feelings of safety that are necessary for them to take risks and critically reflect on themselves and society in ways that challenge their sensibilities and worldviews. In this sense, instructors have a particular kind of investment in, and responsibility to, our students, their processes of learning, and our courses as a whole. Moreover, the pedagogical truly becomes personal since we continually expose ourselves and our views in our classrooms, and these views are held up to additional layers of scrutiny as a result of continually challenging students to leave their comfort zones and reevaluate what they know to be right and good. As well, the pedagogical becomes personalized because our pedagogy is, in a very real sense, a direct outgrowth of our identities, social locations, and experiences in the world. As Gatto (1994) states, "teachers teach who we are"; who we are and what we teach cannot be compartmentalized within this kind of critical pedagogy. As the chapters throughout this book exemplify, the personal and political nature of our pedagogy makes our teaching exciting and impassioned but also scary and lonely at times, engendering feelings of fear, doubt, tension and conflict. As Laubscher and Powell (2003) state, "the personal and pedagogical converge in our efforts as critical multicultural educators" (p. 210).

These convergences, in all of their volatility and tenderness, are at the center of each chapter in this book.

Nieto (1999a) argues that good teaching is about transformation at the individual, collective, and institutional levels. As many multicultural researchers and educators assert, educating students about racism and White hegemony requires a resocialization process which rests on exploring in great depth (and usually with much discomfort) their constructions of race, including Whiteness and White privilege, and of education and society more generally. Further, it is argued that such learning can only happen through rigorous processes of societally contextualized self-reflection (Hidalgo, 1993; hooks, 1994). hooks (1994) argues for educating students for critical consciousness by engaging in "constructive confrontation" and "critical interrogation" of how political standpoints and ideologies shape identity. She asserts that these types of discussions necessitate dialogue about the non-neutrality of all forms of education. Moreover, hooks asserts that such discussions mean that students (and teachers) will need "to undergo a process of unlearning racism, learning about colonization and decolonization, to fully appreciate the necessity for creating a democratic [learning] experience" (p. 93). Teaching in a way that encourages such discourses, shifts in identity and perspective, and, ideally, paradigm shifts, and which crosses over the boundaries of identity, positionality, and experience, takes not only vision and passion, but courage and resiliency. As each of the authors in this book discusses, such pedagogy requires us to continually engage our whole beings—intellectually, emotionally, psychologically, socially, and personally—in our teaching. Teaching within this model is not a tertiary intellectualized activity but, rather, a central and holistic experience that directly shapes our sense of self as individuals and professionals.

In a very real sense, as instructors teach multicultural courses, we bring our autobiographies into our courses in ways intended and unintended, embodied and projected. Our students see us through the lens of their and our social locations and of their and our positionalities and, therefore, our messages are heard and understood differently based on the intersection of these positionalities and social locations. In this sense, both our students and our own social locations map onto the complexities of teaching and learning in ways that lead us to unknown places. Because the curriculum in multicultural courses emerges from the intersection of course materials and the identities and social locations of the participants in our courses, they engender a "radical uncertainty" about how each semester will go. In other words, the dynamics of each course and semester rest heavily on the demographic makeup of the class and even the social tenor of the time. For example, if a course consists of all White students and the professor is White, students often communicate that they feel more comfortable exploring their biases and racism then they would in "mixed company." In contrast, if a class is all White and the professor is a person of color, students often project mistrust and derision and displace their anger and frustration about being challenged on their own biases and prejudices by dismissing the professor as an "angry person of color." If there are only a few students of color or gay and lesbian students in a course, there is a very real concern about them feeling safe and not being coerced into becoming the "spokespeople" for their entire group, which, as has been well documented, can feel both painful and unsafe (Fordham, 1996; Tatum, 1992/1996). Instructors have to manage all of these intersecting interpretations, projections, and transferences (as well as our own countertransferences) both internally and as the facilitators of critical dialogue within a carefully maintained safe space. In addition to the influential variables that affect the tenor of discussions and group dynamics within these classrooms, the larger social and political milieu of the time has a powerful impact on students' worldviews, opinions, and communications. In other words, what is happening in the world around our classrooms shapes students' reactions to the material and structure of our courses. For example, since 9/11, issues of anti-Arabism, anti-Semitism, and racial profiling have become more of a focal point as have issues of patriotism, immigration, and the impact of U.S. foreign policy locally, nationally, and internationally. Additionally, the conservative ethos of our current government combined with the backlash against diversity initiatives and the disdain for political correctness help to form students' resistance against engaging in multicultural dialogue.

One of the major acts in teaching these kinds of courses is making tough yet delicate negotiations: among students' needs, misunderstandings, and issues with each other; between trying to counter students' biases and stereotypes while being supportive of them; between trying to serve both as provocateur and balm in times of conflict; between taking it personally and realizing that students come to our courses with their own histories and have been socialized to believe even some of the most harmful myths and stereotypes. Each class, each reading of a student's paper, and each meeting with a student to process and support is filled with these kinds of intense negotiations. Instructors of multicultural courses continually walk the line between meeting students where they are and leading them somewhere else, somewhere more knowledgeable and critical about society and their locations and choices within it. In these classrooms, instructors take great risks—we risk exposing ourselves and our biases, we risk having to let go of our firm sense of the ways things are, we risk being publicly challenged and ridiculed, and we risk, in very real ways, our reputations and the quality of our evaluations (upon which tenure and promotions are granted or denied). Because of these risks and our level of personal, professional, and pedagogical commitment, because we ask our students to take great risks themselves and must be there to support them, we cannot remove ourselves from these courses or from their processes and outcomes. This kind of pedagogy necessarily invokes our feelings, identities, and our sense of self. It pushes and pulls on our psyches, our fears, and our insecurities (Kagan, 1992). As each chapter in this book exemplifies, the personal and the political indeed converge within this kind of engaged pedagogy, and we must work to define and create safe spaces—both for our students and for ourselves—within the academy.

LIVING OUR PEDAGOGY, TELLING OUR STORIES:
LOCATING THIS WORK WITHIN THE BROADER LANDSCAPE

While much research that supports multicultural education ideals has been published, there is less research available on how these ideals translate into instructors' experiences of teaching within higher education contexts (Ravitch, 2000). As Laubscher and Powell (2003) point out, "Certain areas have been under researched or not examined at all. More attention is paid to the experiences, reactions, and outcomes of learners in the multicultural classroom than to those of educators facilitating the process" (p. 205). Further, as several educational researchers have noted, while multicultural education courses have received much theoretical attention, there are few studies that explore, analyze, and document how teaching and learning happens within these contexts and move beyond evaluative typologies (Grant and Tate, 1995; Ravitch, 2000; Remillard, 2000; Tatum, 1992/1996). Because of its focus on the experiences of both the teacher and the learner, and even more powerfully, on their intersecting experiences, reflections, and dialogues, this book bridges the chasm between multicultural theories and multicultural practices in higher education classrooms. It does so by offering narratives of pedagogies of diversity across disciplines, perspectives, and contexts. The chapters in this book raise questions about how multicultural teaching and learning occur as well as what conditions are necessary for courses to facilitate interruptions to students' Eurocentric and monocultural belief systems and the dominant paradigms of teaching and learning in the academy. Moreover, this book seeks to add a story of complexity about multicultural pedagogy that can serve as a counternarrative to claims that such courses lack substantive content and rigorous intellectual inquiry.

Beyond the significant contribution of this book to the academy as a whole, perhaps its most powerful benefit is that it speaks directly to the instructors of multicultural courses through multiple and diverse voices, perspectives, and experiences. This kind of dialogue about the challenges and triumphs of our situated pedagogies can help us to reflect on our own pedagogy and experiences in ways that are instructive and empowering. Given the range of intense emotions and the kinds of personal and professional concerns that these courses evoke, those of us working toward a more multicultural and pluralistic vision of society require support and camaraderie around our efforts in order to sustain the energy and vision that we need to keep going. Documenting the complex and multifaceted stories of a wide range of instructors' and students' experiences with this type of pedagogy is crucial for making our experiences visible, for gaining support and validation for our work, for having access to models of critical pedagogy and reflective practice, and for helping to develop and support an intellectual environment that allows this kind of pedagogy to be successful. Given the marginalized status of our work within the programs and institutions in which they are situated, supporting and providing guidance to each other is of vital importance.

What is so unique and exciting about this book is that it has both precipitated and nurtured a powerful and complex dialogue between instructors and their students, among colleagues, and among students by providing a framework and a forum for a collaborative, dynamic, and democratic writing process. This collection of pedagogical conversations provides a unique opportunity to better understand the teaching and learning that happens in these courses from the individuals' perspectives as well as across diverse settings and disciplines. This kind of collaborative, reflective writing and honest intellectual exchange between instructors and students—in which each individual voice remains distinct and in dialogue—is unprecedented. The ability to hear the voices of the graduate instructors and students telling their own stories of learning and development in the context of these courses is powerful and has much to recommend to critical discourses of multicultural education courses in higher education. This book responds to the need for democratic, collaborative, and interdisciplinary dialogue that focuses on multicultural pedagogy in higher education and marks an important beginning; a beginning of publicly sharing and valuing the experiences, insights, and stories of critical multicultural pedagogues who work within the academy to transform society.

TO THE NARRATIVES THEMSELVES:
AN OVERVIEW OF THE CHAPTERS

Each of the chapters in this book provides insight into both instructors' and students' experiences of teaching, learning, and collaborating in multicultural contexts. Together, these chapters provide a multivocal narrative of the processes and contents of critical multicultural education as it is enacted in particular relational, intellectual, and pedagogical contexts. These chapters provide a textured and vital collective voice of commitment to the teaching and learning of multiculturalism, pluralism, and counterhegemony. This book, with its collection of pedagogical conversations among and across diverse people, groups, and settings, is an invitation for more critical, collaborative dialogue about what it means to teach and learn against the grain (Cochran-Smith, 1991). What follows is a discussion and overview of each chapter and its unique contribution to the collective voice that this book embodies.

Chapter 2, "Dialogue on Diversity Teaching: Reflections on Research, Pedagogy, and Passion for Social Justice," is coauthored by Helen A. Moore, a noted professor of sociology, and Katherine M. Acosta, Gary K. Perry, and Crystal Edwards, who are doctoral students in sociology and graduate instructors in undergraduate diversity courses at the University of Nebraska. Moore, a faculty supervisor of graduate professional development, offers a critique of how diversity work is allocated, evaluated, and devalued in the academy and provides insight into how critical pedagogical positions "generate contradictions and privileges that make this emotional work as well as intellectual work." The graduate student authors reflect on their own experiences of teaching diversity courses within the academy and also examine how the intersections of race, class, gender, sexual orientation, disability, and age, as well as other stratification dimensions, overlap with their classroom teaching experiences. Their dialogue explores these intersections and makes explicit themes within their teaching and scholarship that "speak to the hidden curriculum and invisibility of identity" within multicultural education.

The authors describe their individual experiences of teaching multicultural courses, identifying their own worldviews on diversity, multiculturalism, and pluralism and how these have been shaped by and challenged in the academy. The authors reflect on how their different social locations even within their shared "minority status" impact their teaching as well as how they must learn to navigate and negotiate the often rough terrain of academia. Deeply embedded in these narratives are reflections about working from "vulnerable positions" as instructors of color who engage in pedagogy that requires intense emotional work. By sharing their insights about their work, the authors create bridges between their teaching and scholarship in ways that engender a dialogue of critique about the "academic minefield" of teaching diversity in a largely conservative academic institution. They also put forth a powerful position of hope about the possibilities of transforming the academy by engaging in diversity work as a source of empowerment.

Chapter 3, "From Silence and Resistance to Tongues Untied: Talking about Race in the College Classroom," is coauthored by Ana-María Gonzalez Wahl, Branden Coté, Keenon Javon Mann, Hattie Latrece Mukombe, and Christina Medina Bach Neilsen. This chapter focuses on the importance of critically reflecting on the kinds of pedagogical strategies and institutional resources that were necessary for the successful teaching of a race and ethnic relations course offered at Wake Forest University. The authors share their own perspectives on the two major strategies employed within this course, strategies they believe greatly helped to create and sustain the kind of safe space necessary to engage in serious dialogue about issues of racism and inequality: the principles and practices of "learning communities" and the development and support of a "critical mass of students of color." This chapter examines the ways that "tongues are untied" and meaningful dialogue is engendered when courses utilize and build on both of these strategies.

Ana-María Gonzalez Wahl, the faculty coordinator for this course, reflects on the relationship between the structure of the course and its influence on her students' experiences of and engagement with the material. The student authors, Branden Coté, Keenon Javon Mann, Hattie Latrece Mukombe, and Christina Medina Bach Neilsen, who are themselves diverse across racial, ethnic, and geographic lines, reflect on their participation in this critical multicultural course which "provided a rare opportunity to generate a provocative and productive dialogue about race." These students explore how their differing social locations and campus experiences interacted with the course content to form powerful learning experiences that shifted their worldviews and helped them to feel safe enough to critically examine their own identities within broader societal contexts. This chapter traces the implications of this unique experience for multicultural pedagogy as well as for institutional practice and policy in higher education with the ultimate goal of ensuring that the commitment to diversity on college campuses becomes "more than symbolic politics."

Chapter 4, "Making Race Matter on Campus: Teaching about Race in the Whitest State in the Union," is coauthored by Jarl Ahlkvist, Peter Spitzform, Emily Jones, and Megan Reynolds. The authors—a faculty member, librarian, and students respectively—were all members of a campus community in rural Vermont in the 1990s. Ahlkvist and Spitzform, who taught courses on Race and Ethnic Relations and co-chaired the Campus Diversity Committee at Johnson State College, a small, racially homogenous, liberal arts college in rural Vermont, argue against the common misconception that race matters only if there is racial diversity in a community or classroom and, focusing on their campus, reflect on how this attitude, and its attendant resistance to engaging with issues of racism, blocked their efforts to make race a relevant issue within their community. The authors reflect on their efforts to "make race matter" on their campus and the unique problems and issues that their college's homogeneity, resistance, and lack of support for diversity initiatives and courses posed for them in the process of promoting multiculturalism and addressing racism as vital aspects of a liberal arts education. The authors highlight the key challenges and approaches to teaching and learning about race in Eurocentric and racially homogenous environments in which explorations of social inequities and issues of racism are not supported or welcomed.

Chapter 5, "The Racial Experiment," is written by Susan C. Warner and Millicent Mickle. These instructors engage in a reflective dialogue on their collaborative effort in developing, implementing, and facilitating an unprecedented and pioneering cross-institutional dialogue about race and racial issues between Black and White students at two racially homogenous rural universities. The instructors brought together students from Wilberforce University, a historic Black college, and from Cedarville University, a predominately White university, several times over intervening years to discuss important issues relating to race and discrimination. Each author reflects on the strategies that she employed in order to critically engage these two homogenous groups of students in an ongoing, critical dialogue about race and racism. Warner and Mickle share their reflections on the lessons they learned from each others' facilitation styles and the pedagogical choices that they each made in the pursuit of interrupting their respective institution's insular, homogeneous populations and helping their students to find common ground and reach deeper levels of understanding, empathy, and respect for each other's perspectives, social locations, and life experiences.

Chapter 6, "Starting with a Story and Sharing the Discussion Leading: Tools and Tasks That Help in a Classroom Dealing with Diversity—Stumbling into an Affirmation of Feminist Pedagogy" by Janet Huber Lowry and Leah Collum describes the value of using narratives, and in this case the use of a satirical story about gender, to introduce difficult theoretical concepts about gender roles and scripts and to encourage meaningful and critical discussion among a diverse group of undergraduate students at Austin College. Focusing on the Gender Studies course she teaches at the College, Huber Lowry examines the ways in which the "mix of genders and sexualities becomes the principal challenge in terms of teaching diversity." The chapter explores the content, material, and process of this course from the perspectives of Huber Lowry, the designer and instructor of the course and Collum, a student and discussant in the course.

Each author discusses how giving different viewpoints a voice through shared discussion leading of multicultural anthology selections constitutes a valuable strategy for enriching the course and the students' understanding of issues of gender and diversity. Further, the chapter shows that diversity is not simply about differences in race, gender, ethnicity, culture, or sexuality, but rather, it also illustrates the various perspectives people use to view these differences, and it shows that diverse intellectual and academic perspectives provide different ways to view issues of gender inequality. Their collaborative discussion shows the possibilities that dialogues on gender and inequality hold for a vision of critical multicultural education and reminds us that issues of gender oppression must remain central to discourses in multicultural education and pluralism.

Chapter 7, "Irritating, Supporting and Representing: Reflections of Faculty and Students of Color," is coauthored by Ana María García and Angela R. Gillem, Dana Szwajkowski, and Lillian West. In this chapter, García and Gillem address the complexities of their experiences as professors of color who are engaged in the collaborative teaching of an undergraduate pluralism course at Arcadia University. They explore their experiences of engaging in dialogue with their colleagues in this teaching collaborative as well as their experiences of teaching and learning with the students in their course. García and Gillem explore their unique perspectives on issues of identity, inclusion, and exclusion as lesbians and faculty of color engaged in diversity work and multicultural pedagogy. Locating themselves as more than educators in a traditional sense, the authors examine social interactions with students and faculty from their positions as advocates and activists for social justice and inclusion. More specifically, they examine the dynamics of being self and other, subject and object with their students and colleagues. They reflect on the "emotional hazards" of continually irritating majority group students, supporting faculty and students of color, and representing the very diversity that is at the heart of the learning and resistance in their courses.

The student authors, Szwajkowski and West, discuss their similar yet distinct perspectives, as a Korean and African American woman respectively, their experiences and reactions to the pluralism course specifically, and their identities and lives generally. The students explore the ideas, assumptions, attitudes, and judgments about race and racism that they brought with them to the course and how these perspectives mapped onto their processes of self-reflection and learning. All of the authors make clear that while they *are* examples of pluralism, they are still challenged by it to continuously rethink their own identities and the world around them.

Chapter 8, "Identity Matters in Class: Conversations in Mixed Company," is written by Jody Cohen, Emily Hayes, Natalie Inozil, Sarah Mendell, and Prerna Srivastava. Cohen is a faculty member at Bryn Mawr College, where the student authors were enrolled as undergraduates. The authors of this chapter collectively address the question: "What are propitious circumstances for generating and sustaining real—that is, honest, fluid, sometimes dangerous—conversations about identity, diversity and power in an undergraduate classroom?" The authors respond to this question from diverse perspectives situated within two writing-intensive, interdisciplinary courses focusing on issues of identity, education, and equity.

In this chapter, the authors reconsider what happened in these courses with the goal of better understanding what it takes to teach and learn diversity. They argue for building community as a prerequisite to engaging in real discussions of diversity and, paradoxically, for engaging such discussions as a requirement for building community. The authors assert that "the challenge of the classroom is to circumvent the belief that trust precede risk, and instead to create the conditions for risk-taking as a medium for engendering trust." Further, they suggest that "the classroom need not and in fact cannot be an isolated, time-bound space." Instead, they argue, students must be supported and challenged to confront real issues involving their emergent knowledge of how to participate in critical dialogue in constructive ways as a part of the ongoing task of building a larger community.

Chapter 9, "Critical Multicultural Teacher Reflections: Counter-narratives to Images of the White Male Blockhead," is coauthored by Sharon M. Ravitch, the professor of a teacher-education course that works from a critical multicultural perspective, and her students, R. Reed Roeser and Brian J. Girard, who are teachers in the Philadelphia area. Ravitch discusses the context, content, and goals of the course with respect to the ways in which it challenges White teachers to critically reflect on themselves, society, and schooling, and assists them in the development of the skills necessary to evaluate their own belief systems, values, and worldviews, as well as to make important changes in their curriculum and pedagogy. Roeser and Girard reflect on their experiences of learning to critically explore and analyze social and institutional discrimination as well as on the impact their social locations have on their identities, worldviews, and ideologies. Their reflections on their learning processes complicate typical notions of White men as ignorant and resistant to learning about their own racism, ethnocentrism, and unearned privilege. These teachers, as students, share their experiences—sometimes painful, often uncomfortable, and, ultimately, transformative—of learning about and then struggling to unlearn the ways in which they have internalized and enacted racism and White dominance in their personal and professional lives. Their reflections help educators to better understand how White teachers who are open to critical reflection make meaning and use of material that provokes them to reconceptualize themselves, their views on society, and their pedagogical choices as teachers as well as to take responsibility for interrupting the oppressive status quo in American society and in their own schools and classrooms.

Chapter 10, "What Lies Beneath: Critical Dialogue for Culturally Relevant Pedagogy," coauthored by Ayala Younger and Bill Rosenthal, is a reflective dialogue between a student and professor who have participated in an ongoing dialogue about race, social class, and culturally relevant pedagogy, which began as an independent study at Muhlenberg College five years ago and developed as Younger became a teacher and Rosenthal changed institutions as a teacher educator. The authors explore how their initial coursework developed into a critical examination of "sensitive and often-silenced issues of race and class in education" that has forced them to re-examine their beliefs, their teaching and the influence that their collaboration has held for their attitudes and ideologies as individuals and professionals. The authors focus on how and why their relationship and exchange of ideas has promoted their self-questioning and has pushed them "toward a raw, critical self-consciousness" in which they have become particularly committed to the "identity work" of increasing their consciousness of themselves as teachers and learners.

From the beginning of their collaborative examination, Younger and Rosenthal discuss their commitment to critically examining the intersections and interactions between their identity work and culturally relevant pedagogy as "White Anglo, suburban, middle-class teachers." Through engaging with major theorists in the areas of culturally relevant pedagogy along with individual and dialogical reflection on their own cultural awareness, the authors explore their process of coming into a pedagogical and ideological stance of critical and contextualized self-questioning. Their collaborative journey reflects their newly developed belief that "essential to teaching students culturally different from oneself is the courage to question—profoundly, relentlessly, and dialogically— one's own beliefs and practices." The authors invite their readers to listen in as they reenact their dynamic discussion over the past five years through the use of a metacognitive approach to their journeys together, their own questioning, and their reflections on the development of critical, multicultural dialogue in which professor and student are truly co-learners.

As each of these chapters will explore, teaching and learning, in their ideal forms, are a mutually empowering co-construction between the teacher and the learners. In learning to co-construct educational spaces of safety, openness to new ideas, and critical dialogue, those of us who teach these courses must become increasingly empowered in our work. But being empowered to counter the systems in which we live, love, and work is a complicated process. Working toward a vision of a critical multicultural education is often impassioned and lonely work. It is inspiring and exhausting and it is never completed. The work of learning, unlearning, and relearning toward a vision of social transformation is not romantic, nor should it be glorified, lest its rendering lose the very real and uncomfortable work that true transformation engenders and requires. The work of teaching and learning must be understood as hard work for everyone involved. In this work, in this discomfort, in this place where teachers and students meet and create places of risk, trust, uncertainty, and possibility, lies the emancipation of future generations. We are all learning to take responsibility for our world. As educators we are learning how to make our students feel safe enough to become uncomfortable and to make sure that we ourselves remain uncomfortable enough so that we can make progress toward our goal of social transformation.

While we have made significant progress in these areas over the past decade, there is always more work to do. As bell hooks (1994) writes:

> The academy is not paradise. But learning is a place where paradise can be created. The classroom, with all its limitations, remains a location of possibility. In that field of possibility we have the opportunity to labor for freedom, to demand of ourselves and our comrades, an openness of mind and heart that allows us to face reality even as we collectively imagine ways to move beyond boundaries, to transgress. This is education as the practice of freedom. (p. 207)

As you will see, the authors in this book believe that classrooms, with all of their limitations and constraints, are locations of immense possibility. And in the work of diversity and multicultural courses—the meeting place of teachers and students as co-learners—the possibility lies precisely in finding, creating, and re-creating the desire to view working toward freedom and equality as an opportunity. The work of demanding—from ourselves, our students, and our colleagues—an openness of mind and heart can help us to face the realities of the less than ideal society in which we live as we strive to move beyond the borders that confine our lives and our work. While the work of social transformation requires considerable focus and energy, our freedom, of mind and heart, is what is at stake. Given the high stakes for everyone involved in this type of pedagogy, this book is a gift—of validation, celebration, and respect— for people who are working toward social transformation one student at a time.

NOTE

1. While there are a variety of approaches that call themselves multicultural, many are superficial and based on a "cultural tourism" model that lacks a substantive critique of social and institutional oppression (Erickson, 2004; Sleeter, 1996). The approaches represented in this book go beyond the mere insertion of multicultural themes into curriculum in an additive way and are therefore referred to as critical multicultural education.

REFERENCES

Banks, J.A. (Ed.). (1996). *Multicultural education, transformative knowledge, and action: Historical and contemporary perspectives.* New York: Teachers College Press.

Cochran-Smith, M. (1991). Learning to teach against the grain. *Harvard Educational Review, 61,* 279–310.

Erickson, F. (2004). Culture in society and in educational practices. In J. A. Banks and C. A. M. Banks, (Eds.), *Multicultural education: Issues and perspectives.* Hoboken: Jossey-Bass.

Fordham, S. (1996). *Blacked out: Dilemmas of race, identity, and success at Capital High.* Chicago: University of Chicago Press.

Gatto, J. T. (1994). A different kind of teacher. Keynote Address at Gate Conference, Omega Institute, Rhinebeck, NY.

Gay, G. (1990). Multiethnic education: Historical developments and future prospects. *Phi Delta Kappan, 64,* 560–563.

Giroux, H. A. (1994). Insurgent multiculturalism and the promise of pedagogy. In D. T. Goldberg, (Ed.), *Multiculturalism: A critical reader* (pp. 325–343). Cambridge: Blackwell.

Goldberg, D. T. (Ed.). (1994). Multiculturalism: A critical reader (pp. 1–44, 325–343). Cambridge: Blackwell.

Gorski, P. (2000). A working definition of multicultural education. http://curry.edschool. virgina. edu/go/multicultural.

Grant, C. A., and Tate, W. F. (1995). Multicultural education through the lens of the multicultural education research literature. In J. A. Banks and C. A. M. Banks, (Eds.), *Handbook of research on multicultural education* (pp. 145–166). New York: Macmillan.

Hidalgo, N. M. (1993). Multicultural teacher introspection. In T. Perry and J. W. Fraser, (Eds.), *Freedom's plow: Teaching in the multicultural classroom* (pp. 99–106). New York & London: Routledge.

hooks, b. (1994). *Teaching to transgress: Education as the practice of freedom.* New York & London: Routledge.

Kagan, D. M. (1992). Professional growth among preservice and beginning teachers. *Review of Educational Research, 62* (2), 129–169.

Laubscher, L., and Powell, S. (2003). Skinning the drum: Teaching about Diversity as "Other." *Harvard Educational Review, 73* (2), 203–223.

Levinson, B. A., and Holland, D. C. (1996). The cultural production of the educated person: An introduction. In B. A. Levinson, D. E. Foley, and D. C. Holland, *The cultural production of the educated person: Critical ethnographies of schooling and local practice.* New York: SUNY Press.

Martin, R. J. (1995). Deconstructing myth, reconstructing reality: Transcending the crisis in teacher education. In R. J. Martin (Ed.), *Practicing what we teach: Confronting diversity in teacher education* (pp. 65–78). New York: SUNY Press.

McCarthy, C. (1993). After the Canon: Knowledge and ideological representation in the multicultural discourse on curriculum reform. In C. McCarthy and W. Crichlow (Eds.), *Race, identity, and representation in education* (pp. 289–305). New York & London: Routledge.

McLaren, P. (1994). White terror and oppositional agency: Towards a critical multiculturalism. In D. T. Goldberg (Ed.), *Multiculturalism: A critical reader* (pp. 45–74). Cambridge: Blackwell.

McIntyre, A. (1997). *Making meaning of Whiteness: Exploring racial identity with White teachers.* New York: SUNY Press.

Nieto, S. (1999a). Critical multicultural education and students' perspectives. In S. May (Ed.), *Critical multiculturalism: Rethinking multicultural and antiracist education.* (pp. 191–215). Philadelphia: Falmer Press.

Nieto, S. (1999b). *The light in their eyes: Creating multicultural learning communities.* New York: Teachers College, Columbia University.

Nieto, S. (2004). *Affirming diversity: The sociopolitical context of multicultural education.* New York: Longman Press.

Ravitch, S. (2000). *Reading ourselves between the lines: White teachers reading, writing, and talking about diversity, inequality and pedagogy.* Unpublished Dissertation Manuscript. The University of Pennsylvania.

Remillard, J. T. (2000). Prerequisites for learning to teach mathematics for all students. In W. G. Secada (Ed.), *Changing the faces of mathematics: Perspectives on multiculturalism and gender equity.* Reston, VA: NCTM.

Sleeter, C. E. (1996). *Multicultural education as social activism.* New York: SUNY Press.

Tatum, B. D. (1992/1996). Talking about race, learning about racism: The application of racial identity development theory in the classroom. In T. Beauboeuf-Lafontant and D. Smith Augustine (Eds.), *Facing racism in education* (pp. 321–348). Cambridge: Harvard Educational Review.

CHAPTER TWO

Dialogue on Diversity Teaching
Reflections on Research, Pedagogy,
and Passion for Social Justice

Katherine M. Acosta
LEAD Center, University of Wisconsin–Madison

Helen A. Moore, Gary K. Perry, and Crystal Edwards
University of Nebraska

INTRODUCTION: MULTICULTURALISM AND MARGINALITY IN HIGHER EDUCATION

Gollnick and Chinn (1986) argue that the concept of "multicultural education" is not new but draws on educational elements in development since the 1920s. Among these concepts are the international and intercultural contexts of curricula, the foregrounding of various ethnic histories and cultures, and an emphasis on intergroup or human relations, especially the reduction or elimination of stereotypes and prejudices (Sleeter and Grant, 1993). Multicultural education emphasizes a range of strategies for increasing student achievement that includes teaching within the cultural contexts of diverse students and providing a dialogue between teachers and students that honors students' experience and "voice" (Hill Collins, 1986). Multicultural educators actively inquire into communication differences between students and teachers, and attend to the mismatch between teaching and learning styles that occurs in a classroom that privileges those who are White, male, middle class, and heterosexual.

Gollnick and Chinn (1986) also identify formal curricular issues that highlight cultural pluralism nationally and internationally, enhance critical thinking, and help students gain a better understanding of the causes of oppression and inequality and examine their own and others' biases and stereotypes. "To educate in a pluralistic society for a pluralistic world" goes beyond dealing with diversity as a "problem" (Smith, 1990, p. 29) and moves toward creating a multicultural campus as its central educational purpose.

One of the most critical elements of the multicultural education definition involves the "hidden curriculum." This concept includes classroom demonstrations of unequal power through institutional rules, the privilege of White, male, heterosexual, and middle-class values and norms in noncurricular dimensions of schools, and systematic efforts to reinforce conforming behaviors. Multicultural education looks to the empowerment of teachers and students as actors even as their strengths are suppressed or exploited (hooks, 1994) through hegemonic curricular structures. This emphasis creates a highly politically charged curriculum which takes place in "a complicated and tense period intellectually" (Sleeter, 1996, p. 3) for both academic faculty and graduate students as struggles continue over what is considered legitimate knowledge and pedagogy inside their disciplines and inside the classroom. Obidah (1999) talks of the "reawakening" to dangers in graduate school "similar to the one in my old neighborhood that threatened my survival" and the danger of "imposed invisibility" (p. 44).

A "diversity" requirement was added to the liberal arts undergraduate curriculum in most colleges a decade ago; at our large Research I campus it is called the "Area H" requirement of the comprehensive education program. As part of our sociological and pedagogical inquiries, we launched a research project to reflect on the experiences of faculty and graduate instructors who teach "Area H" diversity courses. Our goal in conducting and analyzing some sixty in-depth, face-to-face interviews is to understand how intersections of race, class, gender, and sexuality intertwine with instructors' classroom teaching experiences.

As we teach multicultural elements that encourage educational transformations, instructors collide against a curriculum in which students lack systematic linkages to multicultural scholarship before or after this specific course requirement. Instead, it is experienced by both students and instructors as an "add on" that often clashes with the worldviews of the students themselves and those of their other university instructors. As such, 117 hours of hegemonic curricula prepare students for three credit hours of resistance to the scholarship and instructors engaged in "Area H" work. For graduate students and faculty of color who enter a racialized academy, the assignment to teach diversity courses can be a particularly difficult career pathway. Our dialogue seeks to explicate themes within our teaching and scholarship that speak to that hidden curriculum and invisibility of identity within "diversity" education.

DOERS OF MULTICULTURAL EDUCATION

Multicultural education theorists often include a structural critique of the White, Western, and male dominance of the educational labor market itself. "For multicultural education to become a reality in the formal school situation, the total environment must reflect a commitment to multicultural education" (Gollnick and Chinn, 1986, p. 29). This structural multiculturalism includes the pluralistic composition of the faculty, administration, staff, and students; the inclusion of the contributions of all cultural groups in the curriculum; unbiased instructional materials; and the development of faculty members who "understand the influence of racism, sexism and classism on the lives of their students" (p. 33).

Jimoh and Johnson describe teaching in a classroom in which racialized behavior "has now gone underground within the dominant culture" (2002, p.

287). For the instructor of color in a predominately White institution, this poses the "palpable" reality of classrooms as sites where "students might expect to find their intellectual comfort zones challenged and whose Black and female presence potentially may double a student's conflicted response" (p. 288). Gititi (2002) discusses the series of myths that include the "death and disappearance of race as a central and controlling issue in American daily life" as the repeated mantra of White undergraduate and graduate students in his classrooms (p. 180). These myths erase his contributions in the minds of students and colleagues, who assume that he will teach diversity because of his racial identity rather than his scholarship credentials. Other researchers have noted that female instructors "stand in a different relationship to knowledge from men and that makes every difference in education" (Pagano, 1990, p. xvi) as feminist educational praxis assumes a critical-thinking process (Bunch, 1983). The additional legal vulnerabilities of gay, lesbian, bisexual, and transgendered students and faculty, who are not protected by even the thinnest veneer of job discrimination laws, highlight the difficulties in teaching from the academic margins.

The following reflections occur among three seasoned graduate instructors (with a total of eleven years of teaching experience including teaching in "Area H" courses) and one faculty supervisor of graduate professional development (with thirty years of classroom teaching experience, who edits the American Sociological Association journal, *Teaching Sociology,* and regularly teaches "Area H" courses). As we launched our qualitative interviews for the research project, we stopped to identify our own worldviews on diversity, multiculturalism, and pluralism in the academy. The bridge between our teaching and our research scholarship endeavors is set out in the following dialogue.

Transforming the Academy

Helen A. Moore, professor of sociology: Over the past decade, our graduate program in sociology has worked to recruit, retain, and fill the pipeline of future sociologists with people from diverse backgrounds. We have successfully created a demographic profile of race, gender, and sexual orientation that reflects our future as a discipline, rather than our past. However, this shift occurred at a time when the landscape of higher education was expanding rapidly to create new teaching demands. These demands include: more general education courses that emphasize diversity curricula, increased expectations for the documentation of teaching excellence by incoming faculty members and graduate students seeking academic employment, and the recognition that predominately White campuses can be sites of agony (Feagin, Vera, and Imani, 1998) and oppression (Paludi, 1992) for students and instructors from diverse backgrounds.

Sonia Nieto argues that all good teaching is about transformation (1999, p. xvii) "on a number of levels: individual, collective and institutional." The dialogue in this chapter revolves around the experiences of several graduate instructors, doctoral students who are learning the craft of teaching in this changing landscape of higher education, and one senior faculty member who hopes to encourage their, and her own, growth toward critical consciousness in the classroom. Because higher education is a microcosm of even larger societal shifts in demography and politics, we hope to use this dialogue to identify our reasons for "doing" our diversity scholarship projects.

My impetus to join the project evolves out of personal, scholarly, and programmatic (collective and institutional) frameworks. Since teaching in my first classroom in sociology in 1974, I have learned about and reflected on the differences and similarities in my classroom position, compared to other instructors with more or fewer privileged statuses than my own. My background in the sociology of education and my commitment to critical pedagogies leads me to systematically think about how we allocate work in the academy, and the role of faculty and instructors from diverse backgrounds who teach under conditions of resistance, whether that resistance comes from students at a predominately White institution (PWI), from colleagues who ignore the implications of diversity as an attempt to be color- or gender-"blind," or from discipline standards which relegate diversity topics to the margins. My commitment to social change and social support has led me to seek out programs such as Preparing Future Faculty and MOST (Minority Opportunities through School Transformation) as focal points to critique our processes of teaching and learning by, for, and about diversity.

Over the past two decades, I have worked with our campus American Association of University Professors and our Faculty Senate Committees on Academic Rights in faculty appeal processes. In every instance in which a faculty of color or woman faculty member came for a consultation, at least one element of their concerns involved the classroom teaching dimension of their scholarship. They often cited student resistance and low scores on formal evaluations that are mandated at the department or college level. They believed that their pedagogical goals and practices challenged colleagues and students and were misunderstood and misrepresented as they toiled in the classrooms designated to "teach about diversity." In our own department, we have systematic quantitative evidence that both faculty members and graduate instructors are evaluated differently in classes that meet our university general education requirements for diversity content. This has particularly held true for African American graduate students (both women and men), whose student evaluations rise when they teach in more "generic" sociology courses. What are the politics of assigning "diversity" education responsibilities to members of oppressed groups and then evaluating these instructors on the basis of norms and standards calibrated from more "traditional" classroom settings? My own review of the literature on the evaluation of teaching shows that we have little scholarship on diverse teachers teaching diversity topics that can inform our current assessment of colleagues and future faculty members (Moore, 2000).

Research and theory in critical pedagogies place in the foreground the contradictions of teaching critical-thinking skills within conservative institutions such as universities. From the intellectual frameworks set out by Pierre Bourdieu (1988), Freire (1970), and hooks (1994), we learn that class-conscious, antiracist, and feminist educational practices become intertwined with abstract analyses of oppressions carried out in our scholarship. The curriculum is not a "neutral assemblage of knowledge" (Apple, 1993) that sociologists and other college faculty members pass on without sifting through their own biases. How do graduate students working as (cheap) classroom instructors balance ensuring their futures as faculty members with enacting the critical theoretical models that drew them into graduate education? The pedagogy of the college classroom is too often based on a "banking model" of education as knowledge that is received by a passive student body (Freire, 1970). How might these future faculty members help us to envision new models of higher education and enhance student learning?

We are also challenged by intersections of race, class, gender, sexual orientation, disability, age, and other stratification dimensions which are entangled and layered in our classroom lessons. We labor to learn the theories and literatures that edge us toward fully reflexive scholarship and that make us impatient with the hierarchical nature of our work setting. Our own pedagogical positions often generate contradictions and privileges that make this emotional as well as intellectual work.

As a White woman from a fractured class background and a subordinated sexual orientation, I observe and participate in these intersecting inequalities from shifting positions across privilege. Are my emotional responses about teaching as an "outsider within" and as an "insider without" parallel to those of instructors of color, gay men, or heterosexual women? Do I work differently when I teach within my affiliated programs of women's studies or sociology or ethnic studies? What forms of support can I expect from colleagues and what mechanisms of support can I create for others? In my early profession, extending feminist and antiracist analyses to my own classroom work was exhilarating and challenging. Important *faultlines* occur in the disciplines (Smith, 1992), which create new academic identities and practices as we experience and teach paradigm shifts.

My reasons for this research project stem from my scholarly analysis of several concepts: teaching as "devalued" in the world of grants and higher education bureaucracies, work within oppressed groups who are tantalized by the "liberatory" possibilities of education, and empathy for individual instructors who are too often dashed emotionally by the passive resistance of their disciplines and the active resistance of their students and colleagues. These acts of resistance are often micro events that are invisible in the larger academy, but they grind incessantly at the professional identity and self-esteem of those who "deliver diversity" for the core curriculum.

My own typical "sink-or-swim" introduction to teaching in graduate school provided no training in pedagogical strategies, no notion that "teaching" was a dimension for growth in professional career work, and no framework for linking the arenas of stratification and the sociology of education to my everyday classroom experiences. Instead, the teaching we did as graduate instructors was signified as "this is how you earn your keep; this is the work you do in order to have access to scholarship and scholars." As apprentices, we started at the "bottom" to work our way past academic gatekeepers who took little notice of our struggles with diversity. This is a strong message that leaves a residue throughout the academic career: teaching is measured as time spent against research opportunity, and student learning in the classroom is the residual left after putting in your time. Diversity teaching is to be treated by evaluators as if it is a curriculum "without difference," even as it stratifies and often marginalizes the academics who work in this field.

At the peak of their intellectual enthusiasm, I want graduate students to approach teaching as a dignified setting for student learning and a journey for themselves and their colleagues to delve into the complexities of their scholarship. I do not want teaching to be the minefield or the latent excuse that "cools out" the impetus behind ethnic/women/disability/GLBT studies in the academy. Too many instructors of color have been dislodged from the academy because of student evaluations taken out of context, a lack of support for teaching from colleagues, and questions about the "seriousness of their scholarship" when they value teaching and outreach activities. Too many women instructors from all backgrounds have labored in classrooms that are negatively gendered, with gendered pay, gendered promotion, gendered authority, and gendered work (Acker, 1992). Gay and lesbian faculty members and students are still seeking a safe haven in the academy from which to do their work.

Preparing Future Faculty (PFF) is a national initiative to provide graduate students with information and insight into the academies they are entering. Minority Opportunities through School Transformation (MOST) is a program sponsored by the American Sociological Association to transform the discipline of sociology by reflecting on our pedagogical practices in a more diverse landscape of teachers and learners. I want the diverse students on campus and in our programs to have a fighting chance to find the best workplace for their potential growth. This research project grew from the same roots as PFF and MOST, and it offers those involved an opportunity to share the visions, hopes, and agonies of their colleagues and their advisors as gifts to a new generation of scholar teachers. My hope is that these gifts will stoke their sociological imaginations well into their academic careers and contribute to the transformation of the academy toward critical pedagogies that enhance our students and communities.

In the following narratives, the graduate instructors reflect the arguments by social reproduction theorists that structure is a key determinant of social action in the classroom, while joining the critical education theorists in emphasizing the importance of human agency and resistance by themselves and their students and their supervising faculty. As sociologists, we begin our scholarship project assuming that the social construction of reality accounts for the contested terrain of diversity education. Berger and Pullberg (1966) identify the duality of social life that involves both structure and individual agency by concluding that "social structure is not characterizable as a thing able to stand on its own, apart from [the] human activity that produced it [but] is encountered by the individual as a coercive instrumentality" (p. 178). Thus, teaching diversity courses through a multicultural education lens is an individual endeavor that we anticipate will be akin to "dancing through a minefield" (Kolodny, 1980).

At the same time, multicultural education theorists look to the empowerment of teachers and students as actors even as their strengths are suppressed or exploited (hooks, 1994) through hegemonic curricular structures. In the essay that follows, Gary Perry highlights this "minefield" as an African American diversity-centered scholar and teacher of multiple minority identities. His pedagogical work at a predominately White institution is full of challenges and scrutiny that lead him to a deeper understanding of both paralysis and privilege.

Learning to Navigate and Negotiate the Academic Minefield

Gary K. Perry, doctoral student: Ever since the U.S. Supreme Court's 1954 decision in *Brown v. Board of Education*, institutions of higher education continue to experience profound changes. As previously noted by Professor Moore, the subtle and not-so-subtle transformations within the academic curricula, campus demographics, and cultural climate are in part symptomatic of the movements for multicultural and diversity-centered education. At this historical juncture, institutions of higher education have become analogous to "postwar" battlefields, areas wherein *hidden* pockets of resistance and sinister alliances have emerged to undermine such progress.

Learning to navigate and negotiate the academic landscape of higher education is an arduous process. This endless process is the result of the immense sociopolitical changes that have produced today's institutions of higher learning. As bureaucratic structures, many institutions of higher education are composed of multiple roles and varying statuses, all of which are accompanied by a number of written and unwritten obligations. In a social context, an individual's experiences within academe will reflect these sometimes overlapping social identities that one both brings into and acquires within the academy. While everyone, regardless of his or her social statuses and identities, must develop the means for navigating through higher education's minefields, this journey may become debilitating, if not detrimental, for members of many socially disadvantaged groups.

As a twenty-six-year-old, African American, gay male graduate teaching assistant, my journey through academe has been no crystal stairway.[1] More often than not, learning how to navigate and negotiate the academic landscape is *fundamental* to my existence in academe. Unlike more privileged individuals, my journey is inherently underscored by a perpetual state of conflict and vulnerability. Such confusion is primarily the result of my multiple oppressed identities.

Having such stigmatized identities, within the context of a predominately White college, may often present a threat or an affront to the existing social order. In other words, the ongoing struggle between my oppressed selves and the status quo of the academy is what perpetuates such contentious experiences. Another way to view this phenomenon, as discussed by Johnella E. Butler (2000), is to envision predominately White colleges and universities as a boundary-filled or territorial space, which is seemingly resistant toward forces of (progressive) social change. Although this may be an accurate image, aspects of social change are occurring throughout the academy, and with that change comes the need for many oppressed groups to be ever so vigilant of the academic minefields.

Given the previous discussion, it may be apparent why it is central that I learn to navigate and negotiate the academic landscape. What is less apparent, however, are the means by which this process manifests itself. By using my experiences as a graduate teaching assistant of a diversity-centered course at a predominately White college, I aim to capture the essence of this process and to highlight the context in which this otherwise invisible phenomenon may occur.

Teaching diversity: Working from a vulnerable position

Since the beginning of the movement for multiculturalism, particularly in higher education, the classroom has been one arena of the academy where change has resonated (see, e.g., Morris and Parker 1996). As a graduate student and teaching assistant of color, I feel honored to be a part of this metamorphosis. I perceive the classroom, unlike most other arenas of the academy, as having the greatest capacity for inspiring and cultivating social change and cultural enlightenment. My optimism, however, is repeatedly insulted by the reality that such change often comes with severe costs and many unavoidable risks.

While I embrace my role as a graduate teaching instructor, who happens to teach a diversity-centered course on race and nationality, I am also aware that I work from a vulnerable position. My vulnerability, as suggested earlier, stems from a variety of issues: (1) my stigmatized identities; (2) my marginalized presence within the academy; (3) the negative perceptions that my students, fellow colleagues, and faculty/administrators have about me; and (4) my nontraditional ideologies and critical worldviews.

Race continues to matter in U.S. society. As a graduate instructor of a course wherein race and related issues are the central focus, I am constantly reminded of the tension surrounding U.S. race relations. As a minority professor, I sometimes feel as if I have to walk on eggshells. This perception is a result of both the resistance I encounter from most (White) students and my vulnerable position in the classroom.

To begin with, my credibility, as an instructor, and the legitimacy of the course content are often suspect and highly scrutinized by students. More specifically, it is not the authenticity of the material that is brought into question, but, rather, the motives or intentions of the presenter. Such suspicion generally poses a fine line that I must walk. On the one hand, it is my goal to challenge my students' comfort zones and existing worldviews about race. While, on the other hand, I assist my students in becoming more informed and transformed by their classroom experiences. This is not to say, however, that I aim for a "value-free" or an "objective" classroom. Instead, my ultimate goal is one of enlightenment. This task is made problematic when both the message and the messenger are brought into question and deemed dogmatic.

Teaching diversity: Strategizing to survive

Because of my tenuous position in the classroom, I have learned, and am still learning, to become quite savvy in my approach to teaching. Given my experiences with teaching a diversity-centered course, I have learned that there is more than one way to "skin a cat." To this end, my biggest struggle has come from having to learn to see the world through the eyes of my students. If my goal is to help move my students toward a more empathetic and informed understanding of race and nationality, it behooves me to become aware of how they see and approach such issues. This is aided through my use of a student-centered approach to teaching. Unlike more traditional styles, or what Paulo Freire (1970) calls the *banking model*, the student-centered approach often allows the students to feel "safe" in expressing their positions about issues surrounding race. Through gaining such awareness, I have become more equipped to both interrogate and deconstruct many of my students' worldviews. As a result of using their viewpoints and personal experiences as a context to build on, I often challenge the students' positions in ways that are subversive and efficacious. It should not be assumed that student resistance and hostility are eliminated through this approach. Instead, engaging in such a confrontational pedagogical style often breeds more hostility. However, the contentious atmosphere of the class enables us (i.e., the students and myself) to transcend our otherwise polar positions. In other words, by allowing the students, and myself, to struggle with controversial issues in an often nonthreatening and nonposturing demeanor, common grounds and syntheses are more likely to be obtained.

Given that many of my students are White and from racially homogenous and isolated communities, I find visual aids and stories to be a very effective means of challenging their worldviews and ideologies. Although I take pride in preparing and equipping myself with research, facts, and even personal stories to share, I admit that much of this can become lost if not ignored by the students. I have thereby relied heavily on thought-provoking videos and guest presenters, all of which have contributed credibility and support to many of my class discussions. Moreover, these alternative means of teaching have allowed me to expose my students to worlds and lived experiences that they would never have imagined.

Teaching diversity: A source of empowerment

Thus far, my discussion has focused on the challenging experiences associated with teaching a diversity-centered course. These challenges, as already noted, stem from a variety of issues. Nonetheless, my journey through the academic minefield does have its places of relief and excitement. In a word, navigating and negotiating the academic landscape requires that I reconstruct my oppressed selves. This process does not end with mere identity politics, but, rather, entails a process by which I learn to be subversive and ingenious as it relates to teaching from a marginalized and vulnerable place. In some instances, this goal has been achieved by me constantly reaffirming myself that what I am doing is noble and needed for the betterment of humanity. At other times, putting myself in the place of the privileged other often enables me to see potential pitfalls and conflicts that I may experience. Finally, understanding that being an oppressed person does not mean you are paralyzed has allowed me to search for and engage in my human agency. All of these factors, and others, allow me to effectively navigate and negotiate the treacherous terrain of academe.

For most instructors of diversity-centered courses, learning to navigate and negotiate the academic landscape is an "on-the-job" experience. Because so few resources addressing the perils of, and strategies for, navigating the diversity-centered classroom exist, I was drawn to this project out of necessity. At one end of the spectrum, this research project gives me voice and validates my "unique" experiences as a minority instructor of a diversity-centered course in a predominately White environment. At the other end, this project, in my opinion, will place a much-needed dialogue and body of scholarship into the academic discourse.

As the instructor of a diversity-centered course, I have also been forced to learn a process for navigating and negotiating my emotional landscape. In the following essay, Katherine M. Acosta highlights the emotional labor and emotional investment associated with teaching diversity-centered courses. Acosta reflects on the intersections of her experiences as a female, Latina graduate instructor of a diversity-centered course(s) and the trials and triumphs associated with being a minority graduate student in an academic environment that is often hostile and treacherous.

Passionate Pedagogy: The Emotional Component of Teaching Diversity

Katherine M. Acosta, doctoral candidate: My motivations for studying the experiences of those teaching courses that focus on inequality and diversity are varied and complex. To talk about them requires talking about *emotion* in a setting where it is devalued and intellect is privileged. I am motivated by my own personal disillusionment in the classroom. By resentment at our lack of training to do this work. By anger that so much of this demanding work devolves onto graduate students. By fury that the university's nod at "diversity" often extracts unrecognized personal and professional costs from those who actually do the work.

But I am also motivated by hope, by the belief that social change is possible, that this work, teaching these kinds of courses, is crucial to building the kind of society I want to live in, and that there are, *there must be,* effective ways to do it. My hope is that by documenting the experiences of those in the trenches; by making visible their challenges, obstacles, and successes; and by analyzing their ideas and understandings about the work of teaching diversity, we can contribute to creating an environment where this mission can flourish.

When I first entered the classroom as an instructor, the emotional component of the pedagogical process was not a conscious concern. Certainly, I was motivated, as many are, by a passion for social justice. An idealist, I thought that if I simply explained inequality to students they would share my outrage. Instead, I ran into a brick wall of resistance. Like the social scientist I was training to become, I responded with ever more facts, figures, studies, charts, and graphs. I created beautiful slide shows illustrating the increase in the CEO-to-worker pay ratio, wage disparities by race and sex, and unequal educational resources, and I meticulously cited each source. The wall became more impenetrable.

What was happening? I looked out at a sea of stony-faced students, their body language screaming resentment and fury. When they spoke, it was to express cold indifference to the plight of those less fortunate than themselves, stubborn adherence to the American credo that capitalism is the best economic system and gives everyone an equal chance at the "American Dream," and disbelief in the statistics presented. They seemed to really dislike me, too. I often walked away from my first introduction to sociology class feeling as though someone had punched me in the stomach. How could they not *care?*

Looking back, I realize that part of the problem was my lack of understanding of the role of emotion in all this. Student resistance is, initially, an emotional response. Jagger (1989) argues that emotions are closely related to values. In challenging the worldviews of an overwhelmingly White, mostly middle-class student body, I was bound to provoke a wide range of emotional responses. In turn, as a feminist and a Latina, my students' reactions evoked in me what Jagger calls "outlaw emotions"; that is, emotions inconsistent with the beliefs and values of dominant groups, often experienced by members of subordinate groups.

Studying Jagger's work, and in particular, her insight that "emotional responses to the world change as we conceptualize it differently," but that "the ease and speed with which we can re-educate our emotions is not great" (1989, p. 170) would have been enormously helpful to me when I began my teaching career. However, like many graduate instructors, I received little training in teaching (Anderson and Swazey, 1998; Austin, 2002), and none at all in dealing with the emotional aspects of pedagogy. I was therefore unequipped to handle the situation in which I found myself. In that first course, I tried to maintain the illusion that we were engaged in a merely intellectual exercise, and overwhelmed my students with ever more information. Over the years, I groped my way toward solutions, gradually developing some devices for avoiding my early pitfalls, without fully understanding the process I was struggling to master.

Interviewing teachers of diversity courses across disciplines for our study has provided some valuable opportunities for dialogue about these issues that I otherwise would not have had. In one of the earliest interviews I conducted, an experienced African American professor, who is warmly regarded by many students, explicitly articulated the importance of acknowledging and allowing for the emotional responses of students. For her, emotion is inextricably involved in the learning process and an effective teacher learns to channel this in productive ways. Her words expressed a truth I had known at some level.

But why had I not understood this sooner? Certainly, I had long recognized that emotion and reason cannot be neatly separated, and probably should not be. My best intellectual work emerges when I am passionately engaged with the subject. Of course, I try not to reveal too much of that. We learn early in our academic socialization to project that aura of rationalism, dispassionate analysis, and discussion. To behave otherwise invites doubt and criticism of one's scholarly ability and professionalism. I myself was explicitly reprimanded by a professor in a graduate seminar for passionate stances and debate.

I deeply resented this professor's attitude, yet did not allow for the emotional experiences of my own students. Perhaps I was fearful of what I might unleash and whether I could handle it. Certainly I had no role models for this kind of teaching. Teaching diversity courses multiplies the challenges for graduate students. We are not only learning to become teachers; we are teaching the kinds of courses that require us to learn new ways of teaching. We need to develop methods that are often quite different from those we have experienced as students. These pedagogical strategies must address the emotional component of teaching and learning. Laslett (1997) asserts that emotion can provide the energy to pursue our academic projects "even when the way to do so is not clear" (p. 66). For many of us, a passion for social justice fuels our work. However, that same emotional investment can also make us vulnerable to pain when students express racist, sexist, classist, and homophobic attitudes and comments. At the same time, if one goal of teaching diversity courses is to contribute toward the development of a more just society, we need to make constructive use of students' emotions. For Jagger (1989) "emotions are ways in which we engage actively and even construct the world" (p. 159). To critically reflect on emotions, and by extension, the cultural values from which they spring, is a political act that is "indispensable" for "social transformation" (p. 171). A key to successful diversity teaching and learning, then, would involve finding ways to allow for students' emotional reactions, and to manage our own, through a process that promotes intellectual development.

These are the issues and questions that motivate me to take on an additional research project while I am trying to research and write my dissertation. I want to find out whether and how others are handling this emotional component of teaching diversity. Further, I want to know *who* is doing this emotion work (Women? Instructors of color? Graduate assistants and other cheap labor?), and what kind of training, if any, they receive for it. I want to know how this work affects them, personally and professionally. Ultimately, I want to learn what we can do to become more effective teachers of courses I believe are crucial to building a better and more humane society.

In the following section, Crystal Edwards explores the challenge of developing political awareness and a sense of civic responsibility among students when teaching diversity courses. She considers the limited space in which diversity teaching is expected to occur, and the political consequences for instructors who carry out this work. Like Gary Perry, she is acutely aware that she is negotiating an academic "minefield." Like me, she understands teaching as a political act and shares the goal of developing a degree of critical consciousness among students in the hope that this will contribute to the improvement of social conditions. Her concern is with the political nature of multiple aspects of this process.

Political Awareness and Action

Crystal Edwards, doctoral candidate: As a teacher of diversity, I have two goals for my students: To make them aware of how the political process creates and shapes society and to encourage the development of their civic responsibility to engage in the making and changing of society. Consequences of this strategy include student resistance and a heavy load of emotional labor for me. Balancing these consequences with my desire for professional advancement and my commitment to diversity is often painful and joyous.

Political awareness

Exposing students to materials that challenge the validity of "Manifest Destiny," ethnocentrism, and hierarchy enlightens them to the degree of critical learning that is often oversimplified or ignored altogether. When women and people of color began to enter and challenge the ivory tower during the 1960s, they were deliberately challenging the legitimacy of the power of White male academics to define and scientifically report in such a way that excluded women and people of color (Smith, 1987; Hill Collins, 1986). These political actions resulted in the addition of women's studies and ethnic studies across the nation and eventually general education requirements focusing on diversity. Only a small number of departments and programs offer diversity courses and they remain segregated into humanities and social sciences. It is as if only sociology, English, and history can contribute to diversity.

The degree of progress minorities have made on campuses is arguable, but one thing is clear: Of the 120 credit hours required for a bachelor's degree, diversity teachers get three hours to explain how the other 117 hours, and students' prior elementary and secondary education, promoted the political agenda of elite White males. What remains political about these courses is the almost complete isolation in which they are taught. In one semester I ask students to wrap their minds around centuries of political actions which have been either unexplored or presented in such a way as to dilute their meaning.

When I recast "Manifest Destiny" as genocide of Native Americans, I do not find that most students are particularly resistant to this new information. The responses vary and include outrage, acknowledgment, and disbelief. Students respond to this new information about inequality by engaging in a political dialogue. They express political thoughts and demand tools to make change. Some want revolution, some want legislation, and some want charity. As a young instructor, I often waiver from class to class, even day to day, on how best to help them create the change they desire. Sometimes I shrug my shoulders, because I simply do not know. Sometimes I talk about voting rights, lobbying, social action groups, and social movements. I often feel ill-equipped to deal with their demands because I myself lack faith in the current political system's ability to be responsive to the needs of the less privileged.

What I find most offensive about the academy is the almost stupefied way people insist their research, teaching, and service are not political. Once a political science instructor told me that he did not express political opinions to his class; he gave them *both* sides and let students decide what to think. I wanted to tell him that showing students two sides of the same coin hardly qualifies as letting them think for themselves. He was simultaneously reinforcing the hegemonic paradigm and denying any connection to it. Ruth Hsu (2002) encourages us to use self-scrutiny to "recognize that academe is a politicized state apparatus and that the work we do is inherently political" (p. 195).

Diversity courses are political because we ask students to challenge the objectivity of science, explore multiple and simultaneous ways of knowing, and look at what is not there; all of which challenge the basic underpinnings of their education and clash with political agendas of those outside the classroom. Diversity teachers do not have to advance a political agenda to create dismay among students and outsiders. Student evaluations illuminate how perceptions about my politics are polarized. Some students consider me to be narrow-minded while others perceive me to be open-minded. The likelihood that I will be perceived as a raving, ranting political lunatic is directly proportional to how much they disagree with me.

While many students angrily disagree with me, questioning my sanity and my legitimacy, many more are deeply affected by the new critical and sociological perspectives to which I expose them. But either way I find myself in a bubble in which students really do not understand the complexity of creating solutions to social problems. For example, in a discussion about discrimination against homosexuals the students generally want to educate small children, but not challenge church doctrine. They tend to place responsibility onto the individual without challenging the institutions that those individuals participate in. I remind them of the structural forces that extend the argument beyond the individual and link the past, present, and future.

Civic responsibility

I refer to *Webster's* to demonstrate the connections between diversity courses and politics. *Webster's* defines politics first as *exercising or seeking power in the governmental or public affairs of a state, municipality*, and second as *pertaining to citizens' political rights*. I had to look this word up because diversity teaching is often referred to in the context of "political correctness" or "liberal political agenda." The first definition applies to diversity courses because I wish for my students to go on to become community leaders. I know that one day many of my students will be exercising their rights to influence the affairs of the government. I seek to make them aware of how their social location can grant or deny them this access, and to make them responsible for humanity beyond themselves and their own social group.

In our democracy we have freedom to act as a citizen to influence the making of society. Each day we create society through specific actions which are legitimated by specific ideas. I am truly a symbolic interactionist in that I believe it is ultimately through social interaction that we create our own existence and change. We have a system with many openings for the act of creation; we all have the power to choose actions that bring us closer to our goals. If encouraging students to move beyond their apathetic, individualized attitude of "My vote doesn't count" is too political, I do not care. Only in a closed, undemocratic society could the encouragement of individual and social thought and action be considered threatening. Where do you live? Encouraging thought and action does not encourage the adoption of a specific political agenda. I never assume that my students will use the skills that I teach them to advance specific political actions I deem positive. Instead, I challenge them to define their own responsibility to themselves and to others. This encourages a thoughtful, informed, and contextualized democracy, in which students become aware that not only do they have a vote, they have a voice that can and should be used in many ways.

Consequences

As a graduate-student teacher I face a dilemma. I struggle to balance learning academic standards against fulfilling my teaching responsibilities. In addition to this pressure to achieve, reflect, and maintain legitimacy, which are probably normal processes of professionalization (Reinharz, 1992), I carry another burden. I step into classrooms that remain hotbeds of political drama. Diversity courses are the love child of 1960s and 1970s civil rights advocates, and they survive as the only concession to an otherwise intact White male middle-class environment.

An article appeared in the *Chronicle of Higher Education* challenging a women's studies professor's right to create a safe environment for her students by developing discussion guidelines (Bartlett, 2002). Seeing this senior scholar accused of restricting her students' rights to free speech by her own department chair validated the fears I have held since I began my first class. Inexperience combined with the controversy of diversity courses (and sociology in general) lead me to fear litigation from students. I often feel unsafe in the classroom because generating "critical thought" is often interpreted as "anti-American," "anti-male," "anti-Christian," "anti-White," and "anticapitalism." One student told me "love it or leave it" to which I had no immediate answer, but I stewed for weeks before realizing the fallacy of his logic. Another student told me in a written evaluation that the classroom "wasn't the front steps of the capital building." This student resistance challenges my perceptions of my own legitimacy. It is vital that students respect the teacher as a legitimate source of knowledge, otherwise classroom control becomes tenuous.

Professionalization processes often involve a wavering sense of mastery. One day, I am reasonably sure I am a good teacher. I experience my teacher identity as secure and I feel confident in my development as a teacher. I am aware of academic freedom, but have heard informally about those whose use of freedom left them unemployed. Insecurity is the result of my own lack of political power. What remains unclear to me, as an educator, is why in this great land of freedom, asking students to become informed, engaged, and critical citizens is radical.

I joined this research team because we were all concerned about the toll these courses take on our vulnerable minority instructors (myself included). Like the others, I recognized a trend. While I was mired down in the emotional bog we call diversity, my peers were focused on developing their research skills. The more acclimated I have become to the university, the clearer it is to me: A desire to critically examine the discipline and the institution results in less pay and more heartache. I needed to know if my hunch was right.

Dialogic Endings and Beginnings

Our overlapping concerns around issues of teaching diversity motivate us to pursue our research project. A major goal for Helen is to usefully mentor and retain the minority graduate students and professors recruited by our institution. She wants to see due consideration given to students' reactions to minority faculty and the content of diversity courses in teaching evaluations. These concerns directly impact Gary as he searches for ways to negotiate questions of legitimacy that minority instructors inevitably face, and for ways to accomplish his aim of interrogating students' worldviews and developing an informed and empathetic understanding of race and inequality among them. Katherine recognizes that the process involved in developing the understanding that Gary and others seek has an emotional component, requires a significant degree of emotion work by instructors, and receives insufficient attention in an environment in which emotion is conceptually divorced from intellect and devalued. Crystal concentrates on the political implications of a burgeoning critical consciousness among students. How should diversity teachers respond when students ask for advice on taking political action, and what are the political consequences for these instructors?

We have few opportunities for dialogue about these issues within the conventional academic structure. Very little time and few formal mechanisms are built into most graduate programs for teaching development. Consequently, most graduate students receive minimal training and feedback on teaching. In addition, the heavy demands of graduate coursework, preparing for comprehensive exams and writing theses and dissertations, leave precious little time for "extracurricular" activities like teaching development.

The message Helen received as a graduate student, that teaching is something you do on the side, to earn your keep, while focusing primarily on your research, remains substantially the same message graduate students receive today. Our mentors teach us what they have been taught, and what they know to be true of the academy, that we should privilege research over teaching, and that success will be measured by research accomplishments. Material experiences support these ideas; our funding is dependent on our "progress in the program," and future job opportunities on publications, not the time we put in to develop quality teaching. This project, then, has been the major opportunity for many of us to have these dialogues, both through the research interviews with teachers of diversity, and among ourselves as we develop the project and analyze our data.

If rewards in academe accrue primarily through research, and the structure of academic programs provides few opportunities for teaching development, how might we build a "community of teachers" (hooks, 1994)? And why should we? hooks suggests that building such a community begins with "cross[ing] boundaries" to "engage in dialogue" (p. 130).

One idea that emerged from our research is to create a program that would allow graduate students to interact regularly with professors teaching diversity courses in a variety of disciplines. Graduate instructors would have the opportunity to observe experienced teachers in the classroom and to converse about teaching diversity. Our project provided many of us with our first opportunities to meet such professors and to access their insights. Too often we remain sequestered in our various departments, interacting primarily with scholars whose perspectives, though diverse in many respects, are structured by the same disciplinary boundaries as our own. Cross-disciplinary exchanges both expand the community from which we can draw inspiration and offer us different vantage points from which to consider the concepts, ideas, and methods of our disciplines and the ways we teach them. As to *why* we should build such a community, some answers for those of us committed to diversity teaching might be that it is necessary for sustaining multicultural education, for developing methods to promote critical thinking among students, and ultimately, for contributing to the development of a more egalitarian and humane society.

NOTE

1. The notion of a "crystal stairway" is borrowed from the poetry of Langston Hughes.

REFERENCES

Acker, S. (1989). *Teachers, gender, and careers.* Philadelphia: Falmer Press.

Anderson, M. S., and J. P. Swazey. (1998). Reflections on the graduate student experience: An overview. *New Directions for Higher Education, 101,* 3–13.

Apple, M. (1993). *Teachers and texts: A political economy of class and gender relations in education.* New York: Routledge.

Austin, A. E. (2002). Preparing the next generation of faculty: Graduate school as socialization to the academic career. *Journal of Higher Education, 73* (1), 94–122.

Bartlett, T. (2002). Guidelines for discussion or thought control? *Chronicle of Higher Education,* September 27, 2002.

Berger, P. and S. Pullberg. (1966). Reification and the sociological critique of consciousness. *New Left Review, 35,* 56–71.

Bourdieu, P., and J. C. Passeron. (1977). *Reproduction in education, society, and culture.* Beverly Hills, CA: Sage.

Bourdieu, P. (1988). *Homo academicus.* Palo Alto, CA: Stanford University Press.

Bunch, C. (1983). Not by degrees: Feminist theory and education. In C. Bunch and S. Pollack (Eds.), *Learning Our Way: Essays in Feminist Education* (pp. 248–271). Trumansburg, NY: Crossing Press.

Butler, J. E. (2000). Reflections on borderlands and the color line. In S. Geok-Lim and M. Herrera-Sobek (Eds.), *Power, race, and gender in academe* (pp. 8–31). New York: The Modern Language Association.

Feagin, J. R, H. Vera, and N. Imani. (1998). *The agony of education.* New York: Routledge.

Freire, P. (1970). *Pedagogy of the oppressed.* New York: Continuum.

Gititi, G. (2002). Menaced by resistance: The Black teacher in the mainly White school/classrom. In Tusmith and Reddy (Eds.), *Race in the college classroom.* (pp. 176–188). New Brunswick, NJ: Rutgers University Press.

Gollnick, P., and P. C. Chinn. (1986). *Multicultural education in a pluralistic society.* Columbus: Charles Merrill.

Hill Collins, P. (1986). *Black feminist thought.* New York: Routledge, 2000.

Hill Collins, P. (1986). Learning from the outsider within: The sociological significance of Black feminist thought. *Social Problems, 33,* 14–32.

hooks, b. (1994). *Teaching to transgress: Education as the practice of freedom.* New York: Routledge.

Hsu, R. (2002). Where's Oz, Toto? Idealism and the politics of gender and race in academe. In S. G. Lim and M. Herrera-Sobek (Eds.), *Strangers in the tower? Power, race, and gender in academe.* (pp. 183–207). New York: Modern Language Association, 1999.

Jagger, A. (1989). Love and knowledge: Emotion in feminist epistemology. *Inquiry, 32* (2), 151–176.

Jimoh, A. Y., and C. Johnson. (2002). Racing into the classroom. In Tusmith and Reddy (Eds.), *Race in the college classroom.* (pp. 286–298). New Brunswick, NJ: Rutgers University Press.

Kolodny, A. (1980). Dancing through the mine field: Some observations on the theory, practice and politics of a feminist literary criticism. *Feminist Studies, 6*, 1–25.

Laslett, B. (1997). On finding a feminist voice: Emotion in a sociological life story. In B. Laslett and B. Thorne (Eds.), *Feminist sociology: Life histories of a movement* (pp. 48–72). New Brunswick, NJ: Rutgers University Press.

Mish, F. C. (Ed.). (1993). *Merriam-Webster's collegiate dictionary* (10th ed.). Springfield, MA: Merriam-Webster.

Moore, H. (2000). Manifest and latent functions of student evaluations of teaching effectiveness, July, 2000. National Workshop in Scholarship of Teaching and Learning. James Madison University, Harrisonburg, VA.

Morris, L., and S. Parker. (1996). *Multiculturalism in academe: A source book.* New York: Garland Publishing.

Nieto, S. (1999). *The light in their eyes: Creating multicultural learning communities.* New York: Teachers College, Columbia University.

Obidah, J. (1999). Born to roll: Graduate school from the margins, In C. Grant (Ed.), *Multicultural research: A reflective engagement with race, class, gender, and sexual orientation.* Philadelphia: Falmer Press.

Pagano, J. A. (1990). *Exiles and communities: Teaching in the patriarchal wilderness.* Albany, NY: SUNY Press.

Paludi, M. (1992). *Ivory power.* Albany: SUNY Press.

Reinharz, S. (1992). Feminist methods in social research. Oxford University Press.

Sleeter, C. E. (1996). *Multicultural education as social activism.* New York: SUNY Press.

Sleeter, C. E., and C. Grant. (1993). *Making choices for multicultural education.* New York: Merrill.

Smith, D. (1987). *The everyday world as problematic: A feminist sociology.* Boston: Northeastern University Press.

Smith, D. (1990). Embracing diversity as a central campus goal. *Academe, 76*, 29–33.

Smith, D. (1992). The conceptual practices of power. Boston: Northeastern University Press.

Statham, A., L. Richardson, and J. Cook. (1991). *Gender and university teaching.* New York: SUNY Press.

CHAPTER THREE

From Silence and Resistance to Tongues Untied
Talking about Race in the College Classroom

Branden Coté, Keenon Javon Mann, Hattie Latrece Mukombe,
Christina Medina Bach Nielsen, Ana-María Gonzalez Wahl
Wake Forest University

INTRODUCTION

In the minds of many Americans, a gilded image of the college classroom remains alive and well. College classrooms are widely imagined to bring together students and faculty eager to pursue "higher learning" and generate lively exchanges about the most pressing social and political issues of our day. Ideally, these conversations are characterized by a commitment to critical inquiry, civil discourse, and dialogue, widely considered the hallmark of the college classroom.

Unfortunately, courses that focus on race and ethnic relations, or "diversity issues," increasingly seem plagued by a set of realities that runs counter to this ideal. Across the country, both students and faculty find these courses are marked by tension, hostility, and silence rather than civility and dialogue. Student evaluations of these courses are often more negative than their evaluations of other courses, while faculty report feeling exhausted, exploited, and disheartened by these classes (Wahl, Perez, Deegan, Sanchez, and Applegate, 2000). For students and faculty of color, in particular, these courses too often become emotional minefields rather than the intellectually and personally enlightening experiences they should provide.

For many reasons, the Race and Ethnic Relations course in which we participated at Wake Forest University in fall 2003 became an exception to this rule. Together, we forged the safe space necessary for a serious and provocative conversation about race which we sustained across the semester. This was not an easy task, given that we entered the class with perhaps the same trepidation and fears that many students across the country carry into these classes. Our experience, however, suggests that two sets of pedagogical resources and strategies can move us beyond silence to a genuine dialogue in race relations courses: first, the principles of "learning communities" and second, a critical mass of students of color. This chapter examines the way that tongues are "untied" when diversity courses build on both.

Our analysis, importantly, reflects the multiple lenses that emerge from our distinct experiences as individuals whose position in a system of racial, class, and gendered hierarchies differ. Ana-María Gonzalez Wahl, the faculty coordinator of this course, is a first-generation college graduate, part Euro-American and part Spanish, identifying more strongly with the latter. She comes to Wake Forest following eight years teaching at a large state university. Christina Medina Bach Nielsen, a junior transfer student, is similarly a first-generation college student, part Danish and part Puerto Rican. Hattie Latrece Mukombe, a first-generation African American junior, has lived in North Carolina her entire life, though more recently she has reconnected with her father's family in Zimbabwe. Keenon Javon Mann, a first-generation African American junior, has lived all his life in Delaware in a neighborhood that was predominantly Black. Finally, Branden Coté, a Euro-American senior, considers New York home but has also lived in several other large urban areas.

Below, we consider the ways in which a course that brought together a group of individuals who were so different and similar, at the same time, became an effective and important forum for exploring the complexities of race and ethnic relations in American life. We begin with a discussion of the pedagogical theory that guides learning communities and the importance of a "critical mass" of minority students on college campuses.

THE LEARNING COMMUNITIES MODEL

The challenges faculty and students encounter in race and ethnic relations courses are undoubtedly the result of a complex set of factors and dynamics. On the one hand, the hostility and resistance common in many of these classes are undoubtedly rooted in the broader political and cultural landscape of the United States, which continues to deny the realities of racism with calls for a color-blind society that largely avoids a serious conversation about race (Omi and Winant, 1986). However, institutions of higher learning also bear partial responsibility for these problems. More specifically, we can trace many of the challenges facing teachers and students in the "controversial classroom" to the growing importance of the "mass section" on many college campuses. Driven by fiscal pressures and constraints, the mass course section has widely become the way most institutions of higher learning "deliver the goods." With enrollments in these sections often exceeding one hundred, feelings of emotional distance, anonymity, and alienation are almost inevitable. When these courses focus on race and ethnic relations, anonymity often becomes a license for hostility—or dead silence.

In the face of these difficulties, learning communities have emerged as an innovative and important alternative to the mass lecture across the country (Gabelnick, MacGregor, Matthews, and Smith, 1990). Learning communities take several forms, in all cases building on the core principles of a liberal arts education and extending these principles in several ways. First and foremost, learning communities build on the premise that the learning experience should be a *collaborative* one that fosters a community of "student scholars" who share a commitment to critical inquiry through active dialogue with each other and the larger community.

As such, learning communities draw from a number of pedagogical strategies that distinguish these classes from more traditional classes. A *seminar-style discussion* guided by both faculty and students provides the core around which these courses build. Importantly, students are provided the opportunity to take a *leadership role* in these discussions in multiple ways, from setting the agenda and reworking the syllabus to organizing a class session. Beyond this, these courses deliberately and actively draw from strategies intended to build community in at least two ways. On the one hand, most learning communities involve students in collaborative work both within the classroom and outside the classroom to cultivate interpersonal connections among those students enrolled in these classes. These students, for example, may attend campus cultural events as a class, often sharing a meal on these occasions. On the other hand, many learning communities also emphasize the need to forge connections to the broader community beyond campus. Service learning projects, as well as other strategies that literally take students into neighborhoods, schools, and the "real world," serve this purpose.

In many ways, these kinds of pedagogical strategies are ideally suited for race and ethnic relations courses. Building a sense of community among students is certainly important in any course that asks students to discuss "sensitive" issues. Building community, and a sense of trust, is particularly important in race and ethnic relations classes because these courses force students and faculty to acknowledge realities—like White privilege—that are often hidden and emotionally difficult to confront. Building connections to the "real world" similarly seems essential in a course that deals with issues as relevant to current political debates as race and ethnic relations are.

The Importance of a Critical Mass of Minority Students

Race and ethnic relations courses that draw from the principles of learning communities provide an important alternative to traditional pedagogy, but another challenge remains for most faculty and students in these courses: the lack of racial and ethnic diversity all too common on college campuses. Simply stated, learning communities that lack racial and ethnic diversity will typically not generate the kind of dialogue and dynamics that a critical mass of minority students can bring to these discussions. This critical mass facilitates discussion and furthers several other important goals for many reasons. African American, Latino, and other students of color often report a reluctance to speak on issues of race when they are the only minority students in these classes. For good reason, they fear that they will be seen as the "spokesperson" for all Black students, Latino students, or Asian students. A critical mass of minority students can provide a sense of empowerment to these students in the classroom, and across campus more generally. In addition, those who advocate efforts to promote racial and ethnic diversity on college campuses recognize the benefits that diversity brings to all students, providing opportunities to form relationships that cut across racial and class lines and, in so doing, erode the stereotypes and distrust that often unwittingly divide students on college campuses.[1]

Moving from Theory to Practice in a Race and Ethnic Relations Course

The Race and Ethnic Relations class in which we participated in fall 2003 at Wake Forest University built on both the principles of learning communities as well as a critical mass of minority students. In some ways, Wake Forest, like other selective liberal arts colleges, is uniquely situated to bring a learning communities model to the classroom. Classes are typically small, seminar style, discussion is encouraged, and increasingly, service learning initiatives are supported financially and otherwise. While advantaged in these ways, many liberal arts colleges remain predominantly White, lacking the racial and ethnic diversity essential to fully capitalize on the potentially important opportunities a learning communities model would provide in this context. Wake Forest, unfortunately, is no exception. Minority enrollments typically hover around 10 percent of the larger student body, with only 7 percent accounted for by African American students. For a number of reasons, however, our course drew an exceptional mix of students. The department had capped the course at twenty; to my delight, this group included seven African American men and one African American woman, one Latina, and four White women and five White men. Armed with this diversity and the principles of a learning community, we began a conversation our first night that remained dynamic, constructive, and interesting throughout the semester. Below, we explore how the pedagogical strategies we drew from a learning communities model, coupled with the racial and ethnic diversity of our class, contributed to this conversation.

Initiating the dialogue

The content of our course, in many ways, was not unique. Consistent with many leading texts in this area, our academic and intellectual work as a class was organized to provide a historical perspective on race and ethnic relations in the United States, while we considered current debates related to each chapter in this history (see Feagin and Feagin, 2003). Our analysis began with a discussion of the social construction of race, racial identities, and identity politics. We, in turn, moved into the history of colonization and conquest, the industrial revolution and the Jim Crow Era, focusing on the links between racial stratification, economics, and education. We continued a focus on economy and education through the civil rights and post–civil-rights era, touching on such problems as urban education, residential segregation, and the urban underclass.

While similar in content to other race and ethnic relations courses, our class worked from the beginning to deliberately put into practice the principles of learning communities. With this in mind, we devoted our first class session to an explicit discussion of these principles, emphasizing the collective nature of our enterprise. I made clear that I brought a certain expertise to our endeavor, but that the syllabus was a "living document" that should reflect the particular interests and concerns of our class. The students were then invited to introduce themselves and talk about the interests and expectations they brought to the class.

This discussion gave way to a discussion that is widely recommended by feminist scholars and others in all courses that deal with "controversial" issues, namely, a discussion about the broader set of rules that should guide our conversation in these classes (Maher and Tetreault, 1994). In most cases, faculty must deliberately organize students into small groups to initiate this discussion. In our class, this issue was raised by students themselves when sharing their expectations. More specifically, one of the African American men in our class emphatically stated, "I would hope that all of us are willing to openly share our opinions—both our informed and uninformed opinions"—and added that he would rather hear all opinions, even those with which he disagreed, than be faced with trepidation and silence. This statement provided the "permission" needed to push us beyond the reservations we all carried into the class. As Branden Coté, one of the students who wrote for this chapter, noted: "Students need to feel comfortable expressing their thoughts, feelings, and opinions on issues without fear of being criticized and looked down upon. It is only through fully open discussion that any progress can be made." We agreed that this discussion, as much as possible, should be guided by a commitment to "civil discourse," but we also agreed that the realities of racism might generate feelings of anger and frustration that we should feel free to share. In this vein, I emphasized that we might leave some class sessions feeling bothered, and students should feel free to stop by my office to chat and/or send me an e-mail.

This conversation represented an important first step toward making our class a safe space for an open and critical discussion of race in American life. To sustain this conversation, however, we would need to work deliberately to foster a more solid sense of trust and collegiality. To this end, we built on several strategies to forge connections among students and faculty that are the cornerstone of learning communities. In a race relations course, these strategies seem to be the key to unlocking a conversation that depends on a level of trust and collegiality not typically pursued in other courses.

Building trust/building community

Our efforts to build the collegiality and trust which would form the foundation of our learning community began with a dinner organized during the first few weeks of the semester. This dinner, importantly, was paired with attendance at a campus event that addressed issues relevant to our course. Consistent with the learning communities model, the campus event that we attended was one identified collectively by our class. Specifically, several students asked if we could attend a forum that drew together a panel of African American students representing the "Noble Nine"—that is, all nine historically Black fraternities and sororities. The dinner provided an excellent opportunity for students to talk with classmates whom they did not know and, most importantly, cross class and racial lines in these conversations. The forum proved lively and provocative, drawing our class into an interesting exchange between panelists and the audience. Our next class session opened with a discussion of the panel, which provided an opportunity for our class to explore further a theme central to my own emphasis in race and ethnic relations courses: namely, the way that the experience of students of color on predominantly White campuses differs from that of majority students. As importantly, we discussed the value of sharing a meal and taking the time to discuss "nonacademic" as well as academic issues in order to foster an open dialogue about race. We shared several other meals during this semester, pairing these with campus and community events related to our course. Branden's reflections on this as a strategy for building community echoed the sentiments of others.

Branden: Our dinners greatly promoted intraclass relations and raised the students' comfort level with each other. Eating with my peers provided me the opportunity to converse and befriend many students whom I probably would not have talked to otherwise simply because our paths did not cross outside of class. After each of our dinners, I felt more and more comfortable speaking out, particularly with respect to ideas that I knew would not be as strongly supported.

Ana-María: Our comfort level in class was further cultivated by two other strategies that brought us together outside of class. On the one hand, I organized several small group sessions at a local coffeehouse to discuss with three or four students a set of research projects each of us was undertaking. We used these sessions to explore further the intellectual ideas covered in class but, perhaps more importantly, we explored a set of issues that were identified by students themselves as central to their interests in race and ethnic relations. These interests were broad, including issues such as curriculum tracking, hate groups, immigration, identity politics, urban education, and school reform. By using small group sessions to discuss these interests, we fostered a sense of community on two levels. First, our sessions provided us a sense that we really were a community of scholars working together to uncover the forms of racism that persist today. Second, our sessions gave us the sense that we were also a community of "allies" collectively engaged in antiracist praxis.

In addition, I also held one-on-one sessions with many students. In some cases, these sessions were particularly important to work through a set of personal struggles and histories tied to the ways that we live race in American society. Christina and Hattie were among those for whom these sessions provided this sort of opportunity. As an African American woman, Hattie had encountered several forms of both subtle and overt racism that many Black students face in their interactions with staff, faculty, and students on predominantly White campuses. Our course was pushing her to rethink these experiences as well as her academic interests; we used our one-on-one sessions to discuss these experiences and, as much as possible, make sense of these experiences by drawing from the work we were covering in our course.

Hattie: In many ways, my experience at Wake has felt much like a boxing match, as each year seemed like another round in a struggle against a "Whiteness" which I don't think I really expected. Freshman year delivered the wake-up call. My dorm hall consisted of three Black students out of twenty-seven. It soon became clear that many of my White hallmates carried a set of stereotypes I had not previously thought about carefully. I can remember one hallmate noting one day "you're really clean." Of course, I was clean, I thought. Why would I not be clean? She later said that Black people weren't clean where she came from. These and other such comments and actions I have encountered these past few years made me feel for perhaps the first time in my life as the "outsider within" (Hill Collins, 1986).

I have wanted to document my experiences for a long time. I only needed a little motivation I suppose. This class has provided the opportunity to voice myself and vent on an issue I have obviously held in for quite some time. I was initially skeptical about writing my feelings down. I didn't know how my experiences would be received. But then I decided, what harm could there be in simply speaking the truth?

Ana-María: For Christina, the struggle we explored in our conversations outside of class reflects, in a sense, the other side of a "racialized" society.

Christina: The struggle that I face is the struggle to reconcile my White skin privilege with a growing desire to be identified as much Latina as White. With my blond hair, white skin, and green eyes, I am as far as you can get from appearing to be a minority. As we began to discuss the social construction of race in several classes, I saw that race was, in fact, something defined by society. I also realized that what people saw—my white skin—wasn't a completely accurate reflection of who I was. My mother's side of the family, straight from Puerto Rico, did not shine through in my appearance. My looks were clearly dominated by my father's Danish side. As the semester progressed, I came to realize that I was in fact a Latina, but a Latina afforded the privilege of white skin, which made it almost too easy for me to assimilate into White society.

Ana-María: Through our one-on-one conversations, I encouraged both women to recognize the unique perspective that they each bring to any analysis of race and ethnicity and pushed them to share this perspective with our class as well as the broader campus community.

The trust and collegiality that were fostered through these strategies are absolutely necessary if we hope to push past the apprehension and silence so often encountered in race and ethnic relations courses. More broadly, our experience as a class that was more willing than most to engage in an open and provocative conversation about race in the classroom confirms the pedagogical value of the principles guiding learning communities for these sorts of classes. For good or bad, however, we must recognize that a learning communities model calls for an innovative set of strategies as well as additional resources not required in other courses. Institutions of higher learning genuinely committed to diversity must also make a genuine commitment to reducing class size and provide teachers and students the resources necessary to support the kinds of collaborative work and activities that extend the conversation about race outside the traditional classroom setting. In addition, our course suggests that a renewed commitment to diversity on campus is also essential if the conversation about race is to be "blown wide open" as occurred in our class. Below, we offer our reflections on the way that a critical mass of minority students can transform a race and ethnic relations course.

Why a critical mass matters

Few other classes on this predominantly White campus are as racially balanced as was our race and ethnic relations course. Our experience in this class literally brought to life the reasons that diversity is so important on a college campus. We all walked away from this class with a renewed commitment to boosting racial and ethnic diversity at those institutions that remain predominantly White, given the many intellectual and social "payoffs" we observed.

Christina: Our class really did confirm one of the claims most often made in favor of greater racial and ethnic diversity on college campuses: The more diverse a class in terms of race, the easier it is to get broader perspectives and develop a fuller understanding of the ways individuals of different racial and ethnic backgrounds differ in their lived experience and, in turn, their intellectual and political perspectives. The importance of this diversity in opening and fueling a dynamic discussion was particularly evident to those of us enrolled in predominantly White classes that dealt with similar issues. I was taking several courses that focused on issues of race and ethnicity in spring 2003. This was the only class, however, that included more than one or two students of color. Discussion in our race and ethnic relations class came much easier than discussion in these other classes which were predominantly White and female.

Hattie: If the discussion was more dynamic in our course, I think this reflects the simple fact that students of color do not have the luxury of leaving discussions about race and ethnic relations at an abstract, intellectual level. As minority students, we face the realities of discrimination almost daily. For every subject we discussed, I could see a direct relation to a reality with which I had direct personal experience. A discussion of curriculum tracking that explores the class and racial biases embedded in this system reflects my own experience with teachers that doubted my aspirations and ability. A discussion of affirmative action that explores the negative stereotypes that students of color at selective universities face reflects my own encounters with such stereotypes and the need to justify our existence at these institutions. All African American students as well as other minority students have directly encountered—or indirectly encountered through family and friends—the realities of racial profiling, housing discrimination, educational inequalities, and negative stereotypes. Given this, it is impossible not to see our own experience and history reflected in the research and readings that formed the core of our course. If provided a safe space, we feel compelled to articulate these experiences as a way to make the intellectual and academic real.

Ana-María: European American students in our class similarly recognized the value of diversity in pushing the discussion of race and ethnic relations from an abstract intellectual plane to the real world.

Branden: The racial composition of a seminar class can make or break the educational value of the course. If certain ethnic and racial groups are not represented, the experiences of those groups become abstract, primarily in relation to current events. Our class was very fortunate to have a good mix of White and Black students. The experiences that African American students shared about the many forms of racism and discrimination they have encountered provided a real wake-up call for many of us. True understanding comes from experience—and our efforts to connect as much as possible with these experiences. Just as one can study all the available information concerning a particular event in history and never reach the same level of understanding as someone who has lived through the event, we can study all the relevant theories and issues concerning race and ethnic relations but will never have the understanding of someone who has seen or experienced racism firsthand. If we hope to make these experiences real in a race and ethnic relations course, these classes must include students of color willing to share these experiences.

Ana-María: The ways that the voices of African American students facilitated a conversation about the "color line" in American life, I think, is perhaps most clearly reflected in a contrast that became clearer as the semester unfolded. During class sessions that focused on "Black-White" relations, there was a lot of back-and-forth dialogue; however, when we turned to consider the experiences of Latino, Asian American, and other minorities, less discussion occurred. Importantly, our class did not include any students who could be visibly identified as members of these other groups.

The importance of a "good mix" of African American and White students invites more open dialogue for several other reasons as well. The racial and ethnic composition of our class worked against the tendency to treat students of color as "ambassadors" for their group. If there are only one or two minority students, European American students tend to forget that these individuals are, in fact, individuals and not spokespeople for their race. In many classes, White students mistakenly assume that the opinions of a particular minority student represent the opinion of all minority students. In our class, African American students perhaps spoke more freely because they did not have to worry as much that they would be seen as spokespersons for their group. This fear was further eased by discussions that made apparent the diversity of opinions on many issues expressed by African American students in our class. For example, our discussion of reparations for slavery elicited several distinct perspectives, not easily reduced to race. This diversity of opinion encourages a more complex understanding of each person's perspective and opens the dialogue further.

At the same time, these conversations suggested an additional set of goals and pedagogical strategies that must be made central to this course. Most importantly, students made clear that they wanted not only to "talk" about race but also to confront this history "in person" in ways that more fully brought to life the issues we were discussing in the classroom and connected us to local and national efforts to challenge racism. Our course incorporated several opportunities to move beyond talk to "see and touch" the history and realities of racism with these goals in mind.

Taking it to the streets

Service learning projects in many ways represent the most effective pedagogical strategy for providing our students this opportunity—and represent a core component of many learning communities (Gabelnick, MacGregor, Matthews, and Smith, 1990; Marullo, 1998). Since this was my first semester at Wake Forest, I did not have the community connections necessary to effectively incorporate this component. I did, however, include two other activities that literally and figuratively took my class into the "real world" of race relations and laid a foundation for pursuing work in this area through service learning as well as undergraduate research.

Our visit to the Civil Rights Museum in Greensboro, North Carolina, was the first of these ventures into the "real world." From my perspective as a newcomer to this state and the South, North Carolina history was memorable because it included one of the most important chapters in the history of the civil rights movement. Images of the "Greensboro four" who had staged the Woolworth lunch counter sit-ins are images etched in my mind and images that I have shared with students in every course that covers the civil rights movement. In planning this course, I made sure that this class would have an opportunity to see that history in person by reserving one week for a "road trip" to Greensboro. My discovery that none of my students, including five who were from North Carolina, had visited this museum further confirmed the importance of making this trip. Midway through the semester, then, we loaded into a van and made the trek.

Our visit to the Civil Rights Museum provided several intellectual, political, and personal lessons no classroom discussion could provide as effectively. For all of us, the opportunity to sit at a counter where students—

freshmen no less—in many ways like us, sat to bring down segregation was amazing on many levels. Hattie articulates the deep educational and personal significance of the visit for her as an African American woman from North Carolina in this way:

Hattie: Our visit was valuable not only because we had the opportunity to set foot on the actual site of great historic significance but perhaps more importantly because the museum turned on its head the typical representation of this history in text and film. The museum made clear that the sit-ins were an enormous grassroots effort, lead by four courageous young college students, rather than the work of the few national leaders of the civil rights movement most Americans recognize—and the work of these young men and their many allies deserves as much recognition. In addition, the museum highlights the leadership and contributions of "ordinary" African Americans especially, in contrast to many texts and films that emphasize the work of White allies without giving due credit to the grassroots efforts of the Black community. Not to sound ignorant, but no matter how much Whites contributed to the success of the movement, it seems to me that it is the African Americans who initiated and led these efforts who should be paid particular homage. There's just something sacred about Blacks making the difference in the civil rights movement.

Ana-María: Keenon extends this insight to underscore the broader importance of taking the learning experience beyond the classroom when the issue is race.

Keenon: The decision to restrict teaching to the inside of the classroom limits the learning opportunities and possibilities for students. Courses like this need to integrate, as much as possible, firsthand exposure to the experiences of African Americans and other minorities. This is particularly important given the continued failure of many school districts and texts to adequately cover the multiracial/multiethnic history of our country—and the exclusion and discrimination people of color have faced.

Moving forward and bringing it home

The many lessons we drew from our visit to the Civil Rights Museum are testament to the multiple reasons it is important to preserve this history and, if possible, take our classes to see and touch this history. In doing so, we celebrate the most important victories in our struggle against racism. At the same time, it is also important to directly confront as much as possible the challenges and inequities that persist in the post–civil-rights era. To this end, we followed our visit to the Civil Rights Museum with a section that focused on the persistence of segregation across two places we call "home": our neighborhoods and our campus.

To help us "see" this segregation, I have developed an exercise that draws from an outstanding set of resources provided by the Census Bureau. This exercise allows us to map patterns of residential segregation by race and ethnicity for each of our respective "hometowns," including the city in which our campus is located. Specifically, we created maps that highlight the neighborhoods in which African Americans, Latinos, Asian Americans, and Whites are concentrated. In addition, we were able to "zoom in" to examine the racial and ethnic composition of the particular census tracts in which we grew up.

Without exception, the maps revealed the persistence of residential segregation in the cities we examined and generated a provocative and, at times, difficult conversation about the way these realities have shaped our lives. Christina's reflections are typical of the realizations prompted by this exercise.

Christina: The maps I generated really brought home the extreme divide that remains between Anglo-Americans and people of color—and the way this divide has played out in my own life. My hometown, Chester, New Jersey, defines White suburbia. I can't think of a single person on my block that is of minority descent. With only a few exceptions, I was never really exposed to any interactions that cut across race or class lines. All of the people in my church, all of the people that I played sports with, all of the people in my neighborhood were White. This struck me as particularly interesting given that Northerners so often condemn the South for its history of racism, but when we acknowledge the patterns of segregation that cut across the North, you have to wonder.

Ana-María: The maps generated by other Euro-American students similarly forced us to confront a reality that we typically fail to acknowledge: Most White students have been raised in neighborhoods that are overwhelmingly White, affording few meaningful interactions with people of color.

These maps also clarified the diversity of "lived experiences" that African American students bring to predominantly White campuses. Some African American students in our class had grown up in predominantly Black neighborhoods while others had been raised in predominantly White neighborhoods and attended predominantly White schools. This diversity took our conversation in several important directions. On the one hand, students coming from predominantly Black neighborhoods could challenge the stereotypes that have historically fueled residential segregation. On the other hand, Black students coming from predominantly White neighborhoods could speak to the reasons that their parents may have opted for these neighborhoods, the factors that facilitated these moves, and the challenges that they faced.

For all of us, this exercise provided an opportunity to see what C. Wright Mills calls the connection between "history" and "biography," a connection that is too often abstract. We were provided a chance to recognize that residential segregation—a set of historical realities into which we are born—has powerfully shaped our lives, often in ways that run counter to our commitment to integration and multiculturalism. Acknowledging this, hopefully, pushes us to think about the political work that remains for anyone committed to the vision of a better future, which drew us into this course.

As we ended the semester, we worked to bring these lessons "home" by reflecting on the way that these dynamics play out at Wake. This is perhaps a conversation we should have initiated at the beginning of the semester since so many of us entered the class with, first and foremost, a desire to cross racial and ethnic lines on our campus, which remains highly segregated in many ways. This segregation is perhaps most apparent in the racial hierarchies that are tied to the occupational structure at Wake. Most food service workers are African American or Latino, while most administrative support staff, faculty, and top-level administrators are White. Reflecting on this segregation, our class also admitted that many forms of segregation cut across the student body, as is common on many predominantly White campuses. Some saw this segregation as problematic and were disappointed that our course had not done more to foster new relationships that cut across racial lines. They noted that the friendships that were evident in our class reflected the same racial divide that is evident across campus. The course may have brought African American and White students together for an important conversation about race, but new friendships that cut across these lines were not as easily fostered as they had hoped. Several African American students, however, were able to put this reality into a context that hopefully provides both understanding and perspective as we consider the work that remains on our campus and beyond.

Hattie: Most of the African American students who were enrolled in this class were friends before entering this course. The friendships that students of color bring into our class reflect the community that we must forge to survive a predominantly White campus. This is a difficult reality for majority students to appreciate, and we must work harder to push majority students to, if nothing else, symbolically wear the shoes of a minority student. This is not easily done in the classroom. However, we need to, at minimum, discuss these realities, and the race and ethnic relations class provides a forum for doing so, if we are willing to confront highly sensitive topics and struggle through a conversation that is likely to be uncomfortable. We cannot undo all the forms of segregation that occur on our campus in a semester, but we can begin the process and commit ourselves to continuing this work after the semester ends.

Ana-María: This conversation left us with three lessons that I hoped we would take with us as the semester ended. First, much work remains. Second, the skills and perspectives gained from our conversation prepare each of us to make a unique contribution to this work. Finally, we can each pursue a wide range of opportunities available across campus and our community to put these skills to work and remain involved in the broader conversation that we all joined when we enrolled in this course.

CONCLUSION

Race and ethnic relations courses are necessarily challenging for students and faculty alike, forcing us to confront a set of realities that can generate anger, guilt, denial, and other emotions not commonly encountered in other classes. While inherently challenging, my experience teaching this course at Wake Forest suggests several strategies and resources that can facilitate a constructive conversation about race, one which is not weighed down by the hostility and resistance we often face in these classes. On the one hand, the principles that guide learning communities seem to be particularly relevant to this course. Consistent with these principles, three sets of strategies seem to effectively generate and sustain a constructive dialogue: first, strategies that foster trust, connections, and community among students and faculty; second, strategies that provide students the opportunity to shape the agenda; and third, exercises that bring the "real world" into our classes and, conversely, take our students figuratively and literally to "see" the realities of racial inequality and resistance.

The effectiveness of our race and ethnic relations course did not rest only on pedagogy but on two other strengths that distinguished my class. First, the critical mass of minority students who enrolled in this course contributed a dynamic to our dialogue we simply could not achieve in their absence. Second, the group of White students who had chosen this class as an elective rather than to meet a cultural diversity requirement were particularly open to this dialogue and the analysis of "White privilege" as well as other realities embedded in our history of oppression.

If our experience as a class is to provide useful lessons to faculty across a wide range of campuses, we must acknowledge a set of institutional constraints and realities many face. For some, budget constraints pose the key challenge as learning communities call for a commitment to small seminar-style introductory-level classes. At large universities, smaller classes are often labeled less "cost effective" than mass lectures. Even so, some state universities have successfully implemented a learning communities program for incoming freshmen. For others, the attack on Affirmative Action poses the key challenge. Michigan, Berkeley, and other such universities long committed to recruiting a critical mass of minority students have been pushed to abandon those measures. At Berkeley as well as several other institutions, the result has been a dramatic drop in minority enrollments. In the face of these political assaults, universities must renew their commitment to recruiting and retaining students of color. For Keenon, administration plays a critical role in this effort: "Students, no matter how concerned about race-related issues, lack the power to single-handedly bring about lasting change in a whole set of policies and practices that could boost minority enrollments and transform our campuses. Such a transformation necessarily calls for administration to take a leadership role." Without a critical mass of minority students, conversations about race, diversity, and multiculturalism will simply fall short even as cultural diversity requirements become more common.

Faced with these institutional constraints, innovation also becomes increasingly necessary. In short, cultural diversity requirements may be even more pressing in this climate but must be coupled with several strategies suggested by our experience. Strategies that engage students with each other and the community are essential. At some schools, faculty have successfully created small-scale learning communities within the larger classes. Similarly, some faculty have successfully coordinated service learning projects in larger classes. Both depend on institutional support. At the University of Nebraska, for example, students in some intro-level courses are linked through residential learning communities. At the University of North Carolina, a campuswide "service learning center" provides the administrative support necessary to link students to projects and monitor their work. Both represent a serious effort to rethink the way we "deliver the goods" at universities across the country. Race and ethnic relations courses, perhaps more than any other courses, push us to rethink the way we teach at the same time that we renew our commitment to the liberal arts tradition with its emphasis on critical inquiry and civil discourse.

NOTE

1. The University of Michigan's defense of Affirmative Action before the U.S. Supreme Court offers perhaps the most comprehensive statement of the many ways that diversity contributes to the educational goals of any college. Central to these arguments is a long list of scholarly contributions, including Bowen, Bok, and Steele. The evidence and arguments offered in this case are available through www.umich.edu.

REFERENCES

Bowen, W. G., and D. C. Bok. (1998). *The shape of the river: Long-term consequences of considering race in college and university admissions.* Princeton, N.J.: Princeton University Press, 1998.

Feagin, J. R., and C. B. Feagin. (2003). *Racial and ethnic relations.* Upper Saddle River, NJ: Prentice Hall.

Gabelnick, F., J. MacGregor, R. S. Matthews, and B. L. Smith. (1990). *Learning communities: Creating connections among students, faculty, and disciplines.* San Francisco: Jossey-Bass.

Hill Collins, P. (1986). *Black feminist thought.* New York: Routledge, 2000.

Maher, F. A.,, and M. K. Thompson Tetreault. (1994). *The feminist classroom: An inside look at how professors and students are transforming higher education for a diverse society.* New York: Basic Books.

Marullo, S. (1998). Bringing home diversity: A service learning approach to teaching race and ethnic relations. *Teaching Sociology, 26,* 259–275.

Omi, M.,, and H. Winant. (1986). *Racial formation in the United States: From the 1960s to the 1980s.* New York: Routledge & Kegan Paul.

Steele, C. M. (1997). A Threat in the air: How stereotypes shape intellectual identity and performance. *American Psychologist, 52,* 613–621.

Wahl, A. M., E. T. Perez, M. J. Deegan, T. W. Sanchez, and C. Applegate. (2000). The controversial classroom: Institutional resources and pedagogical strategies for a race relations course. *Teaching Sociology, 28,* 316–332.

CHAPTER FOUR

Making Race Matter on Campus
Teaching and Learning about Race in the
"Whitest State in the Union"

Jarl Ahlkvist, *University of Denver*
Peter Spitzform, *University of Vermont*
Emily Jones, *Simmons College*
Megan Reynolds, *University of Massachusetts at Boston*

It's time for aware White people to help, encourage, support,
and even persuade unaware Whites to raise their consciousness
about a reality different from their own. (Ferber, 2002, p. 166)

INTRODUCTION

As members of a campus community in rural Vermont during the 1990s, in most instances where race, racism, or multiculturalism came up in conversation, we could count on someone reminding us that we lived in "The Whitest State in the Union." This phrase says a lot. Yes, Vermont is a very "White state" in a numerical sense according to the Census, but this description of our state was also a coded way of suggesting that "race isn't an issue here—how can it be when we're virtually all White?" This common misconception that race matters only if there is great diversity in a community, state, or country turned out to be pivotal in shaping and sometimes blocking our efforts to make race a relevant issue at Johnson State College (JSC), a small liberal arts college in northern Vermont. It was indeed difficult for many students, staff, and faculty on campus to understand why White folks like us would want to draw attention to racial differences and inequities not readily apparent at the college. But as Mark Chesler recently put it, "A lack of diversity, however dismal on its own terms, does not relieve us of the responsibility to raise and pursue issues of multiculturalism" (2002, p. 47).

In this chapter, we reflect on our efforts to make race matter on our campus, based on our experiences at the time and our current vantage points. While our formal roles at the college differed, we shared a general belief that the "Whiteness" of our state, which was reflected in our campus population, hardly made race a "nonissue." In fact, as we hope to illustrate in this chapter, the lack of racial diversity on campus posed unique and thorny problems for those of us who believed that promoting multiculturalism and addressing racism were vital aspects of a liberal arts education, even in the Whitest state in the union.

There are many things we could discuss regarding our efforts to teach and learn about race during our collective tenure at JSC. We have decided to focus on how we used media and outside experts in an effort to make race and multiculturalism worthy of consideration by students as more than an academic exercise or feel-good celebration of abstract diversity. We have chosen this focus for our chapter because so much of our energy and time at JSC went into simply bringing the experiences and perspectives of people of color to the attention of White students.

Because many JSC students had little direct experience interacting with or living in even minimally integrated communities (this was especially true of students who grew up in rural Vermont), it was vital for us to "import" these "others" onto campus via media representations and expert speakers. Both sources offered an important combination of two aspects essential to teaching about race on a campus where most students viewed the topic as largely irrelevant to their lives and futures. First, they provided the "cold hard facts" and vivid examples of how to conceptualize and analyze tough concepts like racism or institutional discrimination. Second, they illustrated and explained the experiences and viewpoints of people of color in more subjective terms—providing real faces and voices to echo what students may have read in books or heard their (White) instructors say in class. By discussing our experiences using these "outside" sources of information, analysis, and experience, we hope to highlight key challenges to teaching about race in largely Anglocentric and racially homogeneous White environments. Before proceeding to our experiences at JSC, we think it is important to describe the college community we were a part of and introduce ourselves to give the reader some context for what follows.

THE CAMPUS AND THE AUTHORS

Situated in rural Lamoille County in north-central Vermont, Johnson State College is a small, mainly undergraduate institution, with several professional and graduate programs. One could literally count the people of color at the college on two hands. Naturally, as is true the world over, there was much diversity to be experienced in northern Vermont. There was a striking French-Canadian presence (the college is located close to the Quebec border), multigenerational Vermonters lived beside new neighbors (commonly referred to as "flatlanders" by "native" Vermonters) from more suburban or urban places to the south, and wide class differences existed throughout the state. But racial diversity and its accompanying varieties of cultural differences and unequal positioning on social hierarchies were nearly nonexistent on our campus.

Several other characteristics of JSC and its student population are worth noting since they shed light on the prevailing student culture at the college. First, JSC at the time was home to an award-winning and very popular service learning program that offered students a variety of experiential learning opportunities involving helping disadvantaged populations in Vermont and elsewhere. Trips to places like Chicago during spring break exposed students (many for the first time) to racial diversity in the context of material and psychological deprivation via volunteer work. Second, a sizable minority of students at JSC were first-generation college students and many were native Vermonters. Third, many JSC students had grown up in small towns and rural communities in Vermont and elsewhere in New England. Finally, the student culture at JSC was generally culturally progressive—manifested in myriad ways including following "jam bands," liberal attitudes toward drug use, libertarianism, and openness toward diverse sexualities. While hardly homogeneous, we think it is fair to describe the student culture at JSC in the 1990s as infused with a countercultural sensibility.

Jarl Ahlkvist: My tenure as a sociology professor at JSC spanned most of the 1990s. I taught a race and ethnic relations course virtually every year. My experiences teaching a sociology course devoted solely to race and ethnicity were decidedly mixed, and rather than expanding my course offerings in this area, I channeled my time and energy into efforts outside the classroom primarily through cochairing (with Peter Spitzform) the campus Diversity Committee and advising the student Behavioral Sciences Club. I think it is fair to say that my interest and passion for teaching about race and multiculturalism didn't germinate until I found myself teaching this topic in rural Vermont. In fact, I had virtually no prior training or real interest in this area of sociology prior to joining the JSC faculty, having focused on class as the key dimension of difference and inequality in graduate school. As a middle-class White guy who came of age in the Reagan era, I clearly had a lot to learn when it came to teaching about controversial topics like race. Over the years, however, I found that my basic perspective on inequality and injustice (which germinated in graduate school) was a decent fit with what those who had (by choice or necessity) expertise on race and ethnicity had to teach me. While I focus on my race relations class in this chapter, I should note that I integrated race and multiculturalism into most of the courses I taught at JSC, including Introductory Sociology and classes on social theory and media culture.

Peter Spitzform: I grew up in a suburban town on Long Island whose school district was about as integrated as any in the nation—roughly 50:50 Black and White. While it wouldn't be accurate to say that there was a great deal of social integration, people were definitely mixed together, particularly in sports and music programs. To me it was simply the nature of school to live in a climate where race was both front-and-center, and virtually ignored, simultaneously. Uprisings broke out when Martin Luther King Jr. was assassinated. A number of students in the high school were affiliated with the Black Panthers or were attracted to them, and there was even a period of intra-Black conflict, where class tensions were thick between kids who lived on the working-class North Side and those from the more affluent South Side. Despite this visibility of race as a social dividing line, I can't think of a single instance when a teacher broached the subject of race in a classroom. We were never introduced to any kind of dialogue about racism or the dynamics of race in American society, or even about how our experiences in the world might differ. Not surprisingly, I hadn't thought once about diversity when I made out my applications for college and I ended up attending a largely White institution. During college I spent a semester in a Chicago Urban Studies program where the predominant focus was on social and economic injustice in which race was obviously a key issue. Following college, I spent over a decade living in Boston and the Bay Area before becoming the public services librarian at JSC.

Emily Jones: As a sociology and anthropology major at JSC I thought I was starting to understand this thing called race. But once I left Vermont after graduation, I realized how naive I truly was. I grew up in a small town in Vermont where racial diversity was almost nonexistent. After college, and moving to Nashville, I saw an ad in the paper looking for people to join a race issues "think tank." I answered the ad, feeling confident that I would be able to add productively to the group. Upon introducing ourselves at the first meeting of the think tank, I remember saying something about the fact that I was a TA for a class on race in college. One of the group members then began calling me "Doc" since he said I was an expert. Participating in this multiracial group was unlike anything I had experienced in college, and I quickly discovered I didn't have a clue about "race relations" and begged him to stop calling me "Doc." The group was a wonderful way to really delve into the issues of race in a safe space where we could exchange stories based on our diverse backgrounds and experiences— something that was difficult to do on the racially homogenous JSC campus. I will never forget the story told by an African American group member about how when he was young he was walking down the street and a guy drove up in a pickup truck, rolled the window down, and pointed a gun at him. The driver drove alongside him as he walked and eventually rolled the window back up and drove off.

Megan Reynolds: My education about race has been an extended lesson in hubris and humility. I grew up on the North Shore of Boston. It was a relatively heterogeneous area, although I don't really think I was aware of that until I moved to New Hampshire with my family at the age of ten and noticed how few people looked different from me. I remember kids making jokes about people who didn't look like the rest of us. There were only two African American kids at my school. They were twins and the grandparents who raised them were my parents' close friends. I spent weekends at their house and regarded them as two of my best friends. I noticed people shying away from them and couldn't tell if it was because they were quiet or because they were Black. This new reality made me think a lot more about race. I remember at thirteen writing essays in my bedroom on "Black-on-Black violence" to kill the time and defending the rioters to my White friends in the wake of the Rodney King verdict.

I maintained my interest in race issues over the years, so it was natural that, when I began my college education at Johnson State College, I enrolled in Jarl's race and ethnic relations course. In that context I found myself feeling superior in some ways to my classmates. I was well aware that, as a White person in rural New England, race was an issue that one could more or less choose to confront or ignore. It seemed to me that I was one of only a few White students who elected to address race as an issue relevant to us in class and worthy of our attention as a college community.

I am currently a graduate student on the University of Massachusetts' Boston Harbor campus. In this diverse educational environment I often hesitate to express my thoughts about race for fear I might offend someone of color. I question whether my good intentions and "book learning" have sufficiently prepared me to address race. I suppose it is much easier for White people like me to feel ahead of the curve in thinking about race when few people of color are around to humble you. Here, I realize vividly that I am still grappling with race, like most sympathetic Whites.

THE LIMITED POSSIBILITIES OF CLASSROOM TEACHING ABOUT RACE AT JSC

An Anecdote from Peter: "Racism Is Dumb"

Having been involved with diversity issues on campus for a few years, I was asked by a faculty member to speak to her first-year class about some ideas pertaining to race and privilege. I asked the students to read Peggy McIntosh's (1995) "White Privilege and Male Privilege" article to prepare them for class discussion. When I tried to initiate a class conversation about race using the article as a starting point, I hit a wall. "It's stupid," was the predominant opinion voiced by the students. "Judging somebody on the basis of their skin color is stupid." I tried a variety of approaches to help the students grapple with the ongoing problems of race in America, but was met with puzzlement or statements that matter-of-factly dismissed racism as a dumb idea—something only ignorant people were guilty of in this day and age. Through this experience with a class comprised primarily of White students from rural Vermont, I came to understand that these folks had virtually no experience living among people of color and consequently had virtually no idea what McIntosh or I were talking about. The idea that Whites can move through society never experiencing the kind of prejudice a person of color might confront daily was completely foreign to them because of their lived experiences.

Jarl's Reflections on Teaching Race and Ethnic Relations

During my first semester at the college I was assigned to teach a course about "minority groups." Having never taught a course on this topic before, I bumbled through with a standard issue textbook on race and ethnic groups. To my surprise, the course evaluations were very positive with most students indicating that they found the material interesting and relevant. This was in direct contrast to my own perception that the course had largely skirted the important issues and provided mostly a superficial guided tour of "the minority group of the week" rather than a critical sociological investigation of the *relations* between "majority" and "minority." This was the last time I received such high praise from students in this course.

I proceeded to formally change the course title to "race and ethnic relations" and set about redirecting my teaching on this topic toward addressing these "relations" as often problematic for all parties concerned. This shift in direction was accompanied with what I now know is almost inevitable resistance from many White students who preferred the less challenging approach I had initially used. Many of my White students, it seemed, were perfectly happy learning about the U.S. civil rights movement or social-psychological theories of prejudice, because, while perhaps interesting, these were perceived as largely irrelevant to them. After all, they were not responsible for the sins of ignorant White Southerners or previous generations' prejudices, and being more enlightened than their parents and grandparents, they naturally treated everyone the same regardless of skin color. Their enthusiasm waned considerably when I began using a more "relational" approach in which the focus was not simply on "them" (as in "minority groups"), but on race as an issue that implicates even those (Whites) who don't think of themselves as even having a racial identity. When asked to delve into concepts like White privilege and modern racism in a contemporary context and to reflect on these at a more personal level, the predictable pattern of resistance and defensiveness ensued—most students simply did not see the point of "going there" and much of the semester would involve me making futile arguments as to why it was important for us all to do so.

As a sociologist who specializes in media studies, use of music, films, TV, or novels in the race relations class was a given. In this context, however, the primary function of media was to "import" a multiplicity of racial experiences and perspectives into the classroom since those were not readily available among the participants in the class itself. Unfortunately, the impact of many media forms and techniques recommended by colleagues teaching about the sociology of race relations in more diverse contexts fell short in my class. For example, I routinely used the video *True Colors* (1991), which depicts the very different experiences of a Black and a White discrimination tester in St. Louis. Students reacted by condemning the "racist" behaviors of Whites in the film who discriminated against the Black tester, but went on to explain that this was alien behavior to them since "race isn't an issue here." This pattern was repeated with virtually every "imported" depiction of race-related issues that I tried in this class—including Studs Terkel's *Race* (1992), T. C. O'Boyle's *Tortilla Curtain* (1995), Hollywood films like *Mississippi Burning* (1989) and *Do the Right Thing* (1990), and the *Eyes on the Prize* (1993) documentary series. Students didn't resist or challenge me in the way often depicted in the literature on teaching about race. For example, unlike the students in McKinney's (2002) race relations courses at the rural and predominantly White Pennsylvania State University, White students in my classes rarely denied that racism was a major issue or viewed themselves as victims of "reverse discrimination." My students tended to see these as legitimate problems for *other people*, in other places—particularly in situations where there was more racial diversity (such as those depicted in the media texts used in class). It was only when I encouraged them to turn the sociological microscope on White people like themselves that students became resistant and apathetic.

The struggle I experienced each semester when I tried to teach students about race in the classroom eventually brought the realization that work was needed at a broader level if there was any hope of having more than a handful of students ready and willing to study race in a sociologically sophisticated and relational way. It became increasingly clear to me that something had to be done to alter the dominant campus culture, which offered few opportunities for students (or others) to question the assumption that White people in a White state really didn't need to worry too much about people of color's experiences or the advantages of Whiteness. This conviction was reinforced by several instances of hate speech directed against Japanese students on campus, which many students dismissed as reflecting personal disputes rather than racism.

Emily's Perspective on the Race and Ethnic Relations Course

During my sophomore year in college I was a student in Jarl's Minority Groups class. In reading Ronald Takaki's book *A Different Mirror* (1993), I learned a history different from the one I'd studied in high school and it gave me a new awareness of how biased the writers of history can be. Several students echoed this sentiment in class and wondered why they hadn't previously been taught about the Chinese workers involved in the building of the Transcontinental Railroad, Japanese farmers in California, or the Native American civil rights struggle. Despite some enthusiasm about historical gaps being filled, there seemed to be a lack of discussion in the class. I think people were so concerned about sounding politically correct that they would stay silent or only say things that they knew wouldn't be controversial. The sole person of color in the class was an Asian American woman who grew up in Vermont. One day she told the class about some of the racism that she had experienced in Vermont, like getting comments from people that she spoke English remarkably well. This prompted some other students to tell stories about their own experiences of being stereotyped as women, blondes, and hippies. However, when challenged to think about stereotypes about people of color in relation to "White privilege," the conversation shut down. When Judith Levine visited our class to discuss "White Like Me," an article on White privilege she'd published in *Ms. Magazine* (1994), the majority of students seemed uncomfortable and felt that by talking about this issue she was actually engaging in stereotyping herself. Students seemed very self-conscious and worried about being perceived as prejudiced. After all, if this writer on race issues came off this way, the safest strategy was to stay quiet.

Two years later Jarl invited me to be the teaching assistant for his re-named race and ethnic relations class. More than just the class title had changed since I had taken the course. We still looked at race through the lens of sociology, but we spent less time studying the history and culture of different racial and ethnic groups, focusing more on inequalities between racial groups. Because of my experience as a student in the Minority Groups class, I wanted to try to find a way that worked for people to talk about race in an honest way without feeling like they had to be entirely politically correct. I had taken a sociology class on sexuality in which we wrote anonymous reaction papers, so I suggested to Jarl that we try this approach in our class. Unfortunately, the papers didn't work as well as I thought they would. Instead of using them as an opportunity to truly stretch their thinking and perhaps write about things that they weren't quite comfortable saying out loud, most students wrote about the same things that came up in class, and rarely did I come across a paper that addressed issues in a deeper or more personally reflective way.

Once again, there seemed to be a lack of class discussion in the course. Students rebelled somewhat against the idea that they might be racist—to them racism was mostly a thing of the past. They would talk about how things aren't like they used to be and how people today are more educated so they know that racism is wrong. I also got the sense that students believed that racism isn't as bad in the North as it is in the South. Most of the students were from Vermont and other parts of New England, so their experiences with racial issues seemed to be somewhat limited. It is certainly much easier to come at the topic from a detached perspective, thinking that racism is something that other people perpetrate. That racism happens elsewhere. That racism happened in another time.

The students in this class wanted desperately to not be seen as racist or prejudiced. They thought of themselves as accepting of all races and ethnicities. I suspect some students were thankful that they lived in a time and in a state that didn't require them to deal with racial issues on a daily basis. Race was only an issue for them, if out of the goodness of their hearts or as a mostly academic exercise, they wanted to think about it or work on it. I recently read something in *Making a Difference* (Lesage, Ferber, Storrs, and Wong, 2002) that really hit home. In her introduction to the book, Lesage writes: "As a White person, I can elect when to focus on race and when not to" (p. 5). As White college students on a predominantly White campus in a very White state, we had the option to not think about racial issues if we didn't want to. If we did think about race, then we saw ourselves and were perhaps viewed by others as being more enlightened. It was easy to feel morally superior for thinking about race issues, while simultaneously ignoring our White privilege.

MAKING RACE MATTER BEYOND THE CLASSROOM

Jarl and Peter's Reflections on the Diversity Committee

Given the challenges we confronted in the classroom when teaching about race, we hoped that we could make more of a difference as members of the campus-wide Diversity Committee. For several years we swam upstream in an attempt to move the committee beyond the level of an academic window-dresser; that is, a group that "celebrated" difference, memorialized Martin Luther King Jr. one day a year, and essentially allowed the college to put a check in the box next to "held a multicultural event" on the college's annual to-do list. We worried that the approach the committee was taking may well have been causing more harm than good, in spite of good intentions, and actively pushed for a shift in the committee's orientation.

After the administrator who had chaired the committee for several years left the college, we began our tenure as cochairs of the Diversity Committee. In this role we assumed we could "make a difference" in a way that the committee under its prior leadership and our efforts in classrooms had not. While it has come into focus only in hindsight, our commitment of time and energy to campuswide events to raise awareness about race and multiculturalism stemmed from our assumption that, for most Whites on our campus (including ourselves), a shift from denial of racial inequality to the dawning of consciousness about one's whiteness and its relationship to racism and racial inequality would occur out of a more emotionally charged personal experience than we could provide in a college classroom. Therefore, we sought to provide students with a line-up of events that we hoped would encourage progress along Helms's (1992) stages of White identity development. Looking back we were certainly naive about what our committee could accomplish in this regard, but we did make progress on several fronts. Throughout our time as cochairs we took a more or less three pronged approach. First, we sought to educate ourselves as a committee and to foster self-examination among the members about our own assumptions, biases, and political views regarding race, multiculturalism, and the campus climate. Second, we steered away from the "celebration of diversity" approach in an effort to offer the students speakers, films, and events with a more critical slant—reflective of the approaches we used in class. Third, we collaborated with student organizations and clubs on campus that were also engaged in efforts to integrate discussion and activism regarding race and other dimensions of difference and inequality more seamlessly into the campus culture.

It was in this context of trying to reach the hearts and minds of a nearly all-White campus that we turned to the use of film and guest speakers to help us make inroads, albeit modest ones, toward having a meaningful dialogue on our campus about race. It is crucial to emphasize that for a campus that not only lacked minority students, but was comprised of a majority of students who had little or no former exposure to the complexities of racial issues, it was *only* film and outside speakers that could bring the realities of race to bear in a visceral way which in turn might lead to productive dialogue and reflection. Our hope in taking our teaching on race beyond the classroom was that we could help to create a campus climate where race wasn't only relevant during a particular holiday or class, but was appreciated as a multifaceted issue deserving of continuous attention on a college campus, even one as racially homogenous as ours was.

To illustrate our approach to using film and speakers in campus events open to the public we have chosen to discuss our screening of the documentary *The Color of Fear* (1994), which was accompanied by a discussion led by Victor Lewis, one of the key participants in the film. This event serves as a useful illustration of the typical approach we took to "importing" race issues to our campus. *The Color of Fear* documents the gathering of eight men of Asian, European, Latino, and African descent as they engage in an intense, and intensely felt, conversation and debate about race and racism in America today.

As Boler and Allen (2002) point out, the film deftly unearths some deeply rooted issues surrounding racial identity, racism, and White privilege and the exchange between a Black man (Victor) and David, a White man who could be described as a liberal, well-intentioned, middle-class person, is likely to elicit strong emotions in viewers. The heated exchange between Victor and David made the film especially effective on our campus because it so perfectly drew out issues that our students suppressed in class. David puts voice to ideas that many Whites, particularly those who haven't been exposed to people of color or thinking about multiculturalism, believe and express that mirrored the prevailing response of our students to perspectives like that offered by Peggy McIntosh—in effect, "I'm not a racist, and racism is a dumb idea; why would you judge someone by the color of their skin? Everybody is as good as anyone else; we're all equal." Yet David, who maintains that he is racism-free, turns out to embody the kind of racism that others in the film find deeply dangerous and ubiquitous in our society.

The film brilliantly exposes both the dynamics and the consequences of racism at the interpersonal level, which is certainly an excellent starting point for teaching and learning about race. The aim of *The Color of Fear* is to reveal the complex and insidious ways that racism inhabits the consciousness of individuals, which in turn effects interpersonal relations between people, which leads to loss of trust, which leads to the reinforcement of stereotypes, which increases fear. The cycle continues unbroken, except, as posited by the documentary, for the deliberate interruption by interracial dialogues such as is exemplified in the film. It was particularly powerful for our audience to have the lights go up after the film to find Victor Lewis—the man in the film who confronts David directly and ultimately urges him to a breakdown and breakthrough in terms of his thinking about race—standing at the front of the room. The discussion that followed the film was lively and reflected a willingness to grapple with difficult micro- and macro-level questions about how race operates to name, define, constrain, privilege, and alienate individuals in the United States. The most poignant moment in the discussion, however, was a partial replication of the tense, but ultimately productive exchange between Victor and David in the film. In our forum this exchange took place between Victor and several members of the audience who clearly identified with David— the White liberal in the film.

Megan's Reflections on Guest Speakers on Race

In reflecting upon my experiences as a student organizer of campus events focusing on race issues, I am struck by how audiences responded differently to public presentations by two guest experts, both of whom spoke effectively about race issues. During my second year at JSC, I organized a visit from Dr. Sara Willie, the director of Black studies at Swarthmore College. She eloquently expressed her perspective on racial difference and inequality, drawing on her own experiences as an African American woman and grounded in a scholarly critical framework that examined the broader social forces at play in shaping her own and other's behavior and thinking regarding race. I watched the audience as heads bobbed in agreement, as people laughed at her intermittent humor, gave her a round of applause at the end of the talk, and a few participants asked her to elaborate or clarify points she had made.

The following year I arranged another talk dealing with the topic of privilege and its association with race. Deb Cohan, then a doctoral student at Brandeis University, was our speaker. Her treatment of the topic was guided by the use of excerpts from the then-current film *American History X* (1999). The film, detailing the coming of consciousness of a neo-Nazi youth, illustrated many of the points she made about the causes and consequences of racism on an interpersonal level. Her presentation contrasted with Willie's talk not only because she screened scenes from a popular film filled with overtly racist characters, but because she neither addressed racism and privilege in a personal/experiential way (not drawing on her own experiences as a White female academic) nor offered an examination of their origins and perpetuation in the broader social world. The presentation, in comparison with Dr. Willie's, was much more focused on drawing attention to overt racism (in this case illustrated with Hollywood representations of White supremacists), a phenomenon that White students on our campus described repeatedly as "dumb."

Both talks took legitimate approaches in the context of public college forums and both speakers did good work. However, Cohan's presentation garnered significantly more interest and appreciation from the (mostly White) students present. After her lecture concluded, a number of students anxiously awaited their turn to speak to Cohan and then gathered together to carry on the conversation late into the evening. Following her visit, several of the students approached me to express their appreciation and tell me how much they enjoyed having her on campus, an experience I had not had after Willie's talk. Cohan's use of *American History X* offered the audience an extreme and concrete referent that did not implicate the students in racial injustice or racism in any way. In the face of such an example, the analysis Cohan offered posed little threat to the audience, who did not identify at all with the behaviors of these overt racists. For this reason, the second talk proved more enjoyable for our students. Possibly Willie's talk came across as more "threatening" to her White listeners' sense of themselves as nonracist, tolerant, even progressive—here was a Black college professor presenting a "radical" and relational analysis underscored by her personal experiences that didn't let Whites (liberal or otherwise) off the hook. In contrast, Cohan's talk and film discussion may have been perceived by students as "safer"—a White sociologist focusing on images of racist thinking and behavior that students had no affinity for.

RACE ONLY MATTERS "OUT THERE"

Our recollections on teaching and learning about race relations on a predominantly White campus in a largely White state highlight a number of themes, some of which parallel the experiences of others who do such work in more racially diverse settings, and some that seem to deviate somewhat from the norm. Here we will focus primarily on the latter—the aspects of our experiences at JSC that encourage us to pose some less conventional questions about Whites teaching and learning about race. When thinking back on our efforts to make race matter on our campus, the overwhelming feeling we are left with is that for most students, race remained an issue "out there"—something that only had significance and relevance elsewhere, outside of our campus, in other (more diverse) places, in the past. Even seemingly culturally and politically progressive students concerned about social injustice largely resisted considering White privilege (especially their own) as a relevant issue in debate and analysis of race relations.

Jarl's Reflections on Classroom Teaching about Race at JSC

Viewed in light of the literature on teaching about "uncomfortable topics" like race relations, some of the difficulties we describe regarding teaching about race in mostly White classrooms at JSC are hardly unique. However, in my race relations class at JSC I did not experience the sort of resistance, paralysis, or rage highlighted by Davis (1992) as common student reactions in courses on race relations. It wasn't until I taught about race at more racially diverse universities that I truly encountered such challenges, as well as overt student hostility from White students. At JSC, student reactions, when race came up in my classes, commonly fell into two broad categories highlighted by Fitzgerald (1992) who writes about sociology students' tendency to either "blame the victim" and "replace their 'textbook sociology' with their own life experiences and prejudices" or "blame the victor" using a "heavy-handed structural analysis" in which people of color are viewed as "manipulated by a powerful and overbearing structure" (p. 245). The former response usually accompanied my efforts to address race relations on a more personal scale, such as when students were asked to consider Feagin's (1991) analysis of Whites' discrimination against African Americans in public places, which suggests that Whites routinely stereotype and discriminate against middle-class Black Americans—much the same way as depicted in the *True Colors* video. In contrast, students tended to offer more "critical" analyses when dealing with the less concrete and less personal "institutional" aspects of discrimination such as the stereotyping and marginalization of people of color on television or in film. Presumably, students were less comfortable thinking about ordinary White people like themselves committing discrete acts of discrimination in daily life than they were analyzing why Hollywood generates problematic images of people of color—practices they could safely distance themselves from.

The lack of class discussion that Emily describes in my race relations course seems to me more a result of students' sense that race matters were largely beyond their experience or expertise, rather than a belief that this was an unworthy topic being presented to them in a biased fashion. As described above, broaching the question of White privilege in class (or elsewhere) produced the most negative and defensive reactions from students. Gillespie, Ashbaugh, and DeFoire (2002), who teach about race in a program where the majority of students are White women, note that many such students identify with them as White women and assume that they share a similar perspective on race issues. However, when they address White privilege in their classes they note that these same students "disconnect" from them (p. 247). When I came out in class as someone who considers White privilege to be a valid dimension of racial inequality, I may very well have upset students' assumptions that their instructor was essentially on the same page as they were when it came to race issues. Most students were willing to go along with my general critique of our racially divided and unjust social order, but largely refused to "go there" when I raised the possibility that even well-meaning, tolerant, liberal Whites (like themselves) played a part in maintaining such social arrangements. Students reacted similarly to White guest speakers and films in which Whites raised this thorny issue. When Judith Levine visited our class to talk about White privilege from the perspective of a White woman living in Vermont, she was met with "the wall of silence" (Cohen, 1995). It subsequently became clear that most of my White students viewed Levine as using stereotypes about Whites because she rejected color blindness in favor of pointing out that race does make a difference in people's daily experiences, even if you're White and living in Vermont. Students perceived Levine as "anti-White" because she refused to leave whiteness out of the race relations equation.

Like Pence and Fields (1999) I was disappointed with students' reaction to the video *True Colors*. Discussion typically followed a three-part trajectory. First students would dismiss discrimination as an "urban problem"; second, they would "explain" the discriminatory behavior of Whites in the film as a function of ignorance ("racism is stupid") or a lack of education ("they don't know any better"); and finally, they would debate whether these individuals were actually racist or whether they discriminated based on misinformation and stereotypes about African American men (they are prone to violence, theft, laziness, etc.). Contrary to my intentions in showing the video, the issue of the White discrimination tester's advantages in various situations because he is White was rarely of interest to students. There was, as Frankenberg (1997) notes, more resistance to discussing White privilege than racism.

Jarl and Peter on the Challenges of Taking Race Beyond the Classroom at JSC

Discussion in the wake of a public screening of *True Colors* was similar to what occurred in Jarl's race relations class even though the conversation was facilitated by a well-respected expert in multicultural education whom the Diversity Committee had invited to campus for a series of workshops and public lectures. Participant reactions, as Megan noted above, to people of color speaking about their experiences and challenging their White audience to "do the right thing" were typically met with a sympathetic response. Some students at these events would get "fired up" and want to take concrete action to "do something" to help people of color along the lines of the opportunities offered by the campus service learning program. However, the more such speakers or films interrogated White privilege or implicated Whites in the complexities of race relations, the less enthusiastic students seemed to be. The most "successful" events (in terms of turnout and participant enthusiasm during and after the event) tended to distance the White audience from responsibility for the race-related problems discussed. Such events as a "celebration" of Martin Luther King day, a lecture on W. E. B. DuBois, Brent Staples discussing his autobiographical book *Parallel Time* (1995), or a guest sociologist discussing White supremacists were all clearly "less threatening" for the mostly White students present since the issues (while important) were presented at a safe distance as something "out there" or "in the past." In contrast, films like *The Color of Fear* and more radical speakers who focused on Whites' racism or privilege confronted students with the threatening possibility of Whites' culpability for "minority problems." As in the classroom, the challenge we faced in organizing public events related to race was one of moving students beyond observation of various racialized "others" from a sympathetic, but emotionally and experientially safe distance, to thinking about racial inequality in relational terms as something that is relevant for us all since it is a fundamental dynamic in our society with implications for all, not just those who have little choice but to recognize it.

The Diversity Committee did make progress in making race an issue to be addressed on campus, but our efforts were hampered by financial constraints and an uphill battle against the hegemonic student culture that marginalized race as largely irrelevant in northern Vermont. Ferber and Wong (2002, p. 192) describe an "all-too-common trajectory" in which voluntarism in campus diversity work without eventual institutionalization and "a campus-wide commitment to diversity, enacted at all levels" leads to burnout among activists and a declining program momentum. This is exactly the trajectory we followed in our time at JSC. We stepped down as cochairs of the Diversity Committee after several exhausting years due primarily to the lack of any indication that the committee or its work would be institutionalized. The key indicator of a move toward institutionalization and de-marginalization was a committee budget, which was never forthcoming. The Diversity Committee and its projects depended on the largess of the college president. We came to euphemistically refer to the Diversity Committee's "funding" model as the "Dad, can I borrow the car tonight?" model. Our half-joke was unfortunately validated on numerous occasions. With cup in hand, our committee took on the role of the unruly children, while the president was the rational, omniscient, and well-meaning father figure. Ironically, the student organizations and clubs that the Diversity Committee often collaborated with in cosponsoring and organizing events were more institutionalized, receiving funds and official recognition from the student government. It is perhaps telling that after we stepped down as cochairs of the Diversity Committee, no one stepped up to assume the role, nor did the administration feel it necessary to recruit anyone to continue the work of teaching about difference at the campus community level.

The lack of even a minimal institutionalization of the Diversity Committee ultimately led to the unraveling of the committee as burnt-out faculty and staff members turned away and pioneering student members graduated or redirected their energies into other activities on campus. In hindsight we wonder what role our efforts to push the diversity envelope in a direction that challenged our largely White student body to consider race relations in terms of their own privilege may have had on the resistance to the Diversity Committee's institutionalization. Perhaps in focusing on raising awareness of White privilege (without the benefit of the very useful scholarship only now emerging on the subject), we came on too strong, leading some to see us as "anti-White" when our intent was to present ourselves and our message as "anti-oppression." Perhaps a more "liberal" approach, similar to what the committee was doing initially, would have encouraged a move toward institutionalization since such an agenda would have fit better with student expectations about diversity. Of course, in our view institutionalizing such a perspective on race and multiculturalism would have had little positive impact on the campus community since it would simply have reinforced the self-congratulatory attitudes ("we're not racist, we don't discriminate") held by many well-meaning White students, which had been our initial target.

WAS IT ALL WORTH IT?

Looking back, it is tempting to imagine ourselves as an enlightened avant garde of diversity champions at JSC—ultimately doomed, but leaving a trail of converts in our wake to fight the good fight on the foundation we built. Tempting, but ultimately not a self-portrait that we're comfortable with. It is probably accurate to say that during our period of actively addressing race at JSC we did put diversity on the campus community radar due primarily to a consistently high-profile series of well-attended public events featuring quality speakers and provocative films and videos. The Diversity Committee was at the center of this effort, but student organizations and student activists were key in funding and organizing events and drawing student attention. However, with the disbanding of the Diversity Committee it is fair to say that this shift in attention was short lived in the face of a status quo that clearly placed race matters beyond the scope of sustained campus attention.

Producing racial diversity on campuses like JSC is very difficult due to factors like geographic location, institutional apathy or even overt resistance, and resource limitations. While our chapter offers a glimpse at the limited possibilities for teaching and learning about race on predominantly White campuses, we hope that that our experience suggests some fruitful directions for readers working in institutions facing similar constraints. In reflecting on our work at JSC, it has become clear to us that the overarching issue that must be addressed at campuses like JSC is how to encourage White students to "encounter" people of color even when their numbers are limited on campus. For many young people, college is the first time they have any sustained contact with people of different races and ethnicities. The benefits for White students of attending racially diverse institutions with a commitment to multicultural education are well documented. While racial heterogeneity on a campus is obviously not inherently productive for White students (or students of color for that matter), reaping the benefits of a racially diverse campus community is virtually impossible for White students who attend mostly White campuses.

Regardless of our efforts to teach about race, we were working with students who had virtually no opportunities to engage in equal-status, cooperative, interracial learning experiences in class or on campus. Research on the so-called "contact hypothesis" suggests that such cooperative interaction between people of different racial backgrounds is an effective way of reducing prejudice and increasing racial awareness and sensitivity. Had more of our students had such personal experiences with people of color, we believe our efforts to "import" race to campus would have made more sense to them and had more of an impact on their thinking and White identity development. On our campus a key channel for providing such "contact" experiences was the service-learning program. However, a problem in relying on such programs for this purpose is the tendency of service learning to "send out largely European-American students to perform service-learning in communities of color and/or poorer communities . . . with European-American students as 'servers' and people of color as clients" (Myers-Lipton, 2002, p. 202). This dynamic may explain why students involved in service learning at JSC seemed only slightly more ready to address race in a relational way than their peers lacking such experiences.

As we've noted throughout this chapter, we believe that true education about inequity and difference requires those who benefit from membership in overprivileged social categories to, at the very least, acknowledge that such membership has its (unearned) privileges and to consider this in relation to those who lack such membership. To follow the JSC student culture's lead and simply not "go there" was not an option for us, but we can't help but think that perhaps it should have been. Had we not ventured onto the rocky terrain of privilege, the scholarship on antiracist pedagogy (see Gillespie, Ashbaugh, and DeFiore, 2002 for a review of this literature) suggests that our efforts would likely have been better received in the classroom and on campus. Could we have better utilized the progressive inclinations of many of the White students on campus to "do something" about racial inequality and discrimination without challenging them to think about their own privilege and race-based prejudices and assumptions? Perhaps, but what sort of teaching and learning would we have been engaged in had we ignored the (white) elephant in the room?

Michael Schudson (1991) notes that media culture in the United States is extremely good at creating "informational citizens"; people with access to an unprecedented quantity and breadth of information. We think that in teaching about race it is relatively easy to create such informational citizens—students who know a great deal about racially identified "others" and *their* problems. Teaching in order to help students become *informed* about race is another matter though. According to Schudson (1991, p. 265), "being well informed means having a world view that is coherent enough to order the buzz of information around us, and having enough personal involvement with people, ideas, and issues beyond our private worlds to absorb and use information." Our belief that to be "educated" implies being informed led us to put privilege at the center of our teaching about race at JSC, for better or worse.

REFERENCES

American History X. (1999). New Line Cinema.

Boler, M., and K. R. Allen. (2002). Who's naming whom: Using independent video to teach about the politics of representation. *Women's Studies Quarterly 1 & 2,* 255–270.

Chesler, M. (2002). Effective multicultural teaching in research universities. In J. Chin, C. White Berheide, and D. Rome (Eds.), *Included in Sociology: Learning climates that cultivate racial and ethnic diversity* (pp. 26–51). Washington, DC: American Association for Higher Learning.

Cohen, L. (1995). Facilitating the critique of racism and classism: An experimental model for Euro-American middle-class students. *Teaching Sociology 23,* 87–93.

The Color of Fear. (1994). Berkeley, CA: Stir-Fry Productions.

Davis, N. J. (1992). Teaching about inequality: Student resistance, paralysis, and rage. *Teaching Sociology 21,* 232–238.

Do the Right Thing. (1990). Universal City, CA: MCA Home Video.

Eyes on the Prize. (1993). Alexandria, VA: PBS Video.

Feagin, J. (1991). The continuing significance of race: Anti-Black discrimination in public places. *American Sociological Review 56,* 101–116.

Ferber, A. L. (2002). Hate crimes, White backlash, and teaching about Whiteness. In J. Lesage, A. Ferber, D. Storrs, and D. Wong (Eds.), *Making a difference: University students of color speak out* (pp. 153–175). Lanham, MD: Rowman & Littlefield.

Ferber, A., and D. Wong. (2002). Conclusion: This is only the beginning. In J. Lesage, A. Ferber, D. Storrs, and D. Wong (Eds.), *Making a difference: University students of color speak out* (pp. 176–202). Lanham, MD: Rowman & Littlefield.

Fitzgerald, C. D. (1992). Exploring race in the classroom: Guidelines for selecting the 'right novel.' *Teaching Sociology, 20,* 244–247.

Frankenberg, R. (Ed.). (1997). *Displacing Whiteness: Essays in social and cultural criticism.* Durham, NC: Duke University Press.

Gillespie, D., L. Ashbaugh, and J. DeFoire. (2002). White women teaching White women about White privilege, race cognizance, and social action: Toward a pedagogical pragmatics. *Race, Ethnicity, and Education, 5,* 237–253.

Helms, J. E. (1992). *A race is a nice thing to have.* Topeka, KS: Content Communications.

Lesage, J. (2002). Introduction: Conceptualizing diversity. In J. Lesage, A. Ferber, D. Storrs, and D. Wong (Eds.), *Making a difference: University students of color speak out* (pp. 1–14). Lanham, MD: Rowman & Littlefield.

Levine, J. (1994). White like me. *Ms. Magazine, 4,* 22–23.

McIntosh, P. (1995). White privilege and male privilege: A personal account of coming to see the correspondences through work in women's studies. In M. Anderson and P. Hill Collins (Eds.), *Race, class, and gender* (pp. 76–87). Belmont, CA: Wadsworth.

McKinney, K. D. (2002). Whiteness on a White canvas: Teaching race in a predominantly White university. In B. Tusmith and M. T. Reedy (Eds.), *Race in the college classroom: Pedagogy and politics* (pp. 127–139). New Brunswick, NJ: Rutgers University Press.

Mississippi Burning (1989). New York: Orion Home Video.

Myers-Lipton, S. F. (2002). Service-learning and success in sociology. In J. Chin, C. White Berheide, and D. Rome (Eds.), *Included in sociology: Learning climates that cultivate racial and ethnic diversity* (pp. 202–218). Washington, DC: American Association for Higher Learning.

O'Boyle, T. C. (1995). *Tortilla curtain.* New York: Viking.

Pence, D. J., and J. A. Fields. (1999). Teaching about race and ethnicity: Trying to uncover White privilege for a White audience. *Teaching Sociology, 27,* 150–158.

Schudson, M. (1991). National news culture and the rise of the informational citizen. In A. Wolfe (Ed.), *America at century's end* (pp. 265–282). Berkeley, CA: University of California Press.

Staples, B. (1995). *Parallel time: Growing up in Black and White.* New York: Avon Books.

Takaki, R. (1993). *A different mirror: A history of multicultural America.* Boston: Little, Brown & Co.

Terkel, S. (1992). *Race: How Blacks and Whites think and feel about the American obsession.* New York: New Press.

True Colors. (1991). *ABC News Prime Time Live.* New York: American Broadcasting Company.

CHAPTER FIVE

The Racial Experiment

Susan C. Warner
Cedarville University

Millicent Mickle
Wilberforce University

OVERVIEW

Ten miles down a country highway, between cornfields, a different world exists, one my students are totally unaware of, though most could jog to this location. I teach at a mid-sized, Baptist liberal arts university in the Midwest. Fifteen minutes away is one of the oldest historic Black universities in the nation. Both schools have a few similarities: they are rural campuses of approximately the same size that are private and cater to the middle-class student. One other glaring similarity: each campus has very little racial diversity in either the student body or the faculty. This fact alone explains the separate worlds in which students on each of these campuses walk.

My friendship with my African American colleague was forged during a regional sociological conference before either of us started our first full-time faculty positions at our respective institutions. Little did we know we were destined to teach on campuses so close to each other geographically yet so far apart socially. We had each interviewed and accepted full-time tenure-track positions at these colleges the spring we met. Neither of us had much knowledge about what life as a professor would be like, nor did we imagine the impact these campuses would have on our own lives. However, we did know that being a part of these institutions was both exciting and the fulfillment of a dream. We talked excitedly at those meetings about what teaching would be like and agreed to keep in touch since we would be so close in proximity to one another.

Our first year of teaching was filled with the frantic pace of settling into a new teaching position and the year passed with no contact between us. However, the next year we made contact and met for lunch. Each of us was concerned about the lack of racial diversity within our classes and the frustration that accompanies no representation from other voices. During this lunch we devised a plan to bring our schools together. There had never been a collaborative effort to gather students together from these schools, though the distance between them is so short. We knew we were forging pioneer ground. We chose a common book for our students to read, William Julius Wilson's *The Bridge over the Racial Divide*. We agreed to assign this book to our students and picked a date where we would gather together for a dialogue on race. It was agreed that the African American students would come to the White campus for the first dialogue.

As I announced this project to my students, I was met with disbelief and hesitation. They had never been asked to participate in an experience like this. A few of them had Black friends from back home. Fewer still had Black friends on campus, since our African American population was approximately 18 students out of 3,800. It was difficult for my students to read Wilson's book. They found the technicalities of his writing on economics hard to relate to their life. Still, as a class, we trudged through each chapter with various techniques. I invited several interested faculty to join us for the evening with the Wilberforce students. It was a fall evening with severe storms forecasted by the weather services. Mimi Mickle had been in contact with me and was bringing approximately forty students to meet with my class of twenty-eight. The evening was dark and windy as the Wilberforce students arrived by bus. I met them in our student center and led them back to the activities room. My students had set up the room with a large circle of chairs and were ready to participate, though a bit hesitant about what was expected of them.

The evening got off to an awkward beginning. This was the first time the students had met and the greetings between the two classes were cool and reserved. However, it was not long till Mimi took over and broke through that reserve. Mimi deserves the credit for the success of that evening. I stood in awe as she maneuvered her way through the midst of students, getting each student to participate. Her approach was the direct method—she pointed to a student and asked them a question. While this was uncomfortable for my students at first, they began to relax and open up with their thoughts. We discussed issues of race that were brought up by Wilson. Then, Mimi introduced a topic that proved to be the heartbeat of the evening. She asked each student to discuss what they had been taught at home about racial relations. We went around the circle and each and every student had an opportunity to relate to the rest of the group how they were socialized to do race. Emotions ran high as students revealed sometimes hidden prejudices that they had been taught as children. My White students were astounded to hear one African American student after the other relate how they were told that they had to work twice as hard as a White person to make it in the world. They also got to hear personal accounts from the African American students about incidents when they had personally experienced discrimination by the White population. One White student related how difficult it was for her grandfather when one of her cousins adopted a biracial baby. She cried as she told the group how race had divided her family.

The discussion went on much longer than we had anticipated or planned. We finally had to call a halt to the students' dialogue as the hour was getting late. We had a time of refreshments afterward where the students could mingle and socialize. Several of the students sat in small groups and continued the conversation. Some of the students at my institution left, still uncomfortable with the dynamics of the group. Some of the Wilberforce students remained aloof and distant from my students. Interestingly, it seemed the female students had less difficulty relating to each other. As we said our goodbyes, the tornado siren sounded. This proved to be another interesting and unplanned development for the evening. We were all ushered down into the lower level of the building and herded into the inner rooms to await the tornado watch. Students laughed and got to know one another better as we sat for an hour on the floor waiting out the storm. Some sang songs together, some discussed class work, some just told funny stories. It was a nice stress-relieving incident to end a rather intense evening.

Mimi: Actually, I didn't think of this as a "project" when it started. Susan Warner and I met at an NCSA Conference. I was in my first year as an instructor at Wilberforce University, the oldest, private, historically Black school in the country. She had just been hired to teach at Cedarville University, a predominately White Baptist institution about twenty minutes away. We decided to keep in touch. During that next fall, we began to talk about getting our students together to talk about race. That spring, we brought them together in the first of four meetings on race. We assigned both classes William J. Wilson's book, *The Bridge over the Racial Divide,* and told them to be ready to discuss it.

I chose to have my Introduction to Sociology 2 class participate. However, I opened the trip to my other classes and gave them extra credit if they brought two additional students with them. Consequently, approximately forty students from Wilberforce carpooled or took the van to Cedarville.

As I look back on all of the encounters, I must say the first one was the best. I remember quite a bit about it. There were a number of Cedarville faculty members there—more than I had expected. There were two Black people affiliated with Cedarville there—a female student and a member of the Student Affairs Division (either admissions or minority affairs). He was a recent alumnus. Both were excited to have us on campus. They greeted us warmly and expressed their gratitude and joy at "finally" having some Black presence on the otherwise "lily-White" campus. This is not to say that others treated us coldly; quite the contrary, the Cedarville students and staff were gracious hosts. The welcome of the Blacks just exuded the happiness of no longer being alone.

The discussion that ensued was lively. As I expected, the students talked very little about the book. They talked about their experiences and feelings instead. There was more talking going on between people sitting next to each other than there was whole-group dialogue. In this context, that was a good thing because these were interracial dialogues. Susan and I had students sit so that Black and White students were intermingled. In no instances were more than three Black or White students clustered together. Most students were seated next to at least one person of the other race. Even though these pairs were not always talking about the topic, their willingness and ability to open up and find common ground were a positive outcome.

In the group dialogue, Black students were more vocal; they spoke longer and more frequently. Often, the Black students gave different viewpoints on race and the problems of Blacks. Some pointed out the existence of racism and discussed instances when they had experienced discriminatory treatment or attitudes from Whites. Others pointed out ways that Blacks sabotage themselves and spend too much energy "blaming the White man." Most said they thought Affirmative Action was still necessary. Some, even some among those who saw its necessity, however, said they felt demeaned by Affirmative Action. They thought the policy contributed to White people's challenging their competency; a few said they wouldn't accept an opportunity gained because of Affirmative Action. One or two sounded angry; most did not.

Of the White students who spoke, I remember one discussing how her grandparents spoke of Blacks in terms of stereotypes as if they were truisms ("they steal"). She and her parents, however, rejected such thinking. One of the Cedarville students, a young woman from Hawaii, spoke of how the Black-White conflict seemed strange to her. She told us that in Hawaii the racial mix is much more complex (she is racially mixed herself), and yet they do not have the type of racial problems we have on the mainland. As she was speaking, I thought about some of the things I had been reading about conflicts Hawaiians of "native" descent are having with issues of control over some institutions and education and wondered how in tune she really was.

The two Cedarville faculty who spoke brought different views on race to the discussion. One professor seemed to be offended or insulted by the view that the discrimination suffered by Blacks was any different from that suffered by White ethnics or low-income people. He had grown up a poor, Irish kid in a predominately Italian neighborhood. He had survived the insults and deprivation because of hard work and determination; why couldn't Blacks—especially, these young Blacks born after discrimination was no longer the law of the land and Affirmative Action was in place? I had expected to hear this; this is the typical "angry White man's lament." I suspect there were students who agreed but didn't want to appear politically incorrect in front of the teacher who held their course grade in her power. The other professor surprised me. He and his wife had adopted a Black child. He said he had thought giving the child a good home would be enough but had realized soon after the adoption that he would need to do and learn more in order to help the boy deal with issues facing Black males. They expanded their social network to include more Blacks and more Black culture; for example, they joined a predominately Black church.

There were two "unfortunate" exchanges in the dialogue. Both, I felt, had the possibility of shutting down the dialogue. Thankfully, they didn't, but in the one case, I regret that a potential relationship was thwarted before it started. In the first case, one of the White male students was saying that most Cedarville students don't interact with even the few Black students on campus. He told us he was an exception, in that the four Black male students he was friends with spent time with him in his room. Some of the more vocal Wilberforce students jumped on him. They felt his being able to count his Black friends was racist. They missed the point about having the interactions. I wondered if they would have preferred that he had no Black friends at all (then he couldn't have counted them). Most students didn't comment. I think the majority got his point.

However, I was afraid this young man, who was the most vocal White student, would feel shamed and no longer disclose. He kept talking anyway.

The other exchange involved the Black Cedarville student. I don't remember exactly what she said; it was something about her feeling isolated on the almost all-White campus. Whatever it was, some of the more vocal Wilberforce students misunderstood her comment because their reaction was strong and bitter. They accused her of being an "Uncle Tom" and ashamed of being Black. I think she was hoping to form an alliance and get some support; instead, she was scorned. After this, she remained quiet through the rest of the discussion. She interacted less with the Wilberforce students after the session than the White students did.

Our second session was held at Wilberforce in fall 2001. Again, the students were from the Introduction to Sociology class at Wilberforce and the Principles of Sociology class at Cedarville. Because of the time of the conference, there were fewer Cedarville students in attendance. None of the students had participated in the spring discussion. The students attended a panel discussion on reparations, the opening session of Wilberforce's biennial Slave Narrative's Conference. After the panel, we all went to the Wilberforce cafeteria to discuss the program over lunch. As we left the auditorium for the cafeteria, the Cedarville students clustered together and the Wilberforce students drifted away from them. To break that up, we matched them up, one Cedarville student with two or three Wilberforce students. Shock, fear, and anxiety registered on the faces of the White students. Despite the tentative beginnings, however, the interaction between the students en route to the cafeteria and during lunch was friendly and sustained. Again, there was not much talk about the subject— reparations—but students shared with each other and again found common ground.

Susan: Mimi and I both agreed the first attempt to bring our worlds together had been fairly successful. We agreed to try it again the following fall when we were both teaching these same classes again. That next fall, as I prepared my syllabus, I received a call from Mimi. She suggested that rather than read the Wilson book this time, I bring my students to her campus for a program they were having on racial reparations. The title of their program was "Twenty Acres and a Mule." With this topic in mind, my class was required to do some reading on the debate surrounding racial reparations. We then attended the conference in the morning and stayed to have lunch with the Wilberforce students. It was an extremely interesting experience for my students to see African Americans debate among themselves the value and disadvantages of reparations. Many later said they were surprised that there were some African Americans that did not support reparations.

After the conference, my class met with Mimi's outside the building to go over to the cafeteria. Several of my students were unable to stay for lunch, so we were a small White group. Mimi had more students who were able to meet. She and I had previously discussed our desire for the students to mingle during lunch. I was not sure how this was going to happen. I knew my students were out of their element on this Black campus and would be inclined to stick together as a group. Once again, Mimi found a way to overcome this barrier. I stood back in amazement as she took each of my White students one-by-one and sent them off with a group of her Black students. There was no time to argue or hesitate as Mimi took control. She would grab a White student by the shoulders and say to the group, "Now who wants to take charge of this fine Cedarville student?" A few Wilberforce students would step up and volunteer and off my lone White student would go, with a group of Black students. The look in some of their eyes of reminded me of deer caught in the headlights of my car! Still, the afternoon proved to be a huge success in the estimation of my students as they related their lunchtime experiences to the class the next day. The experience of becoming a minority was sobering and eye-opening for them. The Wilberforce students were gracious hosts and the Cedarville students very much enjoyed hearing about life on the Wilberforce campus. Some of the groups continued the discussion on reparations during the lunchtime meeting.

Again, Mimi and I evaluated our joint efforts to produce successful outcomes for the students and agreed to make it a priority to continue finding opportunities to bring our students together. During spring semester, we agreed to meet again at Wilberforce for a presentation on racial relations presented by two amateur filmmakers. These presenters—one White, one Black—had produced a racial dialogue on film concerning the racial riots that occurred in Cincinnati. My turnout for this outing was the least of any of the gatherings. Only two students from my class agreed to participate. However, they each brought a friend with them, so we were a group of five as we made our way down the highway to Wilberforce. This time, we were attending one of the class sessions for Mimi's class. I was struck immediately with the knowledge of difference as we entered the classroom. Foremost was the presence of children and babies with the students. This never happens in classes at Cedarville, but it is a common occurrence at Wilberforce. There was much distraction and noise from the presence of the children. However, it did not seem to distract the Wilberforce students in the same way it did me and my students.

It was a hot spring evening and we moved outdoors after the film to participate in a dialogue on race. The presenters of the film facilitated the discussion. For me, this was the most difficult of the situations we had attempted between our students. I felt apprehensive that our students were being confronted by individuals who were total strangers to both Mimi and me. They began the conversation with the question that they asked people during the film: "What do you hate about Black/White people?" The presenters did not wait for volunteers but rather singled out individuals to confront with that question. If you were White, you were to tell the group what you hated about Black people, and if you were Black, you were to say what you hated about White people. The facilitators started with the Black students. Very few of the first students to speak had difficulty with the question. They had many comments to make about what they hated about White people. Then they asked one of my White students what she hated about Black people. She was embarrassed to answer. She felt uncomfortable wording it in the way the facilitators insisted. Some other Black students also objected to the wording of the question. Still, it did force the students into a dialogue about race.

Mimi: Our third session, again, was held at Wilberforce in spring 2002. This time, Wilberforce's Social Problems class participated. Some of the Wilberforce students in attendance had participated in the first discussion at Cedarville. Two young men from Cincinnati, one Black and one White, conducted a forum ostensibly on the "riots" that had occurred in Cincinnati the previous April. After a brief video presentation and some opening comments, the facilitators tried to engage the students in a dialogue about race. The exchange with the students wasn't very fruitful, especially for the Cedarville students. They remained quiet throughout the session and because of the format, there was little if any interaction between the Black and White students. However, in their comments, students commented on the racial interaction of the facilitators. The Black facilitator was the political conservative; he was, at the time, a Republican party organizer. The White facilitator was the liberal. Often when they presented different viewpoints on the Cincinnati situation, they took the view opposite of what the students had expected. The White man, for example, backed the boycott initiated in response to the riots. The Black man did not. The liveliest part of the exchange occurred when the young men outlined the groups spearheading the boycott. They noted that the Cincinnati chapter of Stonewall Union had joined the boycott during the summer. Wilberforce students jumped on this. Most resented Stonewall's participation and saw it as the homosexual movement's co-option of the civil rights struggle. Most categorically denied the connection between the two disadvantaged groups' fights for equality. At the same time, they expressed curiosity and disgust for homosexuality in general. A few espoused tolerance ("as long as they don't bother me") but most did not.

Susan: I felt this last time together with Wilberforce students was the least productive of the three attempts, though my two students who attended came back to the class with what they reported were changed views on race. One of the facilitators directed the question to me and I did not want to answer it. As a White, privileged person, I could not relate to the "hate" in the question. I realize that is because I have never been the focus of that hate. I wondered if it was productive to center the dialogue on a word with such strong emotions.

Future plans include bringing the Wilberforce students to the White campus next semester. My students will be reading the book, *White Privilege: Readings on the Other Side of Racism,* edited by Paula Rothenberg. Wilberforce students are also reading two of the articles from the book. My students will also prepare for the Wilberforce visit by exercising their sociological imagination. I will show the video *Tuskegee* that documents the hideous experiment imposed on a group of poor, African American men in Georgia when they were used as guinea pigs in a syphilis study. Students will also be required to visit two different websites and participate in an online discussion on what they view. One website is a pictorial tour of the civil rights movement with pictures and information from the key events. The second website is entitled, "Without Sanctuary: Artifacts of Lynching in America." This was a very disturbing website for all my students. The site consists of pictures and postcards of actual lynchings that occurred all over the nation during the turn of the century. These two websites provide students with a firm grasp of the history and biography of African Americans and make them more understanding as we discuss our culture today in regard to race relations. It is my hope to bring them into this world that exists only a short distance from them and help them understand better the racially diverse world in which they live.

REFERENCES

DuBois, W. E. B. (2002). The souls of Black folk. In J. Rivkin and M. Ryan (Eds.), *Literary theory: An anthology* (pp. 873–886). Malden, MA: Blackwell Publishing.

Finch, G. (n.d.) We shall overcome: Historic places of the civil rights movement. Retreived January 20, 2005, from http://www.cr.nps.gov/nr/travel/civilrights.

Matlin, L. (Producer), and J. R. Rost, (Director). (2000) *Tuskegee* [videorecording] (Available from CBS News Productions Imprint, Princeton, NJ: Films for the Humanities and Sciences.)

McIntosh, P. (2002). Unpacking the invisible knapsack. In Paula S. Rothenberg (Ed.), *White privilege: Essential readings on the other side of racism* (pp. 97–103). New York: Worth Publishing.

Peeples, M. (2004). "Without Sanctuary: Artifacts of Lynching in America." Retrieved January 20, 2005, from http://www.npr.org/templates/story/story.php?storyId =1874649.

Rothenberg, P. (Ed.). (2002). *White privilege: Readings on the other side of racism*. New York: Worth Publishing.

Wilson, W. (1999). *The bridge over the racial divide*. New York: Russell Sage Publications.

CHAPTER SIX

Starting with a Story and Sharing the Discussion Leading
Tools and Tasks That Help in a Classroom Dealing with Diversity—Stumbling into an Affirmation of Feminist Pedagogy

Leah Collum and Janet Huber Lowry
Austin College

THE PROFESSOR PONDERS

In 1999, I inherited the Introduction to Gender Studies course. Having been instrumental in the creation of the new interdisciplinary minor four years earlier, I had helped formulate the program and the decision to go for an introductory common course along with requirements of breadth in at least three academic discipline offerings for five other courses at introductory, intermediate, and upper-level courses. A colleague braved the first three years, initially drawing on many faculty members to deliver the first lecture of the week from different disciplinary perspectives. She grew informed and confident so that in the last year the class moved to delivery by a single professor using diverse academic materials to attempt the interdisciplinary task. She taught French; I teach sociology. This juncture of humanities and social sciences still defines our program and provides another level of diversity to work with in the college and classroom.

I had taught something about sex and gender from the time of my first appointment at an innovative women's college in upstate New York in 1975, when the language was sex roles, and the resources, in sociology and most disciplines, were just beginning to appear. I had had no courses and read very little dealing with gender issues, but being a budding gerontologist, I offered to couch the first courses in a life-course perspective. But now it was the eve of the twenty-first century and I wondered how I would select from the vast quantity of material to reflect the diversity of approaches and treatments of this construct for the students of today. My first couple of efforts struggled with balance between sociology and other fields. My comfort level was greater with psychology and anthropology, more than with the philosophy of debates about sexual harassment or literary analysis of novels or poetry. But social scientific discussion of such topics often did not connect to the students' lived experiences. The joy of the intimacy of teaching at a residential liberal arts college to traditional age students in north Texas, where you really do get to know your students by name, is also limited by the lack of diversity in age, class, and race as well as the experience that these dimensions can contribute to class discussion and serious reflection on gender issues. Racial and ethnic minorities represent less than a quarter of the student body, and most students are eighteen to twenty-two years old. But there is gender diversity, both between and within gender groups, as well as sexual orientation diversity. These are topics that have to be addressed in a basic gender studies introduction. How to do it? How to connect?

My basic strategy had been to keep sociology resources to half or less and draw on other disciplines, primarily other social science fields (since there were few full courses offered at the time in the social science division beyond my sociology course). Allen and Kitch (1998) challenge us about the validity of this as a truly interdisciplinary rather than a merely multidisciplinary approach. They believe that without graduate-level interdisciplinary training and funded research, we can only aspire to this goal. At an undergraduate liberal arts college it is certainly easier to interact with colleagues from other disciplines with gender interests, to begin and sustain the dialogue leading to "interdisciplinarity" they advocate despite the lack of graduate research mission. To organize the course I selected a multicultural anthology reader, edited by a sociologist, but containing a wide number of essays and studies. With the reader, once a week, the class members became responsible for reviewing selections and providing discussion-starting questions. I made the initial assignment arbitrarily while the second and third rounds of student leadership were based more on student preference. Surrendering control of the classroom is one step to engaging students and their diversity in the learning process. Feminist pedagogy promotes this while debating the extent to which this is possible in the wider academe's model of effective teaching. The practice also empowers the students' voices and those they are presenting with more active learning. Since students were required to read only half the selections, the presentations each week offered the full extent of contributions in brief. It was hard to get the students to stay brief and really draw out serious discussion, but I tried to keep out of it by just facilitating so that they would have the chance. It didn't work as well as I had hoped until the third year, despite the implementation of such feminist and liberation pedagogy (Deats and Lenker, 1994; McLaren, 2000; Nemiroff, 1992).

I used a theory book that introduced several varieties of feminism, too. Initially it was the first book read, the framing one that we were to reference throughout the course. The difficulty was that it could also be an alienating topic in that early class time before rapport and trust were established when the willingness to identify with the "f" word (feminism) was too risky for some or branding for the brave who got stereotyped and ignored for the rest of the term.

I also attempted to find at least one book each year that focused exclusively on men and masculinity, initially one on growing up male, then a compilation of ethnographic studies of manhood. The biggest difficulty with this material was the lack of enough men in the course to provide commentary that connected the arguments to students' personal lives. Why gang up on the few guys brave enough to take the class with lots of questions about their opinions? As a female instructor with a lopsided gender split class, there is a level of authenticity missing with this well-intentioned selection. Exoticism may be the result or psychoanalysis, neither of which bodes well for a good introduction to gender studies.

Because of the great volume of material available, I also tried one new book on gender each year. This led us through a succession of topics, philosophers debating sexual harassment, social scientists from England who compiled some contributions on sexual harassment, a study of the impact of gender on science careers, the gendered study of child development, and an anthropological examination of the Hijras of India, transgendered male to female individuals with a distinctive community and cultural functions.

Harassment is a tough topic; flirtation is part of the social scene for eighteen to twenty-two-year-olds, not an affront to one's personhood. Gender violence or domestic violence is something that happens to other people. Scientists are scientists, why should gender matter? Childhood is pretty distant, or not yet imagined from a parent's perspective. Men who want to be women in a country on the other side of the world? You see my dilemma.

But things began to change when I started with a story in the third year. The feminists could come along later and help with the classification and clarification of issues that had been identified because the story had gotten under their skin first. And not just any story, a satirical one that turned the world upside down and taught them some early modern women's movement history at the same time. What saved the day for this class and drew the students into a serious consideration of the diversity involved in studying gender and sexuality was *Egalia's Daughters: A Satire of the Sexes* by Gerd Brantenberg. This Norwegian tale, the story of the modern second women's movement, only upside down in a land where women rule and men are willing "housebounds" just beginning to see it as less fulfilling, provided the boost we needed. The story portrays the coming-of-age story from a young man steeped in a culture with language and dress codes and occupational guidance and education and rebellion and love and romance and violence and values so much the same as our own Western world, but opposite, that we began to see the gendered nature of our own reality and could start to find something real about the study of gender and our own identity.

After the story, discussion leading could take on a new authority. References to Petronius hemmed in by cultural expectations of how to behave as a young "manwom" in a "wom-dominated" society provided the common ground for exploring this diversity from the many perspectives that students and academic interests bring to the discussion. Feminism wasn't so strange when "masculist" activities came naturally out of the story. Even sexual orientation became an issue worth exploring more seriously because of the role it played in questioning the dominant paradigm, the hegemonic order.

Having to review something written by a person of color if you are White or vice versa could be handled with greater sensitivity when the class began by turning the gendered world upside down. We learned to laugh at ourselves as well as take each other seriously. Sharing one's unique cultural heritage could become valuable in a class seeing that the viewpoint of the other might actually teach them something important about life and diversity because the story had started giving everyone different views of their own lives as gendered people.

As a teacher looking back over those four years, I can see the improvement and contrasts that came from starting with a story. It wasn't just my teaching experience with this topic that was growing. It wasn't just the class increasing a bit in size and the gender split balancing (adding the story may well have contributed). It wasn't that students led discussions—since they had from the beginning—but that they did it from the common ground of an upside-down view of the world which helped expose our peculiar practices with regard to gender. It got us thinking about what if . . . ? and how about this other perspective . . . ? and what does it really mean to be an embodied human in the twenty-first century? Can't we see beyond the color, the gender, the culture, the carriage, the shock of difference? Yes—if we teach with satirical stories and talk to each other about the great variety of experiences connected with our gendered lives.

THE STUDENT SPEAKS

In the Beginning . . .

One of the advantages of attending a small liberal arts college is that students are encouraged to take classes in fields outside their academic concentration, even in their junior and senior years. When I signed up for Introduction to Gender Studies in spring 2002, I was looking for a fun elective to round out my junior year and offset some of the difficulties I anticipated from taking two courses in Renaissance literature.

When I saw the course syllabus for the first time, I wavered on whether or not I should remain in the class. The professor required five different texts, a subscription to a daily newspaper, essays, a research or volunteer project, individual and partner presentations, and examinations. This certainly wasn't the lighter load I had hoped for when I signed up for an introductory-level, multidisciplinary course! But, not being one to make a rash decision, I decided to forge ahead with an open mind. I told myself I could always drop the class later if the workload became too much for me to handle.

During those critical first few weeks of the semester, with the last date to drop a course moving in closer and closer, our class began Brantenberg's (1977) novel *Egalia's Daughters: A Satire of the Sexes*. As an English major, I welcomed the opportunity to look at gender issues through the lens of literature. The novel turned the gendered world I took for granted upside down by depicting a society that discriminates against males. The satire spoke to the many ways a group of people may be subjugated socially, sexually, and economically. This book, along with an assigned paper on what life would be like as a member of the opposite sex, sparked my enthusiasm and made me think about gender differences and discrimination in ways I never had before.

I enjoyed beginning the course with a novel partially because of the value of the book itself, and partially because it discussed gender issues through the familiar language of my own discipline. As a student of English and French, I am comfortably in my element when learning about the world through literature. Even so, I do not think the gender studies course would have been nearly as effective if the material had been presented solely or even primarily through works of fiction. The very diversity of our course materials, highlighting gender issues through the lenses of history, current events, the social sciences, literature, and accounts of personal experiences, gave us a more complete understanding of the depth and complexity inherent in discussions of gender studies.

Over the Course of the Semester . . .

After reading the novel and making the commitment to follow the course through the end of the semester, I was surprised to learn how many different perspectives there are on gender issues. The course design presented a collection of varied experiences, voices, and opinions for our learning. In addition to studying distinct voices from within the academic world, we also heard diverse opinions on gender from other students in the class.

Class discussions were an integral part of the gender studies course. During these student-led discussions of assigned readings, the professor would act as a facilitator rather than an instructor, allowing us to freely express our ideas, interpretations, and opinions. After presenting his or her assigned material, each student posed a relevant question to the class in order to spark class discussion. Many of the questions touched on controversial topics and inspired lively discussion, if not outright debate, but we always remained mindful and respectful of the diversity of experience and opinion within our classroom.

Though it is relatively diverse for a college of its size, Austin College remains a predominantly White, Protestant, politically conservative institution. Our gender studies class was probably one of the most diverse classes on campus in terms of race and gender, but sensitivity is always an issue when discussing issues of gender and multiculturalism. I believe that our starting materials from different frameworks helped to provide models for our discussions by showing that controversial issues may be approached from different angles in equally thoughtful and sensitive ways. This encouraged me to make my own unique contributions to class discussions, even when my opinion diverged from the views being expressed by many of my fellow classmates. As I gained confidence, I realized that I should not stifle a reasoned opinion simply because it did not concur with the voice of the majority. In fact, censoring my own voice would by definition limit diversity in class discussion.

The professor also encouraged diversity through the written assignments she required. Each paper topic allowed for a certain amount of individual creativity and freedom to explore aspects of the assignment that were of particular interest to the individual student. The assignment on what life would be like as a member of the opposite sex allowed for imaginative and creative engagement of the material we studied. The paper on feminism gave us the option of explaining why we did or did not identify with a particular branch of feminism. As I wrote this paper, I enjoyed being able to express my own unique perspective on the branch of feminism I chose, rather than being limited to a more traditional, objective analysis.

The final research paper topic was entirely our choice. The only requirement was that we find scholarly sources representing a variety of disciplinary perspectives on the chosen subject. I elected to do my final research project on the choice mothers must make to stay at home with their children or try to balance motherhood with a career outside the home. This is a subject of great personal interest to me as I prepare to leave college, enter the world of work, and hopefully start my own family. Researching, writing about, and presenting to the class how women have historically faced this uniquely female dilemma and what societal, economic, and biological factors enter into their decision helped me to evaluate which choice might be best for me and the children I one day hope to have.

A la Fin du Semestre . . .

After completing the gender studies course, I believe that diversity is not simply about differences in race, gender, ethnicity, culture, sexuality, nationality, or socioeconomic status. Diversity also encompasses the various perspectives people have; in essence, it includes the wide variety of ways to view these differentiations. Different intellectual, academic, and even personal viewpoints provide unique ways to analyze the problems of gender inequality. Approaching course material from diverse frames of reference challenged me to stretch intellectually and re-examine some deeply rooted attitudes about gender and society which, before taking this class, I had not even realized I possessed.

The gender studies course was rewarding, but in a different way than I had imagined at the beginning of the semester. I used to think of gender differences as a fact of life that everyone accepts without question: *Of course women are nurturing and men are aggressive—it's obvious!* Now I realize that there are many ways to construct a gendered identity, and that not everyone regards gender in the same ways I had been conditioned to perceive it. I learned that a wide variety of factors—including race, sexual orientation, socio-economic status, and religion, to name a few—can and does have an impact on the way an individual views gender.

Of course, one introductory multidisciplinary course alone cannot give a complete picture of the complex discipline of gender studies. For this reason, I think the starting course materials were absolutely essential to giving the class a well-rounded foundation of knowledge with which we could further examine issues of gender, sexuality, and race in society, either formally or informally.

In the end, what I took from the course were the tools for examining my own previously unquestioned beliefs about gender and the knowledge that there may be no single "right" answer to some of the problems we examined over the course of the semester. I do believe, however, that solutions to problems of gender inequality will be found more readily by embracing a body of diverse perspectives on ways to move forward.

THE COLLABORATION CONCLUDES

Diversity is not just about differences in race, gender, ethnicity, culture, or sexuality. Diversity also encompasses the various perspectives people use to view these differences, especially disciplinary approaches. Different intellectual and academic perspectives provide different ways to view issues of gender inequality. Varied and distinct course materials spark lively class discussions and inspire students to stretch intellectually and view material from diverse frames of reference. Putting students in charge of the discussion of much of the reading selections empowers them and brings their voices into the investigation of gender and all its dimensions.

No matter how well qualified an individual professor is, he or she usually specializes in a specific field and approaches teaching courses from that particular frame of reference. In an introductory-level, interdisciplinary course such as Gender Studies, approaching the course from a single intellectual frame of reference could prove problematic for several reasons. First, students concentrating on a different academic discipline could dismiss perspectives as purely sociological, psychological, historical, and so forth. In so doing, students may easily disregard complexities and diversity within the course material. In addition, omitting or limiting perspectives from a variety of relevant sources by definition limits diversity. Second, and perhaps most significantly, presenting issues from different angles encourages students to view them as more than merely intellectual problems and helps them to internalize the importance of the issues in their own lives. Finally, a professor's specialized expertise alone will likely fail to give students a truly diverse perspective in interdisciplinary courses. For this reason, starting materials, such as books, films, and primary sources providing stories, become essential in allowing students to encounter and evaluate varied viewpoints on gender issues and other issues of diversity.

Begin with a story, something to share in common from the start. Find some assessment of the scene that is not subject to criticisms of limited perspective and manages humor in challenging the taken-for-granted perceptions of the gendered world. With Brantenberg's *Egalia's Daughters*, the course began with a mind-stretching stroll through a very different culture while conveying several important aspects of the second wave feminist's critique of Western society in the late twentieth century. For challenges in an earlier era, Charlotte Perkins Gilman's *Herland* might have done the trick, capturing the dilemma for women of the first wave fighting for suffrage and struggling with the social conventions of turn-of-the-twentieth-century America. Similar success years back in introductory sociology courses occurred in beginning with Chinua Achebe's *Things Fall Apart,* an African account of the impact of colonialism on tribal life. Why did it take two years to try this change again? Perhaps the volume of resources now available contributes to neglecting the stretch required in going beyond one's discipline. Perhaps the "disciplinarity" of the present baby boom professors remains too solidly entrenched.

Dealing with diversity—across disciplines and among people of different gender, sexual orientation, racial and ethnic identity, and age—requires talk across those boundaries as much at the level of instructor and faculty as in the classroom level among students. If diversity is to achieve the magic of its promise, then begin with stories that push the envelope and empower everyone's voice in discussion of meaning and insight from life.

REFERENCES

Abbott, F. (Ed.). (1998). *Boyhood, growing up male, a multicultural anthology* (2nd ed.). Madison: University of Wisconsin Press.

Achebe, C. (1957/1992). *Things fall apart.* New York: Knopf.

Allen, J. A., and S. L. Kitch. (1998). Disciplined by disciplines? The need for an interdisciplinary research mission in Women's Studies. *Feminist Studies, 24* (2), 275–99. http://vnweb.hwwilsonweb.com/hww/results/results_single.jhtml? nn=63, accessed 3/10/2004

Brantenberg, G. (1977). *Egalias døtre.* 1985 translation by Louis Mackay. *Egalia's daughters—A satire of the sexes.* Seattle, WA: Seal Press.

Deats, S. M., and L. Tallent Lenker (Eds.) (1994). *Gender and academe: Feminist pedagogy and politics.* Lanham, MD: Rowman & Littlefield.

Disch, E. (1997 and 2000). *Reconstructing gender: A multicultural anthology* (1st and 2nd eds.). Mountain View, CA: Mayfield Publishing.

Gilman, C. P. (1979). *Herland.* with an introduction by Ann J. Lane. New York: Pantheon Books.

Gilmore, D. D. (1990). *Manhood in the making: Culture concepts of masculinity.* New Haven, CT: Yale University Press.

LeMoncheck, L., and M. Hajdin. (1997). *Sexual harassment: A debate.* Lanham, MD: Rowman & Littlefield Publishers.

Lorber, J. (1998 and 2001). *Gender inequality—Feminist theories and politics* (1st and 2nd eds.) Los Angeles: Roxbury Publishing.

Maccoby, E. E. (1999). *The two sexes: Growing up apart, coming together.* Cambridge, MA: Belknap Press of Harvard University Press.

McLaren, P. (2000). *Che Guevara, Paulo Freire, and the pedagogy of revolution.* Lanham, MD: Rowman & Littlefield Publishers.

Nanda, S. (1998). *Neither man nor woman: The Hijras of India* (2nd ed.). Belmont, CA: Wadsworth Publishing.

Nemiroff, G. H. (1992). *Reconstructing education: Toward a pedagogy of critical humanism.* New York: Bergen & Garvey.

Thomas, A. M., and C. Kitzinger. (Eds.). (1997). *Sexual harassment: Contemporary feminist perspectives.* Philadelphia: Open University Press.

CHAPTER SEVEN

Irritating, Supporting, and Representing
Reflections of Faculty and Students of Color

Ana María García, Angela R. Gillem,
Dana Szwajkowski, and Lillian West
Arcadia University

INTRODUCTION

In this chapter, we will address the complexities of our experiences as women of color both in a faculty collaborative teaching a section of Arcadia University's pluralism in the United States course, and in a student body taking the course. As faculty of color, we hold a unique perspective on identity and issues of inclusion and exclusion. Locating ourselves as more than educators, we will examine social interactions with students and faculty from the position of advocates and activists for social justice and inclusion. More specifically, we will examine the dynamics of being self and other, subject and object with our students and our colleagues. As students, we will discuss our similar yet very unique perspectives, experiences, and reactions to the pluralism class specifically, and our lives generally. Before we took the pluralism class, we had our own unique ideas, assumptions, and judgments about race and racism, and we brought these attitudes to the class. Throughout the class we had certain reactions to the material presented and how it was presented, to the format of the class, and to the opinions and attitudes of the other students. Being the subjects of scrutiny affected us in different ways, one of them being a growth in awareness of the oppression of other groups. Overall, the class changed us greatly in the way we perceive others, but more importantly, the way we perceive ourselves. We are pluralism, yet we are still challenged by it to continuously rethink our own identities and the world around us.

REFLECTIONS OF FACULTY OF COLOR

Over the past several decades, colleges and universities across the country have begun to create and offer diversity and multicultural courses focusing on issues of race, class, gender, and sexual orientation. However, in 2000, the Association of American Colleges and Universities conducted a national survey, which revealed that only 54 percent of colleges require a diversity course. The university where we teach is one of these institutions that require a course on pluralism as part of a student's general education requirements. The course and the faculty who teach it are reflective of the university's racial makeup. That is, it is largely comprised of Caucasian, European American individuals with a small number of people of color.

Courses on diversity challenge both faculty and students on a number of levels. In addition to knowledge-based content, they require a great deal of personal reflection and challenging interpersonal interaction. However, beyond these more universal challenges, as people of color, we are often asked to educate others about race and ethnic issues and to speak for or represent our races/cultures. Thus, for students and faculty of color, the materials and content of these courses are not impersonal or objective. They are personal, and the abstractions of ideas and facts are our experienced realities.

The Western tradition of education has insisted on a text-based, content-driven classroom that privileges objectivity and interpersonal distance. This approach has been challenged by feminist scholars who validate the personal experiences of both teachers and students as knowledge, and who encourage the interpersonal connections that nurture intellectual inquiry and reflection. Feminist scholars and educators have been informed by Brazilian Paulo Freire's liberatory pedagogy, which calls for the transformation of teacher from lecturer to active participant in the learning process. In a pluralism course, this means centering the self as a cultural and racial being with all of the concomitant dynamics of power. Further, it means being open to examining our own conscious and unconscious conflicts that remain unexplored, and which often surface in response to re-engagement with the material through our experiences with students in the classroom (in psychoanalytic terms, this would be called "countertransference").

Irritating, Supporting, and Representing with Our Colleagues

Beyond the sociocultural realities of the classroom and student-faculty interactions, tensions between and among faculty of color and White faculty exist. As faculty of color, we have done the work of identity and racial/ethnic representation in our personal lives and continue to do so within the pluralism courses. This is quite different from many of our White colleagues who have not needed to integrate their Whiteness into their definition of self on both a personal and professional level.

As "faculty of color," a term fraught with both ambiguity and rigidity, we are always struck by the intense and difficult feelings that arise when we are engaged in the discourses of power and privilege with colleagues or students. We are in multiple places: as teachers, we are focused on staying the course and we understand that students take time to learn new material—material that is often in stark contradiction to their ongoing life experiences and current worldviews. As faculty of color, both Latina and African American, we are deeply aware of our responsibility to use ourselves and the course materials to educate and transform others, and we are exhausted by this process. We are frequently disappointed with the resistances and denial that we meet both in the classroom and with our colleagues. Sometimes we are moved to anger by their unwillingness to deal with their own race, culture, and privilege, and that, too, is exhausting..

Ana María García: In the pluralism teaching collaborative, the issues of authority and representation are quite nuanced. We are both the voices of color (the token and politically required representatives who both irritate and support) and the colleague (the supporters). Superficially, all of us in the collaborative are the same: doctoral-level faculty with years of teaching experience who are passionate and committed, personally and professionally, to social justice. On another level, we are different from our colleagues in that we are the "racial experts." We are expected to speak as the voices of color and to give insight as to how students might learn the course material. However, sometimes, we are too visible, pushing too much for our White colleagues to claim their Whiteness and make it central to their teaching. At these times, we are expected to behave as tokens: to be seen but not heard, to legitimize the pluralism course and the university's multicultural mission without pressing for change, to be polite and applaud our colleagues' progressive ideas and values, to avoid making them feel uncomfortable by pointing out their inconsistencies.

For both of us, it was stimulating to work with a group of faculty who were thoughtful about the issues we covered in the course; in many ways it was validating. We felt fortunate that we were working with a group of White colleagues who were to some degree sensitive to and aware of diversity and social fairness issues in more than just a superficial way. And they wanted to be doing it—it was, for the most part, voluntary.

Angela R. Gillem: I felt numb as I began to write this paper. It parallels my experience while teaching these kinds of courses. As I teach them, I need to send my own feelings into the background in order to express even-handed sensitivity to students who respond with skepticism to the issues of cultural diversity and cultural, racial, socioeconomic, sexual, and gender sensitivity. We both had to do this with our colleagues on the pluralism collaborative in order to make a comfortable space for them to explore their issues as they came up in our work sessions. At the same time, we felt the need to be a catalyst for them to change, not only for the purpose of making the pluralism course better but also to engage their friendship. Here is an excerpt from my journal during one of our summer planning workshops:

> I just got home from the first pluralism meeting and I feel agitated and frustrated. We tried to talk about issues among ourselves and we kept getting off track and being interrupted. We can't have a serious conversation about issues in that group without ending up joking and moving into more pedagogical issues and leaving the difficult issues. I feel bad that I kind of ignored [my colleague's] request not to talk about the difficult stuff. I feel like I was kind of insensitive to

her. I feel angry and frustrated with the group, though. We are avoiding the very issues that we want our students to grapple with. . . . I really don't know what I want to do. I don't feel like thinking about it any more. I'm beginning to hate the pluralism meetings because the joking and distraction are so frustrating for me.

As faculty of color, teaching about issues of color and sexual orientation means managing a whole host of emotions that are engendered in the present but that also reverberate with past experiences that are part of our social histories. Primary among these emotions is a feeling of frustration that stems from a multitude of life experiences wherein folks have rendered us or the issues invisible or have trivialized their importance. While we understand that our colleagues of majority status (read White and straight) also feel frustrated by student reactions or attitudes, we also understand that they are primarily frustrated by pedagogical setbacks. That is, they are frustrated by a student's unwillingness to see the relevance or importance of race and sexual orientation, of stigmatization, of the "other" status. They are not, however, rendered personally insignificant by those same student attitudes.

Irritating, Supporting, and Representing with White Students

Ana María: Faculty of color who teach pluralism in the United States courses must navigate the difficult social position of being in dual roles and realities. We are both subject and object in very complicated ways. When we speak with the class about the culturally held stereotypes around Latinas and African Americans, we are the "other" that is being studied and read about as well as the "self" that is present in the room. This duality of presence and representation means that when the validity of the "othered" experience is challenged as not real, or contrived, our own identity and experience is challenged. When our majority/White students express the belief that racism and sexism are a thing of the past, that people are people and we are all the same, they are directly questioning and invalidating our history, our social realities, and even our sense of self and identity.

We feel that we are always walking a fine line. When students say that people of color complain too much, we need to try to understand where they are coming from, and not take it personally. When they say that gay and lesbian folks flaunt their sexuality, we need to understand where they are coming from, and not take it personally. Here is the problem: it *is* personal. We *are* those people of color and those gay and lesbian people. We represent them. By denying the significance of identity and the prominence of race and ethnicity, White students reduce people of color to one-dimensional characters. That is, we are just like them—"people are people"—and therefore we are not of color. For a person of color, denial of this important identity dimension and its centrality to the integrity and cohesion of self is painful.

As mentioned earlier, the question of expertise or authority, in feminist perspective, can be established through personal experience as well as empirical data. However, in the multicultural course, this authority from faculty of color is juxtaposed with the majority students' ideas of a racial other that is inferior. Although Hendrix (1998) found that Black professors' racial status enhanced their credibility in courses dealing with cultural/racial issues, we have found quite the opposite: many times White students will reduce our presentation of social science data and of our lived experiences to the status of opinion, thus diminishing their credibility.

Maybe we should not take it so personally. Mostly we try to avoid doing so. Instead, we support because we do understand their limited experience, their fear of change and introspection and of personal responsibility for sociocultural and political change. Jackson (1999) has characterized students' anger, denial, isolation, reaction formation, projections, mistrust, hostility, and ambivalence as normal resistance reactions to the anxiety and vulnerability provoked by the uncomfortable and unfamiliar course content. She suggests dealing with these reactions with empathy and that they should not be prevented or avoided. She also warns teachers not to blame or pathologize the students for their resistance, but to use it to enhance their learning. Thus, we must manage our counter-transferences so that we remain open to our students and so that they, in turn, can remain open to what we have to teach them. We have to support them even as we "irritate" them.

However, we suffer a lot of stress teaching these courses because of the personal nature of the material and the stress each week of going into a classroom full of students who doubt the validity of research on the experiences of people like us. Perhaps our efforts as teachers to have our students understand our experience by encouraging a perspective consistent with ours *is* counter-transference. Our students become every White person, every heterosexual person, every man who has doubted our experiences. So now that we have "power" in the classroom, we use it to try to convince our students of the veracity of our subjective experiences. There is a fine line that we walk—when we explore cultural norms and traditions and the *isms* of our world—between imposing our ideas on others and exposing others to them for conscious awareness and for critical consciousness. We always find ourselves walking this fine line and tripping occasionally on our own good intentions and counter-transferences. Perhaps this is how we learn, but, goddess! How painful and burdensome the lessons!

One of our colleague's discussions of her feelings at one of our meetings was very powerful to both of us. It felt honest and real. It was revealing to us about the fear and discomfort that White folks have about the issue of race. We appreciated it and it worried us. It gave us a good perspective on how hard it is for Whites (and other privileged groups—heterosexuals, men, the wealthy, the able) to deal with this diversity stuff, and it clued us in about why our students resist so much. We believe that we should still push them to struggle with it, but we also need to take their cognitive and social identity development levels into perspective (Chan and Treacy, 1996). In so doing, we must also take into account the fact that they might be unwilling "victims" of our efforts to enlighten them.

As Chan and Treacy (1996) suggest, it is normal for students to respond emotionally to the destabilization of their social identities. They are afraid. Like good therapists, we as teachers need to create "safe" spaces for them to discuss this material and even then, they won't feel safe. When we are in supporting mode, we realize that their resistance should stimulate our curiosity, not our disdain. It should stimulate our concern, not our distancing from their struggle as if we've never been there. We need to remember that we have struggled in much the same way that they do. Who are we to act as if we are above them? We were once clueless ourselves. *"Why can't we all just get along?" was a genuine, heartfelt question for me (Angela). "Why can't we just take each individual for who s/he is?"* We should not let ourselves become so distanced from who we were that we cannot see what our students can become. We notice every day the ways that we have internalized racism, ethnocentrism, homophobia, sexism, classism, and ableism. It makes us feel ashamed every time we notice it. Oops, now we're back to representing. . . .

Irritating, Supporting, and Representing Students of Color

Less attention in the literature and research has been focused on the presence and experiences of students of color in these courses. For students of color, as with faculty of color, the materials and content of these courses are not impersonal or objective. It is personal, and the abstractions of ideas and facts are their experienced reality. In relation to students of color and gay/lesbian/bisexual students, we are "self." That is, we are like them in that we, too, hold minority status. So we have to irritate and support in just the right balance while, at the same time, to all who are White and come in contact with us, we represent our races, our cultures, our group histories, a whole diverse people whose reputation rests on our every move, each verbalization, each gesture of word or body.

Angela: At one point, during a period of time when I was particularly stressed and depressed by teaching pluralism every semester plus a cross-cultural counseling course in the spring, I attended a session at the American Psychological Association convention in which the presenter discussed Claude Steele's theory of stereotype threat. The theory suggests that students who identify with the academic domain are threatened by the possibility of being negatively stereotyped based on beliefs about the group to which they belong. This threat can have impact regardless of whether one believes in the stereotype or its applicability to oneself. Specifically, research has shown that stereotype threat depresses standardized test performance for women in the mathematical arena (Spencer, Steele, and Quinn, 1999) and for African Americans in the general intellectual domain (Steele and Aronson, 1995), and that it leads to disidentification with school. The research also demonstrates that these negative academic effects can be ameliorated by practices that reduce the stereotype threat (Steele, 1997). This presentation was my first introduction to the theory. However, I immediately resonated with the idea that activation of a stereotype about the group with which I identify could affect my performance and my stress level. I came back to the pluralism collaborative excited to tell them about my insight into the depression and stress that I had been experiencing while teaching the courses. Specifically, teaching two courses about cultural, racial, and sexual differences activated my internalized stereotypes about myself as a Black lesbian woman and seemed to lower my energy and motivation level as a teacher.

Retrospectively, this makes even further sense when I recently received feedback from some students of color that I was not a notable presence in the course outside of my small group section, and that I hadn't done a very good job of defending students of color from the assaults on their veracity by the White students. I also don't remember many incidents that happened in the course— outside of the big picture of events—that some of my colleagues remember. I think that this is what I do when stereotype threat is activated for me: I zone out or, to use a more psychological term, I "dissociate" from the experience and remain in the experience in only a marginal way. This is how stereotype threat affects me. Unfortunately, what happens then is that I don't adequately irritate or represent. I don't effectively speak up for students of color or for my colleagues of color when they are experiencing the "assault" of White students' resistance. In effect, my performance is impaired. Like Kate Rushin in her "Bridge Poem" (in Moraga and Anzaldúa, 1981), I grow weary from the responsibility of irritating, supporting, and representing:

I've had enough
I'm sick of seeing and touching
Both sides of things
Sick of being the damn bridge for everybody . . .

I'm sick of filling in your gaps
Sick of being your insurance against
The isolation of your self-imposed limitations . . .

I'm sick of reminding you not to
Close off too tight for too long
I'm sick of mediating with your worst self
On Behalf of your better selves (pp. xxi–xxii)

Every summer at the faculty workshop we discuss the course and the particular process for that year. For years we have struggled with what additional burdens are carried by students of color who must represent their entire race or ethnic group. Often these students are asked to explain what it means to be of color, to validate that racism exists, and to forgive White students for their ignorance or prejudice. Students are vulnerable—after all they must live with each other after the class ends—and so they are in a very difficult place when they are in a minority of one or two in a class section. In the past we have tried to respond to this situation by dividing up the ten or twelve students of color among the six sections so that there would be more than one in any particular section. Of course, this assumes a sort of homogeneity of students of color that is completely false. Nonetheless, we struggled to create "safe" spaces and this particular summer we took the plunge and assigned all students of color to two classrooms that were taught by the two faculty of color, us. The remaining four sections were all White. Our rationale for doing this was multiply determined. Students of color might feel emboldened to speak up in an environment in which their section leader and a large number of their peers were also of color. Having critical mass would mean that no one student would have to represent his or her race or ethnicity. Also, White students could profit from all white spaces in which they could speak freely without worrying about offending students of color.

Some of the reactions from the faculty after teaching like this for a semester are enlightening. A few felt exhausted and upset by their role as the spokesperson for people of color, and felt unqualified to do so. Others felt that White students profited less from this arrangement because, after all, "without students of color, what was there to talk about?" Predictably, we, as faculty of color, enjoyed this arrangement because we did not have to work as hard to protect the students of color. There was the opportunity for intense interchange between students of color and White students. And White students had the unique experience, if not the luxury, of being less dominant in a place where dominant status could be explored gently and in a nonthreatening manner. Clearly, this was also true for students of color as they found themselves to be among a significant number of students of color for probably the first time in their university experience. They felt that they could expose more of their feelings and experiences in a classroom where others like them had their backs and where the White students, now with less power over the classroom, were less adversarial.

REFLECTIONS OF STUDENTS OF COLOR

Lillian West:
Scene I: Three African American students including myself are congregated in the dormitory's lounge. They are seated upon the practical yet uncomfortable blue and red lounge furniture that can be found in almost every dormitory in America. You know, the kind that would make you break something if you sat down too hard on it.
Me: Did you guys sign up for pluralism yet?
Lil'Bit: Yeah! (with indignation written all over her face)
Tae: We Black! Why we gotta take this class?

Lil'Bit: You don't have to take nothin' because you aren't going to be here next semester.

Tae: Yup. You right. That's why you have to take pluralism. (in a teasing manner)

Me: Shut up! I don't see why colored folks need to take this class.

Lil'Bit: Yeah. We've had hundreds of years of slavery and a couple more hundred years of oppression so what are they gone tell me that I don't already know? White people are scared of us and we don't particularly like them either.

Me: Child you' crazy. I don't see why we gotta take this class. Shoot, me and Lil'Bit are living the class. She has a White roommate and I got an Asian one and we all are friends. What more do they want?

Tae: That's why y'all have to take pluralism.

Lil'Bit and Me: Shut up!

Cut!

As an African American I saw no point in taking pluralism. I already knew what racism was, I already knew that we needed to have open minds and accept everyone. So what else did they want? I already had bad vibes from the class because I'd heard that they were separating the classes by color. There were going to be five classes with all White students and professors and two classes with professors and students of color. We would all come together as a big group at times but would usually stay in our small groups. I heard that they were doing this so that all the students could be comfortable and feel free to really speak their minds. I wasn't feeling that theory. The only thing I kept envisioning was *coloreds* over here and Whites over there. I guess I still had the *coloreds*-to-the-back-of-the-bus syndrome. (I wasn't born then but I still felt the repercussions). I also took this theory with a grain of salt because I am normally the only person of color in my classes so I was already used to that kind of environment.

My roommate and I signed up for the class. We had hoped we would be together because we are both colored and there were only two colored classes, so we knew we had a 50–50 chance. I personally couldn't wait to see the professor's face when she called out my roommate's name, Dana Szwajkowski, and saw the demure hand of a Korean student rise in the air. I always get a kick out of that. Most professors will look at her as if she was purple with green stripes all over. My small group professor was a feisty, strong, and very independent Latina woman. She spoke her mind and didn't mind making you challenge some of your core beliefs. She and I clicked instantly, which is surprising since she is a lesbian and I am a traditional Christian. You see I already had that open mind, was accepting and all that good stuff which brought me back to my core question, *Why did I have to take that class?*

The class seemed to focus a lot on the issues between Blacks and Whites. It did touch on the problems that Latinos, homosexuals, persons with disabilities, Asians and Native Americans faced but its primary focus was Black and White. That really irked me. Any time I've read or talked about diversity, its primary focus was Black and White. African Americans like myself are so sick and tired of always having to validate our existence. I am also pretty sure that White America is tired of being seen as the only group of people who have to lift their veil of ignorance and is tired of being seen as these oppressive monsters that still believe in Manifest Destiny ready to destroy the *poor weak coloreds*. I hated having to read all the negative things that people thought of me. I hated being that nigger, coon, slut, whore, single, uneducated, teen mother who is also a welfare recipient. I was tired of hearing my friends and people I knew say obviously racist and biased comments and then watching them become indignant when you try to explain to them the offensive nature of their comment. I loathed hearing my friends say that things aren't as bad as the professors and the readings made them seem. I wondered what planet they were from. In essence they were saying that my experiences as a Black woman and the experiences of Black America/other coloreds did not exist, or in their words, "wasn't all that bad." How do you respond to that?

Large group was like stepping into the pits of hell. How do you try to validate who you are and your experiences to a group of over one hundred people, 80 percent of whom are White with 70 percent of them never really knowing another Black person? How do you try to make them see the world through your eyes without becoming known as the angry Black girl? How do you survive in a class where your soul feels as if it is being put under a microscope and left for all to examine at their leisure? How do you leave with your soul and sanity intact? Going to class was unbearable at times because I was always Black girl first and Lillian second. Have you ever wished you could crawl out of your skin just so that people would see you for who you are and not your race, sex, or economic level? White people just don't know how good they have it.

Scene 2: I'm at work and a friend of mine who has taken the class already stops by to chat.

Jenn: Hey, girl. What's going on?

Me: Nothing much. I'm just doing one of my many readings for pluralism.

Jenn: I know what you mean. How's it goin'?

Me: Fine except for the fact you actually realize how many people hate you. You hear every prejudice, racist, and biased remark that is specifically made just for you.

Jenn: I really can't say that I know how that feels. I can't even imagine what that would be like.

Me: It sucks. (I feel myself beginning to cry so I start to laugh.) I can't even imagine in my wildest dreams what it would feel like to be White: to walk around as if I owned the world, knowing that my every move won't be seen as a reflection on my race. I can't imagine walking around knowing that there isn't a racial slur in almost every language just for me. (By this time I am laughing and crying almost hysterically.)

Jenn: Are you saying that you don't like being Black?

Me: (The crying stops immediately.) Child, please. I love being Black. I love this chocolate skin, luscious lips, and big old ghetto bootie.

Jenn: Oh good. I thought you were saying that you didn't want to be Black.

Me: Girl, I love who I am and I love my people. I just hate how people judge me by it and this class is just putting it all up in my face.

Jenn: I got you. Well, I need to go and do some work myself.

Me: Okay. See you later.

Cut!

Small group was like a haven. Since the class was predominately colored I felt as if I had a shared experience with the other students. Even the few White students got a chance to see what it felt like to be a minority. My professor, Ana María García, was the angel of our haven. She set the classroom environment up in such a way that we were free to vent, we were able see that colored of the same race do disagree, and you didn't feel like you were a specimen under a microscope. That is where we talked about issues between the races and in the races. That is where I was Lillian West first and then the intelligent, beautiful, chocolate, big girl from around the way. Even though we talked about things that disturbed me, I felt that I could be just me.

I loved the days when I came in and did not have to be the "White man's victim" or the "poor ghetto girl." Those were the days we talked about Native Americans, homosexuals, and all other *colored* folk. I know that they were probably feeling the way I did, but I was happy to take the focus off of me for a while. Besides, my heart was being burned due to extended exposure to the microscope light. I really felt sorry for the mixed colored homosexual female. She just never got a break. These were the days that made me focus on how I affected others. Being the lower socioeconomic colored that I am, I did not think that I had any privileges. As an exercise in class, there was a list of, let's say, thirty White privileges and you had to mark off those that applied to you. I marked off two (my professors sure knew how to make us *coloreds* feel special). After that experience of feeling like you were the bottom of the barrel, would you think you had privileges?

Before I took this class, I did not know that a person would use me to discriminate against a homosexual. Bottom of the barrel me! I did not know that Asian Americans are still seen as immigrants by many people even though some of them have been in the United States longer than most "Americans." Remember, some of them were brought here to build the railroads. I also did not understand how Native Americans felt about being made into sports team mascots and cars like the Red Skins and Jeep Cherokee. I didn't see a problem with it until I read an article and watched a movie by a Native American that explained that the term "red skin" was used when Whites would skin Native Americans and sell their skin at a store. The author also asked would I mind a sports team being called the Coons, Crackers, Fairies, or Kikes. Ouch! Now you should see how they feel.

If you are wondering about the title and why I used the word "colored," it's because that's the way the class made me feel. I did not feel like Lillian RaeVonne West, an intelligent, funny African American female college student. I felt like someone colored on me with a Black marker—stamped oppressed, repressed, depressed, poor, second-class, coon, nigger, fast, victim, subhuman— over my body, mind, soul, and being. Stains like that don't come out with soap and water. "What did this class want from me?" I asked. They wanted me to sit there and worry about if the White people got it. Did they get it? I don't know. I do know that I felt that at the end of the semester my experience, my soul, was put away with the other colored slides into the box labeled "pluralism" ready for next semester's viewing.

Dana Szwajkowski: For most of my life I have been White. I had a white name, white family, white mentality. So that makes me White, right? After all, Whiteness is as much a state of being and an attitude as it is a color—or lack of color.

When I was younger I hated any mention of race or ethnicity. I hated the "Chinese eyes" taunt of grade school. I hated the shape of my eyes and the eyes on me whenever anything Asian was mentioned. My parents wanted me to love my Korean heritage, but it was much easier said than done. Together we read an illustrated book called *Chinese Eyes* (Waybill, 1974) about a little girl like me. The moral of the story: we are all different, yet the same. Be proud of who you are. Very nice and touching.

So I was supposed to be proud of who I was, but what was I? I did not know any other Korean children. I have never had a Korean friend. I don't know the language. I don't know the culture. I didn't want to know. Everyone I knew, admired, and loved was not Asian; therefore, I wanted to be not Asian. So, I stopped being Asian. It wasn't as hard as you might think. Many people wanted me to be White. Many people thought of me as White. No, they didn't look at me and think that I was White, but I was "just like them." I thought that was a good thing.

Now I'm White. Of course, I'm not, really. Even though some people went along with it, others didn't. Why? Because I am not White. I have these almond-shaped eyes. It's amazing how important a single part of your body can be. Other people see me as Asian, and rightly so, but I wasn't seeing myself or anybody else. At least not until the pluralism class.

I was actually looking forward to the pluralism class as an intellectual endeavor. I wanted to learn about different races. The first blow came when I found out that there were going to be two mixed classes and five White classes. I criticized this intensely. Why do we need to be reminded of our race? The school is a White school as much as it tries to seem otherwise, and I felt that I would be unfairly singled out. They obviously didn't understand that I am a White person trapped in an almond-eyed, yellow-undertoned body.

The class challenged my carefully pieced together identity. At heart, I felt that there was something wrong with me. I knew that I wasn't White and I would never be White. But I "wasn't really Korean" either, as other people tell me when they discover my ignorance of Korean culture. So, what am I? There is no box for me.

Asians are the forgotten ones. Most race-talk deals with White and Black. People assume that Asians don't have issues. They are considered the "good" race—intelligent, obedient, brilliant, hardworking—the people who deliver your Chinese food or do your dry cleaning. All Asians look alike: "You look like Michelle Kwan, Lucy Liu, or Lisa Ling." People ask you where the good Chinese restaurants are or how long you've been playing the violin. In your lifetime, you will be from China, Japan, Taiwan, Korea, Cambodia, Vietnam, and the Pacific Islands, but mostly from China.

Just because the class didn't talk about Asians that much, it still blew me away completely. I finally began to understand the unrest that I had been feeling for so long. But I still couldn't put it into words. Like a deep wound reopened, it was often painful. I was open and exposed and afraid a lot of the time. I found help from my roommate and my professor—the only people I could really talk to and who could relate to my struggles. I deeply appreciated the mixed class; it allowed the people of color to find support and commonality, an impossibility in most classes.

The large group, comprised of over 80 percent White people, was very hard at times, almost unbearable. Often, White students made obviously racist remarks. The professors rarely challenged them. Yet, they would often put students of color on the spot when they made comments. Just imagine—you are surrounded by maybe two hundred people, many strangers, most of whom are different from you. They make comments about you. Do you say anything? What do you say? How do you talk to an entire auditorium of skeptical and fearful people about how you feel? I felt lost, confused, and angry. I desperately wanted to say so many things, but the words wouldn't come. I was angry with the professors. Here they were, coolly telling me to tear open the wounds I had made tolerable, while they (the three White professors) returned to their comfortable White lives, leaving me to clean up the mess alone.

I think that I've finally managed to turn the pain into action. You have a choice: curl into a little ball and hide or doing something about it. I've worked hard at becoming articulate and masterful with words. When you are the majority or hold majority views, you can say whatever you damn well please, no matter how ignorant it is. The sad truth is, when you are the minority, you must be brilliant so that the others will even consider listening to what you say. You must construct a powerful defense against the piercing attacks. Words have the ability to pierce the thickest skin. It is you they are attacking, not some abstraction or theory, and detaching yourself from your race or heritage is nearly impossible to do and harmful, too.

The work in pluralism was painful, but for me, it was necessary pain. I don't want to live the rest of my life in turbulent, dissonant ignorance, only fooling myself. White people can choose to walk away, learning a lot, or nothing at all, as can any person who is privileged over another, such as heterosexuals and men. It is the others who are again given the burden of examining the injustice of their everyday lives, educating others, all the while in a White, male, heterosexual, educational system. People ask if White people "get it." I don't know if they do, and sometimes I really don't care. I'm afraid that it is we, the others, who "get it" and have been "getting it" all too well.

EPILOGUE

All of this takes a toll on those of us who teach and take these courses. It's exhausting to constantly be moving back and forth between irritating majority group students with discomforting information and supporting them at whatever level they receive it, while also trying to support students of color and gay/lesbian/bisexual students by how we personally represent women of color and lesbians in our teaching, our responses to resistance, and our active guidance of class discussions.

Ana María: I am facilitating a two-part class on *The Laramie Project* where students view the film, complete a structured set of questions about their reactions to the film, and then participate in a large group discussion. As I begin the facilitation process and ask the students to articulate what they heard and saw in the film and their reactions to it, I am deeply aware of being a lesbian and alone in the front of the room. I am exposed. I continuously remind myself that I am the professor, and as such, have to take a weirdly reserved stance around the topic. About a third of the way into the discussion, students are comfortable enough to say what they really think about Matthew Shepherd, about gays and lesbians. It starts: "he was an idiot to get into the car," "he should have known better," "he probably came on to the other two guys," and "all murder is about hate, to label this a hate crime is to want special privileges." These responses are fairly typical and actually allow some pretty deep conversation about what exactly is a special privilege (safety, civil rights) and the gender issues involved in the violence enacted by Shepherd's killers. Okay, so far so good.

And then the questions and reactions begin from fundamental religious students. They say gays are "disgusting," that the Bible says "it is a sin," that the use of angels by gays protesting Fred Phelps is insulting because "angels are from God." I ask which God and they say *the* God. And it goes on and on. I am an abomination to these students. I represent the sinner, the unholy, the bad. A colleague of mine steps in to challenge their selectivity in what rules they follow from the Bible. I use this opportunity to gather myself and figure out where to go. It is at this point that I notice that sitting several rows above the religious group are four students who are somewhat out as gay and lesbian. They are literally leaning on each other, and they seem to me to be hugely vulnerable. I am enraged. Their pain and their exposure to such hate speech galvanize me. I must act—not just for myself, or for the group, or for the edification of all, but specifically for these four students. I must support them because I represent them.

REFERENCES

Baldwin, D. (Producer), and M. Kaufman (Director). (2002). *The Laramie project* [Motion picture]. United States: HBO.

Chan, C. S., and M. J. Treacy. (1996). Resistance in multicultural courses: Student, faculty, and classroom dynamics. *The American Behavioral Scientist, 40* (2), 212–221.

Hendrix, K. G. (1998). Student perceptions of the influence of race on professor credibility. *Journal of Black Studies, 28* (6), 738–763.

Jackson, L. C. (1999). Ethnocultural resistance to multicultural training: Students and faculty. *Cultural Diversity and Ethnic Minority Psychology, 5* (1), 27–36.

Rushin, D. K. (1981). The bridge poem. In C. Moraga and G. Anzaldúa (Eds.), *This bridge called my back: Writings by radical women of color* (pp. xxi–xxii). Watertown, MA: Persephone Press.

Spencer, S. J., C. M. Steele, and D. M. C. A. Quinn. (1999). Stereotype threat and women's math performance. *Journal of Experimental Social Psychology, 35* (1), 4–28.

Steele, C. M. (1997). A threat in the air: How stereotypes shape intellectual identity and performance. *American Psychologist, 52* (6), 613–629.

Steele, C. M., and J. Aronson. (1995). Stereotype threat and the intellectual test performance of African Americans. *Journal of Personality and Social Psychology, 69,* 797–811.

Waybill, M. and P. Cutrell (Illustrator). (1974). *Chinese eyes.* Scottsdale, PA: Herald Press.

CHAPTER EIGHT

Identity Matters in Class
Conversations in Mixed Company

Jody Cohen, Emily Hayes, Natalie Inozil,
Sarah Mendell, and Prerna Srivastava
Bryn Mawr College

Ironically, it seems as if the process of speaking openly on the sensitive issues of different experiences comes with the shared experience of dialogue to do with those different experiences.—Sarah Mendell

INTRODUCTION

What are propitious circumstances for generating and sustaining real—that is, honest, fluid, sometimes dangerous—conversations about identity, diversity, and power in an undergraduate classroom? As a way to address this question, the co-authors of this chapter set out to explore what happened in two writing-intensive, interdisciplinary courses offered as part of the College Seminar (CSem) Program for first- and second-year students at Bryn Mawr College.

College seminars are designed to invite students to engage as readers and writers, speakers and listeners in significant questions that cross disciplinary boundaries. Classes are small (15 to 18 students) and discussion based, to facilitate the creation of a community of learners who stretch themselves and each other in the interest of building and deepening individual and collective knowledge. Students discuss shared texts and do frequent drafting and revising of papers. Professors meet biweekly with students to discuss their works-in-progress, and students also read and respond to each other's texts. In College Seminar 1: Identity Matters, in fall 2001, a class of first semester students used printed and visual texts to examine issues of identity through such disciplinary lenses as anthropology, psychology, and literature. In College Seminar 2: In Class/Out Classed, in spring 2002, first- and second- year participants took on issues related to education, identity, and equity. Students in both courses were all women and represented diversity along other dimensions. Both courses were designed to provide opportunities for exploration of identity politics in the nested contexts of classroom, campus, city, and world.

In this chapter, we reconsider what happened in these classes, with the goal of better understanding what it takes to teach and learn diversity. In this vein, we argue for building community as a prerequisite to engaging real discussions of diversity, and, paradoxically, for engaging such discussions as a requirement for building community. Thus, the challenge of the classroom is to circumvent our wish that trust precede risk and instead to create the conditions for risk-taking as a medium for spawning trust. Further, we suggest that the classroom need not, and in fact cannot, be an isolated, time-bound space. Instead, as students take on real issues involving their (evolving) identities and differences over time and across (college) contexts, they bring their emergent knowledge of how to participate in constructive ways to the ongoing task of building a larger community.

The process of coauthoring this chapter became itself an attempt to generate and sustain real conversations about identity, diversity, and power in the undergraduate classroom; as such, this chapter both employs and extends some of the same premises and structures as the courses.

ESTABLISHING THE BACKDROP AND THE FOREGROUND

To promulgate a rich, if still partial, picture of participants' experiences, we write and negotiate meanings from our several perspectives: Jody Cohen, a member of the college faculty, designed these college seminars with colleagues and taught both courses. Sarah Mendell and Emily Hayes were participants in both courses as freshwomen, while Natalie Inozil was in CSem 1 only, and Prerna Srivastava was in CSem 2 only. To offer a poly-vocal understanding of the ways that these courses did and did not open up compelling explorations of pluralism, we embarked on this opportunity to investigate differences as well as convergences in our perspectives.

This group went through several iterations: As we met, talked, and wrote—in the student dining hall, on the sofa and chairs in Jody's office and via e-mail—the "we" changed, literally as we subtracted (those unable to make the commitment) and added (those we realized we needed in the conversation) and figuratively, as we articulated, questioned, and stretched our understandings. Our first conversations were broad, in terms of how we conceptualized both the literal and the theoretical terrain. Not having all shared a single classroom as context, we were quickly drawn to exploring the ways diversity was constructed on the campus. A diverse group in terms of race, ethnicity, sexual orientation, age, and role at the college ourselves, we may have reached for a theoretical underpinning that would acknowledge our diverse perspectives while not putting ourselves in an untenably uncomfortable relation to each other before we had our bearings.

We use the format of speakers in dialogue to highlight where we were coming from as we began the project and how we experienced and thought about these issues. Following our initial dinner, Prerna sought to articulate what we'd discussed and to move us to the next step.

Prerna: How do we define diversity? In *Webster's*, the term "diverse" is defined as "composed of distinct or unlike elements or qualities." If this is the case, then why does the term "diversity" take on such a different meaning in real life, specifically on the college campus? When we speak of diversity, it does *not* include the majority. Case in point: The purpose of the Office of Institutional Diversity is here to promote "diversity" on campus; that is, support the minority cultural groups on campus and ensure that the campus is not homogenous in composition. Who are we talking about when we talk about "diversifying" the student body or "diversity-sensitive" issues? Do I contribute to the "diversity" on Bryn Mawr's campus, and another person doesn't?

Let's address those who diversify the student body due to their cultural/ethnic/racial differences. The term "minority" not only affords a disadvantage in terms of numbers but it is also a political term, since minorities struggle against a layering of historical biases. Members develop the feeling that "This is my reclaimed space, and you have no right to encroach upon it," and "I refuse to be the iconic mouthpiece for the group you expect me to represent." They forge an internal solidarity upon mutual recognition of what being "Indian" or "African American" means, a tenuous cultural cohesion forged upon wrongs committed by the group seen as "not diverse," who in turn tends to further this exclusion by building their own walls of protection. Anna Deveare Smith (1996) introduces the concept of "identity houses," which we enter in order to be with others like us. A "them/us" dichotomy emerges, and the further individual identity is concretized along these lines, the harder it is to break through this barrier and foster real dialogue. Given all this, how do you set a ground for effective, dialectical dialogue rather than monologue within the classroom?

Questions for the classroom: When students from different "identity houses" meet in a single space, what kind of dynamic emerges? Should political correctness be checked at the door, and at what risk? What forces are employed to protect this space? What is the value of rupture?

Jody: We discovered that in order to truly open up, listen, challenge, and extend ourselves and each other, we needed to conduct inquiry in which we probed not only our theoretical understandings but also our own and each other's specific experiences. In generating this kind of dialogue, we needed to be able to name the social locations of various players on campus and in the classroom. We also needed to name uncomfortable and usually unspoken dynamics, such as the self-censoring that Sarah describes in her e-mail below. Finally, we needed to be able to explore what constituted "successes" and "failures" in the classroom, despite our different stakes and experiences. Thus we began to expose our vulnerabilities and hopes, to take risks with each other as we sought to understand the role of risk in the classroom. Sarah moves us in that direction.

Sarah: Studying multiculturalism in a liberal arts college today is dominated by what I will refer to as students' or even professors' "justification of experience" (that is, each of us feels entitled to speak only when we share the "identity house" under discussion). Of particular interest to what this chapter will explore is the fact that CSem 1 was quiet and reserved, with the exception of a few outspoken women, while CSem 2 was dominated by enthusiastic dialogue and daring comments. I believe the "failure" of the first course may be attributed to a general lack of experience in discussing such sensitive issues as race and ethnicity, particularly in light of the events that took place during only its second week on September 11. Lacking the academic experience of engaging in risky dialogue, students in this class remained quiet until the conversation became one they felt they could contribute to legitimately because of their own personal experience. As a simple example, during a conversation to do with African Americans in the United States, only African American students would speak.

But the second class, In Class/Out Classed, was full of students who spoke out loud about points of difference not their own. I am currently accounting for this contrast by considering the students' academic experience as part of their personal experience. The women who spoke frequently and relatively uninhibitedly during the fall course had experience in other settings where they dealt with pluralism, and those in the spring course were either sophomores who had been immersed in the study and culture of multiculturalism, or freshmen, like myself, who had taken Identity Matters. If students had previously participated in similar dialogues, then they would feel the same sort of legitimization speaking about some point of difference as they would speaking on behalf of that point of difference themselves, and the justification of experience would essentially disappear. The quiet students were less often disinterested than they were following that elementary talk-about-what-you-know recommendation that instills fear and a sense of danger in everything you don't know. Today they are often center-stage participants in similar identity-marking conversations. Only when college students are exposed to classes like these and become comfortable putting multiculturalism into academic, as well as everyday, language, may they join others in paving the way for a more diverse and better integrated community at large.

In attempting to understand the difficulty we had in opening up the very issues that Identity Matters was designed to provoke, we cannot declare a lack of words as a lack of thought; we can, however, try to understand why someone might not articulate their thoughts during a classroom conversation. We should not assume that silence is "bad" because in trying to understand why someone is silent, we come across many answers and questions. Conversely, is intense emotion necessary for good class discussion? An outspoken class—those who put issues on the outside, visible and expressed—is not better or worse than a class where individuals keep issues inside, invisible and silent. The real success of the class comes with the thinking that the individuals develop and produce over a greater period of time.

Jody: Although we continued to value the importance of viewing diversity on the campus and in our respective lives beyond the campus, we also noticed that our exchanges deepened as we delved into specific, sometimes troubling dynamics of classroom life, especially those spaces some of us had shared. It was from plumbing the meaning of particular people, texts, and interactions that we began to envision what might be possible.

I am thinking of real and often specific moments in classes where issues of diversity came up—and these seem to me both preeminent teaching moments *and* unpredictable, potentially painful moments that could lead to shutdown. So, for example, when a majority/dominant culture person makes a comment like "race is not (or should not be) important," does this mean something different, and/or provoke a different response from others, than if a minority person makes the same comment? These kinds of questions seem essential to considering the paradox of safety and risk in the classroom.

As a (White) teacher, I feel a commitment to contribute to campus dialogue about "diversity" and I argue for the importance of the classroom as a site for this work on several grounds: First, human identity and difference are foundational to investigation across the disciplines. Second, in the world right now we are experiencing the profound ramifications of differences as these play out in geographic, cultural, and ideological conflict; dealing with identity and difference is of critical importance. Finally, the classroom is a space that is diverse by fiat; that is, as a space not designated as a forum for an identity group, the classroom becomes a place where people have the call to emerge from our various "identity houses" to meet, exchange views, reach for a deeper and more complex understanding of ourselves and one another. On the best days, I imagine this as an act of creativity and risk, the classroom as a place of intersecting personal and political meaning.

I am most interested in fostering a classroom space that encourages participants' development of what I'll call "imaginative capacity," which I'm defining as the capacity to enter as far as possible into someone else's experience of, and perspective on, the world. My goal as a teacher is to cultivate people's capacity to both know and stretch themselves, and in so doing to challenge the boundaries between "self" and "other." I see this as a lifelong task, and consider myself also engaged in this challenge.

A WORKING THEORY: DEALING WITH DIVERSITY IN THE CLASSROOM

The working theory we present here emerged as we wrestled with the meaning of the particulars—with the paradoxes of safety and risk, "success" and "failure," capacity and actuality. Below Sarah sketches this collective understanding of what it takes and what it might mean for individuals to talk about hard and complex issues in a real way in the classroom. Then we elaborate this working theory, weaving in classroom stories from several of us that nuance and texture our understandings. We consider how individuals' processes necessarily implicate the group—within a given classroom and in the fluid and evolving context of the college community.

Sarah: I'll begin at the *establishment of a safe space*, which is not necessarily the beginning of the process of discussing diversity because the process is a circular one. This includes the role of facilitator in terms of how the space is introduced: what ground rules are put out there and what happens when there's a violation of safety. The immediate goal of establishing a safe space is to allow for . . .

Risk. Risk involves pushing borders and crossing boundaries that have been constructed on an individual and group basis. To put something out there that others have not ever thought of or that goes against previous assumptions or standards or that challenges what we're comfortable with is to . . .

Challenge assumptions and offer diversity of opinion concerning those assumptions. Though it's often difficult to define a group since the nature of identity is so unique, it must be true that a congregation of similar people do not push each other to think in ways that challenge their current thinking. Once radically different ideas are thrown into a diverse mix of people, the group as a whole is forced to go through the process of . . .

Conscious reversal. This process asks that individuals internalize statements made by others so that they may better understand them. This requires that these individuals hear clearly what the speaker is saying and relate that statement to their own life. For instance, if a Black student gets angry at having to defend her race because she is the only Black person in the class, I apply that same example using criteria specific to me. In this case, I would imagine myself the only lesbian in a room full of straight people having to serve as a representative of the entire sexual subgroup. This process is dependent upon the imaginative capacity of the individual to enter as far as possible into someone else's experience and perspective. The use of this capacity for experiencing this conscious reversal is a mark of success in a classroom dealing with diversity. The outcome of this step of the process is therefore the fulfillment of this capacity, to . . .

Promote entering as far as possible into someone else's experience and perspective on the world, in other words, to increase awareness and widen scope of perspective, which will ultimately lead to a . . .

Closeness among the group. Such closeness within the group closes the circle by serving to enhance the already established . . .

now, *reestablished safe space*, thereby opening up greater opportunity for the sharing of diverse perspectives.

Establishing a Space/Taking (and Not Taking) Risks

Since it is the teacher who "intends" the course, often selecting focus and/or curriculum materials, planning the syllabus, and even arranging the chairs in the room, we might assume that the part of the teacher's role is to "establish the space," especially for a course like CSem 1, which is co-designed by teachers for entering freshwomen who carry little prior experience with either the college or the others in the room. Further, the word "establish" might suggest that the nature of the classroom space gets defined early and rather definitively. However, we want to argue for the establishment of space in the classroom as mutual and reciprocal, as in dynamic relation with taking risks and challenging assumptions.

As we discussed what kind of space we thought encouraged openness and growth in relation to issues of diversity, we found ourselves returning again and again to the continuum and coincidence of safety and risk: for example, we recalled spaces in which the development of a certain closeness allowed for risk, defined as generating "something you haven't already thought that threatens something you need." We pose this question: What type of classroom space is conducive for encouraging people to emerge from our "identity houses" and become aware of our "blind spots"?

Both safety and risk are critical for this work. Safety is necessary to nurture the recognition and articulation of our own perspectives, which in turn provide us with a stance or position (an identity house) from which we can then stretch beyond ourselves to try to see/hear/comprehend others' experiences and perspectives that are different from our own. But to take that step out of our own stance/position to try to understand the world from someone else's position requires a risk, a letting go of self, preconceived notions, guarantees. In traversing this distance between self and other, we have to risk letting go of political correctness, of the power and/or voice we're accustomed to. This groundlessness can be frightening, whether it's going on internally or more externally, and whether the scene plays out in intellectual or more personal terms. These variations are the plot, so to speak; the real classroom drama—the development of imaginative capacity as a kind of leap from "self" to "other"—is going on where there is intent to create and sustain a conducive space and where individuals make the decision to take on this work. It might further be the case that when a critical mass of individuals takes on this work in a classroom, it galvanizes a kind of collective development that participants recognize and share; but this doesn't make the less public and collective work of individuals inside a classroom without such a critical mass any less valuable.

We are always and continually establishing the space of the classroom, in relation to simultaneous trajectories that are always in play:

1. Who we are as individuals is always in flux, especially given the transitional phase that most freshwomen experience and the subject matter of Identity Matters, which is indeed intended to respond to this transitional moment.
2. Who we are in relation to each other is likewise in constant flux, and this occurs as relationships form and shift both in and out of the classroom. This is true of the teacher's relationships with students, and also of students' relationships with each other. In this regard, the classroom space may be more contiguous and profoundly entangled

with campus life than is often recognized when we consider the classroom as a place with clear boundaries. Further, the teacher's knowledge is likely limited in this arena.

3. The world itself is in flux—from the smaller world of the campus and surrounds to the globe. This was especially evident in CSem 1 (2001), a school year that opened with 9/11 and its aftermath.

In the stories of this section, we recall our several entryways into the classroom of CSem 1. Entering as a disparate group of individuals with no intrinsic reason to trust and engage with each other, how do we take up the work of creating a space where trust and risk, stretching and knowing become a shared possibility?

Jody: Curriculum itself—especially for a course with a primary subject of diversity—presents a paradox insofar as we understand materials/texts and participants as essential and interdependent components. Strangely, then, the teacher is set the task of selecting material for a group of students whom she may not yet know at all, and thus she is working in the dark from the beginning. This notion of working in the dark is a powerful metaphor for considering what the teacher does and does not know from the first day onward. Not only does she bring only her single perspective to the classroom, but also her role and even her desires—for example, that this constitutes an effective and enjoyable course for students—further separate her from knowing her students' experiences of the course. The teacher's apparent role as course architect both enables her to establish certain purposes and processes that define the "space" of the classroom and specifically delimits her role, highlighting the crucial roles of other participants in doing this work.

In fall 2001, Identity Matters was a new course I had designed for the College Seminar Program. The focus of the course was on the nature of group identity in light of contemporary and historical constructions of identity, difference, and power. Due to the knowledge and interests of those of us who designed the course, there was particular emphasis on racial and ethnic identity and on issues of expression and representation of identity. As a group, we were all women: thirteen White students (including several Jews), a Black student, an Asian American student, a Japanese exchange student, and a student who identified as half European and half Muslim. My section met Tuesday and Thursday mornings at 10:00 A.M. On the third day of class, before we knew all of each other's names, we walked in to find the towers burning on a television set pulled to the front of the room. Like much of the rest of the world suddenly unified in real-time, we struggled to process what was going on, opting at some point to turn off the TV, stay together, and share something about ourselves with one another. This fragile hour, in which we told each other mostly small, daily things that would not ordinarily ever be the stuff of the college classroom, held a tenuous promise. And yet I had little notion of how students were experiencing the opening of this class.

Natalie: Walking into CSem class Tuesday morning at ten o'clock, I felt out of place. First let me formally introduce myself and give you some background information. My name is Natalie Inozil. At the time of this course I was a freshman at Bryn Mawr. I was born and raised in Boston. The neighborhood I live in is made up predominately of West Indians, Africans, African Americans, Dominicans, Puerto Ricans, Mexicans, and Vietnamese.

The main reason I'm at Bryn Mawr College is because of the Posse Foundation. Posse is an organization that partners up with the best colleges in the country and sends ten diverse student leaders to these premier learning institutions. Posse sends groups of students together to provide support systems for themselves and to diversify the campus. Bryn Mawr Posse I is made up of eleven amazing women leaders from all walks of life. We went through extensive training for eight months to prepare us for issues inside and outside of the college classroom. After our training we arrived on campus and were given a mentor, Cynthia, the director of institutional diversity. We met once a week as a group and separately with our mentor. This background should help you understand where I'm coming from.

I felt out of place that day because of the makeup of the class. In my other classes, the previous day, I knew at least one person from my Posse, so I felt somewhat comfortable, but I was the only Black person in Identity Matters class, in which the dominant kind of identity we looked at was race. I felt uncomfortable. The racial makeup of the class made me aware of my race. Not that being at Bryn Mawr itself doesn't make me aware. But being the only Black person in that class I definitely felt like all eyes were on me. I have always been taught that you do not talk about race in "mixed company." I don't know where I learned this, maybe it's one of those commonsense things because when I asked my Black peers where they learned it they couldn't remember, but they all said that talking about race in "mixed company" is not the smartest thing to do. To avoid conflicts and those uncomfortable feelings you don't talk about race in front of people that are not the same race as you. To talk about race you have to get out of your personal space/circle and I can't do that with people I don't feel comfortable with. I feel a level of comfort with people of the same race; even if we don't agree we can understand where the other is coming from. But you don't have that when you're in front of a group of people that you don't feel a historical bond with through the struggle you had to endure due to the color of your skin. So I refrained from voicing my opinion during discussions because of the "mixed company" and because I felt like whatever I said, I would be talking for all Black people, and I don't represent all Black people. I had yet to feel comfortable at Bryn Mawr itself, never mind feeling comfortable enough to talk about these topics in class.

Jody: While Natalie feels exposed, too centralized in terms of how the Identity Matters curriculum is constructed to highlight certain dimensions of identity, Emily quickly feels left out of this curriculum, as if her identity were invisible and thus by implication does not *matter*.

Emily: Going into Identity Matters, I was excited about the course, and the prospect of exploring and sharing my identity with other students. I felt since I was in a new environment where people had not previously known me, I would not be judged for what had happened to me, but instead would be seen for who I was. I went into Identity Matters with the mindset of being ready and willing to share about myself.

But something happened: on the first day, when given the opportunity to share about our identities, I hesitated and lost my courage. We did an activity the first class in which we had to write about identity/something we identified with, and then share our writing. I had the desire to write what I was truly feeling, but it felt too risky to reveal those things about myself right away. So instead I wrote vaguely:

> Identity: part of what I identify with includes being a woman. And also with the need to become more independent. I find my identity changing; the last three years have brought about so much change, it's sometimes hard to believe my identity was ever so different; I feel I have become someone unlike who I once was. Some of these changes have been conscious decisions, while others have been forced upon me. I have come to realize that even though I did not choose some changes, they became a part of me.

I can remember sitting in class, wanting to share, yet scared to open up; I did not want to reveal my true identity. I felt that my identity, and things I identified with, were too different from other people, and that my type of diversity was not important—an odd way to feel in a class entitled "Identity Matters." That first day set the tone for the rest of the semester.

I think the course material and the fact that I felt everybody else was going to write about her ethnicity or gender made me hesitate. Also, experiences outside of class influenced how I acted in class. While I had arrived on campus ready to share, after some meetings with the administration of the college I felt vulnerable and on the defensive. The message I felt I was getting from the college was "you are too different, and are not worthy of being here." Where before I had had pride for overcoming so much to get here, I now held fear that I would not be allowed to stay. This made me less eager to share. If the administration, who before my arrival had assured me they would support me in every way possible, was already giving me these messages, how would the students react? I was not sure, and was scared to find out.

Jody: Natalie and Emily entered the class with awareness of their own identities, which was attenuated by the perceived fit, or lack thereof, with the curriculum and the identities of others in the room. Although differently situated from each other, they both describe a tension between the urge to speak openly on the one hand and the call to protect themselves and proceed cautiously on the other. The process of establishing a space for open communication puts demands on participants, requiring that students consider speaking in "mixed company," as Natalie says, and in the absence of any certain knowledge of having compatriots, being understood, or finding acceptance, as Emily reminds us. And yet it is also in this early experience of campus life that these students have the opportunity to listen to their inner dialogue and to dare to engage in outer dialogue—to take a leap that might engender trust and make sustained conversation possible. Below Natalie and I recall moments when we felt the class to be in the midst of this challenge.

Jody: I remember one class discussion, about halfway through the semester. We had read about and condemned Gobineau's eighteenth-century European racism (Augstein, 1996), with some embarrassment, I thought, and I'd asked us all to consider for the next class whether and in what ways we were inheritors of that very racism. That day I pushed, doubting myself all the while. At one point in the rather halting acknowledgment of racism in our current lives, one young woman said that she'd considered going to the Sisterhood dance but had been concerned about perhaps being the only White woman there. Others nodded, shared this concern. The Black student exploded (not loudly but as if she were surprised to hear herself speak): "There *were* White people there! And how do you think it feels to be the only Black person, here (in class) and lots of places on campus!" As the period ended and we all headed on to our next locations, next personas, I worried for both of these students—for their public display, for the ways that we understood their positions incompletely at best. And yet I also delighted in their willingness to risk, and in the energy and vulnerability their risks touched off, which I thought essential to moving us past disembodied appreciation of texts. It was fall break. We returned after a week to gaze and smile again across our circle, puzzled that we were again strangers, coming up against what felt to me like complex barriers to real engagement.

Natalie: Looking back now on the times I chose to voice my opinion in class and when I chose to keep my opinion to myself, there were many factors that dictated my decision to talk or not. First I must say that I'm an introvert. I take in everything and process it before I speak. Some people talk to process their thoughts/opinions, but mine are already formulated when I articulate them. Second, I'm shy and I felt somewhat intimidated by a few students. Some of the girls in Identity Matters were very talkative and were using these big words that I didn't understand, which made me feel like their social class gave them this education that I didn't get in my Boston public school. Third, I felt like I was the only one in the class that had the "double consciousness" that W. E. B. DuBois (1953) talked about in the reading we did. I saw myself and I saw myself "through the revelation of the other world" (p. 3). At times that was a factor in my talking or not. The makeup of my audience, in this case the class, and their vision of me really affected what I said or didn't say because I took that into account before I spoke and after I spoke.

Reflecting on the class now, I think it was a success. Conferences with Jody helped me open up more in class. Cynthia's [Posse mentor] words of encouragement were also a factor in me gaining a voice in the class, not only in that class but in all my classes. As time went by I felt more comfortable and I voiced my opinion more frequently; others might think it wasn't a lot but I never was a big talker. I think more than I speak and when I do speak, I get the whole class's attention and I make an impact on their intellectual space. I walked out of the class many times with something to share with my Posse and Cynthia, whether it was a comment a student made or a new perspective I had gained in the class. If the class was more diverse then maybe I would have talked more but that's not a guarantee. In the African History class I am taking now there are an equal number of Black and White students and my voice is heard when I feel like I can bring insight to the discussion. I don't talk because I like to hear my voice. Some students always have something to say, which I guess was good because they propelled me to voice my opinion on issues of diversity in a nondiverse class. The success in the College Seminar class was my gaining a voice. I learned to put aside my difference and speak my mind; in order to feel more content in the class I had to voice my opinion and deal with the outcome of my opinion instead of leaving the class feeling offended by someone's opinion and not being able to express mine. At the beginning of the semester I didn't speak at all, and by the end I spoke whenever I felt I had something to add to the discussion.

Jody: There's a temptation to believe that classroom space is accomplished once and for all, resulting in a stable and coherent situation. Even when the space may not be all that participants might wish for, there is a comfort in the known. However, the work of establishing the space is never over, and in fact a different kind of opportunity may present itself toward the end of the semester, as participants may be again on the brink of becoming "strangers." Perhaps there are lapses—moments outside of our usual conception of the classroom as an encounter in time and space—that represent the chasm, the leap. . . .

It was almost the end of the semester. On mid-semester assessments I'd heard from several students that we'd done enough on race, and indeed I'd backed off, framing issues in economic and other terms. I scheduled a video viewing in the final weeks, and was debating a few choices when, to my surprise, several students requested that we see Spike Lee's *Bamboozled*, as one of the other sections had done. I agreed. In my re-viewing of this film before class, I was convinced of its brilliance and also that it was too daring, even painful a choice for this group at this time. Although I usually love teaching, I didn't want to go to class that day. I couldn't think how I'd possibly facilitate a useful discussion of this film with this group. The class took off: We critiqued all racial representations, from the Black entrepreneur to the White audience in black-face, and acknowledged the nuances of our own varying complicities in these representations. We spoke from ourselves and with each other, listening, learning, allowing questions to sit. I left class with a more intricate and profound appreciation for the film, and also for the sixteen human beings who had just unraveled my assumptions about our work together.

Challenging Assumptions/Catalyzing Conscious Reversal

When the space has been established for the fluid interchange and cross-fertilization of ideas between public and private "thought-space," the next step is toward "conscious consciousness reversal," a heightened sense of critical consciousness which entails "being conscious of, not only as intent on objects but as turned in upon itself in a Jasperian 'split'—consciousness as consciousness of consciousness" (Freire, 2002, p. 79). This process of active introspection in relation to one's context, however, is never fully complete, the space never fully fertilized, as it is precisely these "limit-situations" (p. 113) in the form of unchallenged mental blind spots that lay the fertile ground for the dialectical and cyclical processes of action-reflection and lead to the further development of imaginative capacity. "Student-teachers" and "teacher-students" are perpetually in the process of "becoming"—"as unfinished, uncompleted beings in and with a likewise unfinished reality" (p. 84).

This spiral downward and outward toward heightened critical consciousness and the establishment of fertile ground for internal development, however, does not occur in simply one step, but rather in a series of "states of consciousness." At each subsequent stage, the recognition and subsequent action upon one's blind spots progresses deeper into oneself, digging deeper into one's consciousness and allowing for the fertilization of thought by allowing for absorption and the critical evaluation of opposing ideas.

The first state, which we will refer to as "sterile consciousness," is one where the very existence of blind spots is unbeknownst to the student/teacher, and no allowance is made for the penetration of opposing ideas into private thought-space. This state of consciousness is often marked by sterility of thought in that no assumptions are challenged, and mental traffic remains static.

In the second state, referred to as static "fertile consciousness," the subject, though conscious of his or her blind spot(s), makes no attempt at "conscious consciousness reversal," and these blind spots, instead of being acted upon, fester and stagnate within one's consciousness, thereby arresting the cyclical development of critical consciousness. As Freire (2002) suggests, consciousness that is not in dynamic tension with the world is uncritical and "detached from reality" (p. 72). This state of consciousness is often marked by a facade of political correctness, which smothers the process of attaining critical consciousness as it deliberately shrouds one's unchallenged assumptions in verbiage, an indication of the lack of depth of one's understanding.

As we grow accustomed to a classroom in which we've struck certain bargains about what of ourselves we will share and what of others we will be open to, we may reach a plateau in which our internal awareness outdistances our present capacity for exposure. As the coauthors of this chapter returned to the subject of silence over the course of our conversations, we became increasingly intrigued with the notion that, like the color black, silence was not absence but rather a complex mix of "presences" or experiences that might later reveal themselves. It may be that in silence we each bring to consciousness the sensitivities and uncertainties that will later bear the fruit of shared insight.

Emily: I figured that as Identity Matters progressed, I would have the opportunity to share my thoughts about the aspects of my identity. But instead of becoming more comfortable and able to share, I retreated, isolating myself from my classmates and the possibility of sharing. I was looking forward to investigating a myriad of different aspects of identity; but it seemed as if we were on a pre-set course of what differences constituted issues of identity. Race and ethnicity were the key components we studied. I enjoyed and wanted to investigate those aspects, but I also expected us to touch on other aspects of diversity and identity. I waited for other issues of identity to surface in class readings and discussions. When they did not, I distanced myself from the class and the material. Although I thought about aspects of my identity, I did not talk about them in class. Although I identified with the readings, the aspects by which I identified with them were different from those of the class, and therefore I did not voice my thoughts. The semester drew to a close, and still I did not share in class.

Jody: In some senses, static fertile consciousness can actually be seen as a regression, for the acknowledgment of these blind spots leads to deliberate inaction.

A next and significant state of consciousness, though by no means an "end" to the cycle of consciousness, is "dynamic fertile consciousness," wherein both the necessary components—reflection and action—continue indefinitely in a mutually reinforcing dialectic, catalyzing cross-fertilization of internal thought-space. At this point, one both recognizes and takes action upon conscious reversal of one's blind spot(s). A person experiencing true dynamic fertile consciousness recognizes her/his own incompleteness and the inexhaustibility of her/his blind spots, and is never complacent about reaching a perfect state of consciousness. As is the case with this state of consciousness, which fosters fertile ground for the fluid exchange of ideas, "true dialogue cannot exist unless the dialoguers engage in critical thinking—thinking which does not separate itself from action, but constantly immerses itself in temporality without fear of the risks involved" (Freire, 2002, p. 92).

For the participants in these College Seminar courses, time itself played a critical role in learning, as students moved through the weeks that became a semester and then a school year. Further, students experienced the sheer force of being *in the mix*, of sitting with themselves and others in spaces where people were deliberately recognizing difference—silently and out loud—in texts and in the room. As participants coalesced, dispersed, and recoalesced across campus contexts, they called up more frequently the conditions for challenging assumptions, locating blind spots, deepening dialogue. Natalie, and Emily reflect on moments of blindness, sudden insight, and the emergence of community in diversity below.

Natalie: I remember talking to Jody during one of our meetings about how when I spoke that day in class about the Alvarez reading there was total silence after my comment. Usually after someone makes a statement in the class I felt like someone always refuted, agreed with their point, or brought a new angle to the discussion using the previous point. In my case I felt like since I was Black and my comment was about something that only I would know, then I was right. But Jody pointed out that it was because what I said was so profound that everyone was quiet after I talked. I brought an insight into the discussion that no one had seen. By stepping out of my comfort zone to make that comment, I made the discussion more fruitful for everyone else. Looking back now, the only reason I made that one comment is because a comment was made about the distinction between light skin, dark skin, nice hair, and bad hair in the Dominican Republic. The comment propelled me to express my point of view on the difference in differentiating between light- and dark-skinned Dominicans and racism in the United States. I come from the neighbor country, Haiti, which, just like the Dominican Republic, is made up of one race. When a distinction is made between light and dark skin it doesn't mean that one gets advantages over the other. If a light-skinned Haitian/Dominican gets on a packed bus, a dark-skinned person doesn't have to get up and give their seat away. We use these characteristics to distinguish between a group of people who are the same race. But that is not the case in the United States, where the distinction means a better life for one race at the cost of the other race. My added input is what the class needed for the discussions to be fruitful, and that's why my classmates were quiet after my point.

Emily: By the time the second semester rolled around, I had proved myself to the school, and they had backed off; I no longer feared being forced to leave. Without this threat, I became more comfortable and self-confident, and vulnerability transformed into anger at how I had been treated. I began to share, to drop my defenses and guard, although it took time and experience for me to become comfortable doing so.

   As we sat around in a circle on the first day of class for CSem 2: InClass/OutClassed, Jody had us do an activity similar to the one we had done in CSem 1, but this time the prompt was to write about a time in school when our cultural needs did not fit with what the school provided. I remember sitting there, looking down at my blank paper right after Jody had given us the prompt, and wishing I could sink into the floor. I tried to think of something to write, besides what immediately came to mind. I had flashbacks to CSem 1, and was hesitant to open up and share personal information with the entire class on the very first day. I desperately searched my brain for something else, but nothing came to mind, so with my heart beating in my throat, I wrote what I felt was a risk to write:

After my brain injury, my culture needs did not fit in with what my school was used to providing. My high school, having practically no experience with someone in my position, did not know what to do. In the beginning, when even I did not know my own needs, I was placed on home instruction, and tutors were assigned to cover my subjects. They were not prepared in the least for the task that lay in front of them; they had simply been handed my work and expected me to fly through it. They did not understand the fatigue, headaches, dizziness, nausea, and everything else I was experiencing; they were not prepared for my limited cognitive abilities. The first thing my school did was kick me out of Honors classes; they were trying "not to stress me"—they did not understand how they only succeeded in hurting me. I went from being a top Honors student to *bottom* in their eyes; they did not understand that brain injured does not mean stupid. My (cognitive) processes have been altered, but my intelligence has emerged unscathed.

It was not the writing that bothered me so much; I had written about my brain injury and its effects on me on numerous occasions. But when we were asked to first talk with the person next to us about what we had written and then to participate in a read-around, that made me uncomfortable and nervous. When it came time to share with the student seated next to me, I was nervous but at least I knew her. She had been in CSem 1 with me first semester, so I felt I would not be judged as much on what I said to her now. Still, I summed up what I had written, and left out parts. During the read-around, I was the second person to share. I felt so different from everybody else in the class; I thought that their cultural differences would be similar, or at least there would be a few common ones, and mine was so different. I guess from previous experiences with people's reactions, I half expected them to get that "oh" look on their faces, shake their heads in pity, and from thereafter view me as not as smart. I did not say much, I summed it up in about a sentence, saying something short like, "my culture needs were not met in high school after I received a brain injury."

As the read-around continued and I heard the other students' responses, I was amazed; there were such a variety of responses, I was shocked! By the time the last person spoke, I found myself wishing I had been on the other side of the circle—if I had been one of the last to go, and not one of the first, I would have shared more.

The reason sharing my thoughts felt so risky to me was that I felt that nobody else had gone through anything similar to what I had experienced. My view was that I was different from them, not that we are all different from each other. I looked at what made me different from everybody else and saw *only* the differences. Still, I took the leap. And even though I was hesitant, it felt good to do so, and I did not regret taking that risk. As the issue at hand was education, we all stood on a common ground, so my experience, while I felt it was very different from everybody else's, had that similarity.

I left class that day with a renewed sense of self. This was the beginning of a change in me, and I began to approach my differences in a different manner, viewed others and myself in a different light, and felt myself becoming more open-minded; and the learning and growth that resulted were incredible. No longer closed off as I had been in CSem 1, I found myself voicing my thoughts and taking more risks, not just in CSem 2 but in other places on campus as well. I had come to realize that everyone has their own difference. I was no longer scared or intimidated by others or the school, and I felt anger and pride instead of fear and embarrassment.

My blind spot was that I viewed myself as being so different from everybody else. While I recognized that each person had a distinct personality and identity, I viewed it as a "me versus them" situation. I saw all the other students as having something in common, and myself as being the odd woman out. What they had in common was something I did not have, nor would I ever have. I perceived everyone else at Bryn Mawr as having had very similar high school experiences: the honors track all the way through, lots of advanced placement (AP) courses. Me, I was different. My injury had taken me off that path, and my last two years of high school were the antithesis of what I imagined to be their experience: junior year I was on home instruction while in rehabilitation, and senior year I went back for three classes, none of which were honors or AP. So this was the difference I saw: although I knew each of their high school experiences had had slight variations, they were remarkably similar. But mine looked nothing like theirs.

This "me versus them" thinking limited me and was my blind spot. It was not until that first day of CSem 2 when we did the read-around that I began to realize the way I had been viewing others and myself. I had perceived diversity in a skewed sense, either you had it or you didn't. I failed to consider that everyone, in their own way, in some way, has diversity, for we are all different from each other. Once I came to this realization, I began to see how viewing others through that lens was holding me back, that it was limiting my growth and learning. As the semester progressed, I not only became more willing and able to share my own experiences, but I also became a better listener and learner. As I sat in class, I took in all my classmates had to say; I listened to their thoughts, processed what they said. Now in class, I also responded to what my classmates said. I did not hold back.

TOWARD A CONCLUSION

Henry David Thoreau (1983) talks about the process of spiraling downward, digging and unraveling until some place is reached that seems more real, if only as a result of having slushed through the muck of all that was not so real—opinion, prejudice, assumptions.

> Let us settle ourselves, and work and wedge our feet
> downward through the mud and slush of opinion, and
> prejudice, and tradition and delusion, and appearance, that
> alluvion which covers the globe, through Paris and London,
> through New York and Boston and Concord, through church
> and state, through poetry and philosophy and religion, till we
> come to a hard bottom and rocks in place, which we can call
> reality, and say, This is, and no mistake; and then begin,
> having a point d'appui, below freshet and frost and fire, a
> place where you might found a wall or a state, or set a lamp-
> post safely, or perhaps a gauge, not a Nilometer, but a
> Realometer, that future ages might know how deep a freshet of
> shams and appearances had gathered from time to time. (p.
> 142)

We think this describes the cyclical and cumulative nature of our work dealing with the layers and complexities of diversity in the undergraduate classroom. We speak in this chapter for the difficulty, and, at the same time, the necessity of taking on this challenge in the classroom early in students' undergraduate experience. While students may enter without having engaged in such dialogues in "mixed company," giving rise to pockets of silence as well as dialogue, we see this as a crucial opportunity for creating the conditions for the risk-taking, both inward and outward, that is necessary for real dialogue. We argue for crafting an undergraduate trajectory in which teachers and students engage such dialogue early on, as in CSem 1, and then again in other courses and contexts in their college careers. This kind of trajectory scaffolds individuals' evolution and encourages individuals to work collectively to create a truly diverse college community.

REFERENCES

Augstein, H. (Ed.). (1996). *Race: The origins of an idea, 1760–1850*. Bristol, UK: Thoemmes Press.

DuBois, W. E. B. (1953). *The souls of Black folk*. Chicago: A. C. McClurg.

Freire, P. (2002). *Pedagogy of the oppressed* (30th anniversary ed.) New York: Continuum.

Lee, S. (Director). (2001). *Bamboozled*. Special ed., widescreen. Burbank, CA: New Line Home Entertainment.

Smith, A. D. (1996). *New traditions compendium forums and commentaries, 1992–96*. http://www.ntcp.org/compendium/artists/ANNA.html (accessed Dec. 2002).

Thoreau, H. D. (1983). *Walden and civil disobedience*. New York: Penguin Books.

CHAPTER NINE

Critical Multicultural Teacher Reflections
Counternarratives to Images of the White Male Blockhead

Sharon M. Ravitch, R. Reed Roeser, and Brian J. Girard
Arcadia University

INTRODUCTION:
CONTEXTUALIZING MULTICULTURAL TEACHER EDUCATION

As America's student population grows increasingly diverse, the teaching force is becoming steadily more homogenous. Currently, approximately 86 percent of American public school teachers are White, middle to upper-middle class, and monolingual and approximately 36 percent of American public school students are people of color (National Commission on Teaching and America's Future Report, 2003). Research confirms that the percentage of White teachers will continue to increase as the student body grows more racially and culturally diverse (Cochran-Smith, 2000; Howard, 1999; National Commission on Teaching and America's Future Report, 2003; Nieto, 2004).

The social, political, and educational implications of these statistics have become the subject of much study and debate in current multicultural education discourse. Many multicultural researchers and educators discuss the issues that arise from the "cultural mismatch" between these two populations. Furthermore, they examine the possible negative ramifications associated with White teachers teaching students of color, given issues of racial inequality and the pervasive ethos of White hegemony in American society (Delpit, 1995; Sleeter, 1995a, 1995b, 1996). Research in multicultural education overwhelmingly asserts that White teachers tend to embrace conservative views of schooling and teaching, lack awareness of structural and social issues affecting student achievement, believe in deficit theories about students of color, and feel ill-equipped to relate with, and effectively teach, students of color (e.g., Delpit, 1995; Hidalgo, 1993; hooks, 1993; Howard, 1999; Ladson-Billings, 1995; Nieto, 2004; Sleeter, 1993, 1996).

Clearly, concerns about issues of diversity and inequality in education are crucial for teacher educators. Less straightforward and more contested, however, is the issue of how these concerns should be addressed in teacher education courses. Current debates in teacher education focus on how teacher educators can help their students to develop the knowledge, attitudes, and skills necessary to work effectively with children from diverse racial, ethnic, and social class groups (Delpit, 1995; Ladson-Billings, 1994; Martin, 1995; Schultz, 1997); whether or not teacher education students retain and use what they learn in their courses (Brown and Borko, 1992; Ladson-Billings, 1995); and what preparing teachers to address student diversity entails (hooks, 1993; Ogbu, 1995; Remillard, 2000; Schultz, 1997; Sleeter, 1995b). Many educators concerned with multicultural issues in teacher education argue that meaningful multicultural teacher education entails more than helping teachers learn to make pedagogical shifts. They argue that it requires challenging and inspiring teachers to make paradigm shifts—shifts in worldview—which will then lead to significant changes in their teaching (Hidalgo, 1993; hooks, 1993; Giroux, 1994; Martin, 1995; McCarthy, 1993; Nieto, 2004). Even among teacher educators who agree on the practical value of facilitating such paradigm shifts, questions remain about what this type of instruction involves and what forms it should take within teacher education courses.

This chapter focuses on two teachers' reflections on their learning experiences in a teacher education course that is based in a critical multicultural perspective.[1] These teachers, both White men, reflect on their experiences as graduate students learning about issues central to multicultural teaching and describe the processes through which their individualized learning and self-reflection occurred. Through centralizing the voices of these teachers, the primary goals of this chapter are to complicate the picture of how White, male teachers learn about issues of culture, racism, and structural and social inequality, and to explore what conditions are necessary for White teachers to make the kinds of shifts in their beliefs, perspectives, and pedagogical philosophies that are necessary to become multicultural educators. This chapter presents and contextualizes the complex and unique experiences these two teachers had as they learned about and engaged in critical self- and societal reflection. The chapter is structured, in part, as a response to the need for what Brookhart and Freeman (1992) refer to as a sub-group consideration of White teachers, who they (and I) argue are not as homogenous as teacher educators are typically led to believe.

I teach at Arcadia University, which is located in the suburbs of Philadelphia. I teach a course called "Cultural Foundations of Education," a master's level education course for students enrolled in a variety of teacher education programs taught within the university's Graduate Education Division. The central course concepts are structural and social inequality, prejudice and bias, social justice, educational and social critique and reform, critical self-reflection, and culturally responsive pedagogy. The course is mandatory for most teaching certificates as a result of a state requirement that teachers enroll in at least one course with multicultural content. Each semester, there are approximately twenty-two students enrolled in the course with an even split between pre-service and experienced teachers. Across semesters, the students are typically all White, middle- to upper-middle-class, heterosexual, nondisabled, European Americans. I have taught this course for over seven years.

This chapter emerges from these seven years of learning, firsthand, about the importance of working to see each student as an individual and to meet students within their own constructions of the world even as I actively encourage them to try to see and live in the world differently. In this chapter, I discuss the context of the Cultural Foundations course with respect to its goals of challenging White teachers to reflect critically on themselves, society, and schooling in ways that help them to evaluate their own values, belief systems, and worldviews as well as issues of social justice in education. Two former students from the course, R. Reed Roeser and Brian J. Girard, reflect on their experiences of learning about themselves as White, upper-middle-class men in our racist, hegemonic society and about the impact their social locations have had on their identities, worldviews, and ideologies. Reed's and Brian's reflections on their learning processes challenge typical notions of White men as ignorant and resistant to learning about their own racism, ethnocentrism, and unearned privilege. These teachers, as students, share their experiences— sometimes painful, often uncomfortable, and, ultimately, transformative—of learning about and then struggling to unlearn the ways in which they have internalized and enacted racism and White hegemony in their personal and professional lives. They do so with an honesty and sensitivity that hold promise for those of us looking for ways to help our White students make paradigm shifts away from their Eurocentric ways of looking at the world and toward a vision of a more equitable and pluralistic American society in which they both take responsibility for their participation in a hegemonic system and locate themselves as advocates for social justice. Particularly for those of us teaching teachers, Reed's and Brian's reflections help us to better understand the ways in which White teachers (who are open-minded) use critical reflection to make meaning and use of material that provokes them to reconceptualize themselves, their views on society, and their pedagogical choices as teachers. These reflections help us to see opportunities for engaging in critical pedagogy and, hopefully, ways to create learning environments that help White teachers come to terms with who they are and how our society functions to marginalize, invalidate, and oppress people of color, gays, lesbians, bisexual and transgender people, non-European immigrants, second-language learners, and people with disabilities.

Context of the Course

Cultural Foundations of Education is designed to create a learning environment in which pre-service and experienced teachers are guided through a critical analysis of the relationship among society, ideology, schooling, and pedagogy. Students are challenged to rigorously explore issues of race, culture, social class, and educational and social inequality and how these relate to education, teaching, and schooling. To achieve these goals, students engage in intensive reading and discussion of interdisciplinary texts which focus on how issues of race, culture, social class, sexual orientation, gender identity, disability—social location broadly defined—bear upon philosophies of education and pedagogy, views on student achievement, curriculum development and implementation, and culturally responsive teaching. Moreover, students are challenged to locate themselves with respect to large-scale social issues and to critically reflect on their own autobiographies and the inextricable link between their personal and professional identities. The course is designed to create a structure in which students examine their identities and belief systems and in which they can practice new ways of thinking in relation to systematic self-reflection grounded in social critique. Further, the course is structured to create a learning environment in which students critically explore their ideologies and belief systems in a reconstructive rather than additive way (Banks, 1991; Nieto, 2004; Perry and Fraser, 1993). This means that students are challenged not only to learn new information to add to their existing views, but to make substantive changes in their perceptions of society and perspectives on schooling, teaching, and learning. Therefore, the focus is on exploring the value, importance, and potential implications of engaging in the exploration of one's self and "personal social constructions" (Hidalgo, 1993).

The main goal of the course is to problematize teachers'—both pre-service and experienced—understandings of American society, the U.S. educational system, and, ultimately, the practices of teaching through engaging with them in a critical analysis of the relationship between society, ideology, and pedagogy. The perspective upon which this course is structured is that in order for teachers to engage in pedagogy that works against deficit models and that is culturally aware and responsive (and therefore effective), they must make paradigm shifts that complicate and influence their conceptualizations of themselves, society, and their teaching. As much of the current research on multicultural teaching indicates, teaching teachers to shift away from mainstream educational perspectives—which are based on Eurocentric and monocultural views of society, culture, schooling, and learning—is a necessary goal in helping them to become multiculturally competent (Erickson, 2004; Martin, 1995; Nieto, 2004; Remillard, 2000). Creating such a significant shift requires engaging teachers in processes through which they learn to acknowledge, deconstruct, and critically reconstruct their knowledge base and make shifts in their belief systems. Within this context, making shifts in one's beliefs about self, society, and the way the world works requires that students gain tools to critically analyze the structure of American society, schooling, and education. As well, making such shifts necessitates that teachers, as students, learn to critically reflect on themselves as people who live, and teachers who work, within a society fraught with inequality and structural discrimination.

Since learning is assumed to be about engaging critically with concepts rather than uncritically accepting them, students are encouraged to actively question the concepts and issues raised in the course and to critique the course material (including ideas espoused by the professor) both in their written and verbal communications. The course is structured so that students bring their own experiences and life histories directly into the course in order to explore their views on all of the issues and concepts presented throughout the semester. Just as students are encouraged to challenge the course material, the course, in return is designed to challenge their blind spots and biases as they become visible within the process of writing and engaging in course dialogue. However, while I believe that challenging White students' perspectives is crucial, I argue that this must not be done through an approach that disregards or essentializes their perspectives and lived experiences. Therefore, I take a stance that the "critical interrogation" (hooks, 1993) of students' perspectives on their identities and social locations, society in general, and education and teaching, specifically, requires that they be actively supported as they are asked to engage in critical self-reflection.

To support a pedagogy that begins with one's self and prior knowledge, students write "cultural autobiographies," which are intended to create a conscious starting point for the location of their identities within the discourse of diversity and hegemony as well as an exploration of the wider spheres of influence on their individual lives and perspectives on teaching. Students are then encouraged to reflect, in writing, on these autobiographies at carefully selected points during the semester in order to take perspective on the shifts that occur in their understanding of their identities and histories as a result of the course discussions and readings. Early discussions in the course, as well as students' weekly reflective writings about their perspectives on selected issues, serve as a basis for engaging in an ongoing dialogue about how they as individuals fit into larger social realities and the picture of schooling and education.

Carefully designed early course discussions on issues such as critical self-reflection, social constructions, and the pervasiveness of racist socialization and deficit theories jumpstart a semester-long conversation about how we, as White people, have biases and hold discriminatory attitudes toward marginalized groups given the way that society is structured, and further, that these biases are not to be feared or concealed, but rather to be brought into the light and reflected upon so that we become aware of them and actively challenge them over time (Allport, 1958; Nakkula and Ravitch, 1998). Throughout all of the reflective writing assignments, students are encouraged to unearth and explore their biases and stereotypes rather than to fear or hide them. This exploration is framed as a way of learning about themselves rather than as an attempt to attribute blame about the views they hold. Throughout the course, I discuss my own struggles to confront my privilege and the ways in which the status quo of hegemony benefits me as a White, upper-middle-class, heterosexual, nondisabled woman as well as my biases and how they affect my teaching, as a way to model reflective practice and to create a constructive framework around examining our prejudices as teachers. Through each of these teaching modalities, entry points to issues of social justice, which are at the center of the course, are created since students are required to read the course through the use of critical autobiography as White people in a White-dominated social structure.[2]

Interrupting and Interrogating White Privilege: Teaching within and about Whiteness

Given the whiteness of the teaching force in America, research on White teachers' learning about issues of racism and inequality is of central importance for teacher educators who wish to teach White teachers about issues of hegemony, oppression, and social justice (Howard, 1999). However, within current research in the fields of multicultural education and multicultural teacher education specifically, White students tend to be considered and described as a monolithic entity. Within most discussions of White teachers, they are described as at best naïve and ignorant about the meaning and implications of their whiteness and their participation in a system that privileges Whites and, at worst, as irresponsible, racists who become harmful teachers. Further, research in this area tends to assert that White teachers lack the ability and awareness necessary to engage in meaningful discussions about their own cultures and identities as well as issues of multicultural education and culturally responsive teaching (Ravitch, 2000).

I strongly agree with the assertion that the hegemonic system in American society is based on normative whiteness, and that within this system, whiteness translates into cultural capital and social control (Erickson, 2004; Giroux, 1988). I also believe that White people do not generally realize this and, even when they do, they most often do not wish to acknowledge the power of being White in a racist and hegemonic society (Goldberg, 1994; McCarthy, 1993; McLaren, 1994; Turner, 1993). Further, I agree with assertions that White teachers tend to lack awareness of structural inequality, discrimination, and educational inequities and that this has potentially harmful implications for their students and for education more generally (hooks, 1993; Martin, 1995; Sleeter, 1995a, 1996; Soto and Richardson, 1995). However, my experience of teaching this course for seven years has shown me that White students learn in relation to their whiteness in individualized ways that cannot be neatly typologized and, further, that many White students show a profound willingness and ability to engage in critical explorations of issues of culture, race, and multiple forms of inequality *when provided with the conditions necessary to foster critical exploration* (i.e., a systematically developed and maintained safe space; the active development of trust and a sense of community; challenging but not alienating readings; rigorous, ongoing autobiographical writing; and the ability to think out loud about their own racism, biases, and social constructions without fear of judgment or reprisal). Therefore, it is my strong belief that the picture of White teachers' learning about issues such as racism and whiteness should not be painted with the flat, lifeless strokes that it has been thus far. Such a rendering of this population lends itself to pedagogy that is judgmental and pedantic and which is as generalized as the understandings upon which it is based.

In previous work, I have argued that doing a whitewash—glazing over individual differences and ignoring intragroup variability—over a classroom of

White teachers, either as a teacher educator or as a teacher researcher, leaves a lot to be desired in that it loses very real, complex aspects of students' identities, experiences, and learning trajectories (Ravitch, 2000). As a teacher educator, losing sight of who White students are by viewing them solely through the lens of their race and their presumed lack of understanding of social inequities means obscuring students' individual realities and learning processes. The result is that possible points of connection with students are lost, which precludes the possibility for engaging in meaningful, critical dialogue in which students feel at once challenged and understood. To be clear, while I strongly believe in the value and importance of educators engaging in what hooks (1993) termed "interruptive pedagogy"—pedagogy that interrupts the status quo by challenging students to move beyond their myths and misconceptions—I assert that this must not be enacted from a position that ignores students' individuality and denies their complex processes of learning.

What follows are the narratives of two teachers who were students in the Cultural Foundations course that I teach. While both of these students are White men from upper-middle-class backgrounds—a group typically viewed as resistant to critical self- and social reflection—each has a unique perspective on the course (and the world) and moved through the course in particular, individualized ways. Their reflections on their journeys through the critical multicultural terrain of the course provide a textured picture of the ways in which students bring their autobiographies into the course and how the course material maps onto, and then challenges, their identities and social locations. It also shows the importance of teachers making connections between multicultural material, critical self- and societal reflection, and their pedagogy. Moreover, I believe that their stories serve as counternarratives to sources that posit that White teachers, and White men in particular, are resistant to, or incapable of, critically reflecting on themselves, society, and their positions of privilege and dominance. Such counternarratives are important so that teacher educators have access to examples of what critical multicultural learning looks like for White (male) teachers.

In the following section, R. Reed Roeser, who teaches fourth grade at Thomas Fitzwater Elementary School in the Upper Dublin School District, reflects on his experience of the course. Reed's reflections focus on his realizations about his own biases and prejudices as well as on the meaning and implications of his social status within a racialized and oppressive society. His reflections explore his unlearning process; he examines what it feels like to unlearn the ways in which he has been socialized and privileged as a White male. Reed's deeply emotional, critical process of self- and societal reflection is marked by profound inner struggle and discomfort with his own blind spots and biases as well as excitement and inspiration about new possibilities to realize his full humanity. His journey through such multicultural learning sheds light on the complicated and dynamic processes that can happen when White teachers are given a structured and carefully maintained critical learning environment in which they are challenged to develop the skills necessary to reflect on themselves, their emerging worldviews, and their pedagogical philosophies through a critical multicultural lens.

From Silence to Recognition to Engagement to Change and Back Again

Reed: I came to the Cultural Foundations class five years ago after deciding to make a career change from businessman to teacher. The main reasons I left the business world were that I wanted to work with children and I was troubled by the competitive, stratified business world. I wanted to focus on the natural, not the comparative. I wanted the opportunity to think about and discuss my thoughts and feelings in a safe learning atmosphere. Cultural Foundations provided those opportunities and more. The course gave me a foundation, a basis, an orientation, and an underpinning for examining my thoughts and actions and how they would relate to my future as a teacher. The content of Cultural Foundations set me on a path of critical reflection and understanding that I still follow today as a practicing elementary school teacher.

The course provided several conceptual tools that helped to deepen my learning and thinking about myself, society, schools, and teaching. First, it was made clear from the outset that we would be discussing complex, sensitive issues that would result in a wide range of perspectives from participating students. The course required that we, the students, provide a safe classroom community for discussion and Sharon Ravitch was very specific about what that meant and what it entailed from each of us. Second, Sharon quickly established herself as a facilitator of understanding rather than an imposer of it and told each of us that we brought expertise into the classroom based on our life experiences. Since I was not yet a practicing teacher, I was encouraged to draw upon my experiences as a shop owner and stay-at-home dad and use them to gain a deeper understanding of myself as a person, and how that "self" would interact with a future class. Third, Sharon established an individual relationship with each of her students. I will never forget getting back my first reflection paper and finding substantial comments, reflections, and "think about" questions. It was clear that Sharon had considered my work carefully. I was so thankful to receive her comments as a way of challenging me to make further meaning of my thoughts. By establishing a reciprocal dialogue, Sharon modeled for me effective multicultural teaching that is part of my pedagogy today.

Five years have passed since I "finished" my coursework in Cultural Foundations. I am now an elementary school teacher in a local school district. Everyday I carry with me a philosophy that was focused, cultivated, and deepened in the course. The reason I put "finished" in quotation marks is because this course helped me to see that living and teaching in a multicultural world requires dynamic, *ongoing,* and even painful critical self-reflection. The coursework was not the beginning of the end of this type of approach, but rather the end of a beginning. As I look back now on my reflections from the class, I find that I have put into practice what was then only theory, with my experiences in the classroom, the readings, my own reflections, and Sharon's teachings at my side. What follows is a discussion of some of the core lessons that I learned in Cultural Foundations.

Reflecting on my own identity: Learning for myself and my teaching

One of the key and lasting aspects of the course was the idea that in order to provide a positive learning experience for all students, teachers must be in touch with who we are and what we bring to the classroom with respect to aspects of our own identities such as race, class, gender, and ideology. In my first reflection paper I wrote the following:

> Growing up White, upper middle class, and male had given me a sense of safety from which I thought I had learned tolerance and inclusion. That illusion was shattered the first time two young Black males entered my newly opened retail store. Instead of regarding them as potential customers, I saw them as a potential threat. And, indeed, they were a threat, not to my person or my goods, but to my self-concept.

When I initially wrote the above quote, I came to a deeper and important understanding about myself. It was powerful. It was painful. It was productive. Previously, I had "substituted my lack of knowledge and understanding with myth" (Wehmiller, 1992). My myth was that I had a well-developed relational self and that I viewed others based on who they were rather than who I thought they were because of my own assumptions and stereotypes. As I made these realizations about myself, it seemed to me a classic battle of theory and practice. Thinking about these issues was easy, taking action would be harder. I have used the deeper understandings of myself gained through the course as a way to create a classroom in which students' race, religion, economic status, gender, and sexuality are an unmistakable part of their stories, but don't define them. Cultural Foundations helped me to give this way of thinking some structure and a context so that I could use it productively in my career. Sharon's insistence on "changing lenses" and seeking new and different perspectives has stayed with me. I use this approach to create a personal, individual relationship with each student in much the same way Sharon did with each of us. This relationship building helps to create a safe, democratic learning environment in which student commonalities are stressed at the same time that differences are represented, acknowledged, and celebrated. As a student, I valued this approach in the Cultural Foundations class; as a teacher, I use this approach to empower both the teacher and student in collective learning.

Looking back, the class discussions we had about issues of White privilege and racial inequality and the articles by Olson (1998) and McIntosh (1990) were particularly meaningful and poignant. This was sensitive and really uncomfortable stuff! I remember thinking that I didn't want to feel badly about myself even though I had come to the realization that these articles really pertained to me, a White man who grew up with a knapsack that I felt was given to me by chance. As McIntosh states, "White privilege is like an invisible weightless knapsack of special provisions, an invisible package of unearned assets that I can count on cashing in each day, but about which I was 'meant' to remain oblivious" (McIntosh, 1990). As we read the readings and I was challenged to think, talk, and write about the relevance of these issues to my life, I kept struggling with the fact that I felt that I was not a prejudiced person, but according to Olson, McIntosh, and our class discussions, I had to realize and acknowledge that I have benefited from privilege in a myriad of ways that were previously invisible to me and that I do carry biases and prejudices by virtue of growing up in a society that is set up to benefit people who look, think, and act like me. These realizations were powerful, painful, and pregnant with possibilities for changing my perspective on the world, myself, and my future as a teacher.

During classroom discussions of issues of White privilege and racism, we focused on how constructs like privilege and power relate to us, our lives, and our perspectives of others, while de-emphasizing the need to assess blame or create guilt. This was powerful for me on two levels. First, it provided a model for guiding a classroom to an honest, constructive, respectful, and safe discussion of sensitive, important, and provocative issues. Second, the material itself helped me to think more deeply about myself as a springboard for deepening my understanding of others. The course discussions helped me to view the idea of the knapsack as a vehicle for understanding my own identity and how I relate to others, rather than as something to feel a personal sense of guilt about. I was encouraged to use my experiences, my ideas, and my reflections to go beyond what the articles said and to concentrate on what they meant to me as a person and a teacher. What made this critical learning experience possible is that instead of denying or judging our individual experiences, Sharon invited and embraced them. She showed us that the process of operating in a multicultural world is not static and absolute; it is dynamic and ongoing. In my own life, both professional and personal, I have used her model, drawn on her encouragement and support, and made reflection an indispensable part of my teaching. As a result, I try to fill the knapsacks of my students with advantages that are of value to all of them, with particular attention and sensitivity to how issues of race, class, culture, sexuality, gender, and disability can have an impact on their educational and life experiences. I know it has made my classroom a better place; one that strives toward the respect and appreciation of all students. What follows is a statement about how I began to integrate my newfound understandings into my thinking about life generally and teaching specifically by the middle of the semester:

> Since I am not currently teaching, I have largely remained in
> the theoretical realm when thinking about how I will operate
> my classroom. In some ways, this is a positive because it
> allows me the freedom to develop a classroom in my mind

incorporating all the ideas we've considered. At the same time, I am concerned about translating all my reflections into a positive classroom atmosphere. I feel that I have made great progress in bringing multicultural issues into my everyday consciousness rather than just an occasional point of view. Though I have not tested this new thinking in the classroom, I have tried to practice it in my everyday life. My belief is that as long as I am progressing along a continuum of learning based on the concepts we've considered, I will be better prepared to face the realities of the classroom. In sketch form, I see the continuum in this way:

Silence → Recognition → Engagement → Change

When I wrote the above statement, it helped me to organize and make sense of the many issues I had been thinking, talking, and writing about in class. At the time, I was not yet teaching. I felt it was important to set a goal that would keep me thinking about multicultural issues. As I look back, I realize how powerful this continuum model has been for me and how my experience in the course shaped my progress along it. When I came to Cultural Foundations, I was mired in the silence stage. Metacognitively, I was thinking about these issues, but I had yet to bring them to the forefront of my thinking. I had not yet given my ideas a texture or a voice. Sharon was able to access these ideas and draw them out. During the course, I felt that I was moving beyond the silence stage and into the recognition stage. Today, I feel I am even further along the continuum, clearly engaged and trying to affect change. The role of Cultural Foundations in this transformation was critical. The power of the class was that each of us was developing new ideas, gaining deeper understandings, and sharing personal experiences that were of benefit to all of us. As I look back five years later, I realize that what Sharon led me to understand was that teaching in a multicultural world is about ending silence and becoming involved in a deepening cycle of recognition, engagement, and change. And this is good. It also has implications for my own model of five years ago. My old continuum suggests a linear progression from point to point. Cultural Foundations showed me that real learning—learning that truly becomes integrated—is more than that. It has more dimension. It is not linear, but builds through reflection, action, and successes. Eventually, the spin of the cycle pushes off silence, which stands increasingly alone. By the end of the course, I had revised the model (see Figure 9-1).

Throughout the course, I engaged in intense and challenging introspection. This introspection has continued long after I left Cultural Foundations and is an important legacy of the course. Cultural Foundations encouraged me to make introspection lasting and productive—to take my agitation and actualize it. In the past few years this has become an integral part of me.

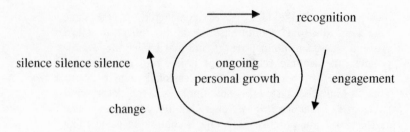

Figure 9-1: The role of autobiographical writing in the facilitation of my personal change and growth

As I look back on Cultural Foundations, I recognize that I was engaged in a personal struggle to make meaning of all the issues we considered and that central to this struggle and to my learning and reflection was a process of critical writing. Clearly, the core of my struggle was rooted in the idea of White male privilege. It was difficult, even painful, to come to terms with myself in terms of race, gender, sexual orientation, and class privilege. On each of these points, I am part of the dominant group. As a White male from an upper-middle-class background, I had not functioned in other societal arenas though I believed I had thought quite a lot about others. When I read McIntosh and Olson, I was angry that I fit the description of an advantaged person. Harder still to accept was the idea that a person in my position was often ignorant of that reality. It was me the authors were talking about when they suggested that members of dominant groups have the luxury of ignorance! In my first reflection paper, I had recognized that, even though I thought I was open-minded and engaged on issues of race, gender, culture, and class, I had deep-rooted feelings that, while they were not overt racism, were reflections of the societal constructs in which I operated: biases, stereotypes, deficit theories. When I viewed young Black males as a potential threat, I realized that thinking about multicultural ideas at arms length was much different than acting in a way that valued and considered cultural, ethnic, religious, and economic differences. Writing my cultural autobiography helped me to get in touch with my story, while at the same time helping me to understand that the stories of others would be vastly different. By getting in touch with my own story, I was beginning a transformation from my cultural island to becoming engaged with my responsibilities in the larger context of functioning as a teacher and an empathetic, ethical human being.

In my second reflection paper, I considered my own K–12 schooling experiences as a basis for thinking about how students who are marginalized might feel in the classroom. As an elementary student, I found the classroom to be a safe place. As a White, Christian male from an upper-middle-class background, my race, religion, gender, and class were reflected throughout the school. I saw similar faces in our textbooks. I found it easy to identify with the material we studied because, in general, it reflected my story. Again, my school ideal was being undermined by the fact that we did have people who were culturally and religiously diverse in class but that I never was provided the opportunity to value those differences. I remember writing about a girl from India who joined our class. Instead of learning how we were alike, I found that we focused on how she was different. Our teacher, though well meaning, was not a "mediator of culture" (Grant, 1977). The teacher did not give me the tools to help me interact with this student on a safe, relational level. Because the course required me to reflect critically and write extensively about my own classroom experiences, I began to see the societal constructs in schools that were reflective of larger societal ills and that tend to marginalize groups that are different from the dominant group. Writing about these experiences was central to deconstructing them because I was challenged to re-experience social realities in ways that were personally relevant.

As I moved deeper into the course and analyzed my own place in the world, it became evident to me that I was going to have to "shift my center." I needed to examine what I brought into this new teaching career and how I wanted to construct my understandings. In my third reflection paper, I talked about the responsibility of teachers to become community builders within the classroom. This was during the sixth week of the course. I really believed that my mind was open and that I was accepting of the fact that I had much work to do. Indeed, I had made much progress, but as we considered the idea of White, male privilege, I struggled. My confusion and dissonance sent the walls back up again. It was only writing about these issues that involved unlocked doors to my consciousness.

In my fourth reflection paper, I wrote about how the concepts of White, male privilege and the ignorance of the dominant group began to make sense to me. I acknowledged how I have personally benefited from this "aura" that I didn't see but others saw all around me. However, when it came time to discuss this in class, I shut down. I didn't talk in class that day. I didn't share any of my feelings or experiences. I felt somewhat under attack. Here I was thinking that I was empathetic and fair-minded, but our readings and discussions seemed to focus on my failure in society. At the time, I wrote in my journal that I wanted to be a listener that day and fully hear varied points of view. Looking back, I recognize that I was angry. I hated the idea that I was "advantaged" and, even more so, I hated the idea that I didn't recognize it in a way that would help to transform society. Identifying examples and anecdotes that illustrated White, male privilege was easy; changing it, and myself, would be much harder.

A corollary to my agitation about my privilege as a White man was the notion that I needed to start a move from talk to action. After my night of silence, I came to an important conclusion: I was long on talk and short on action. In my fifth reflection paper, I began to explore and understand that as a member of the dominant group, my inaction is a luxury that others do not have. Clearly, as a teacher, I would have to pop my theoretical bubble and begin to take action. Nieto (2000) helped me to understand that action must be considered incremental, that any steps we take are valuable, and that there are many different forms of activism. I felt myself beginning to move away from anger and confusion and into a realm of acceptance and action. I had begun the transformation from "passive activist" to an engaged, action-oriented member of society. At the same time, I began to see how others felt about societal and educational constructs such as White privilege. I remember distinctly a class discussion about meritocracy. The guiding question was: Is meritocracy a myth? The discussion was framed as a debate in which class members argued either side. At the beginning of the course, I think I would have argued that our country and our educational system were indeed a meritocracy. Instead, I wrote in a later reflection that our system were the ideal of a meritocracy, but not one in practice. I provided a metaphor of meritocracy as a running track in which meritocracy was the "finish line." Advantaged groups started on the inside track so their path to the finish was much shorter than those in the outside lanes. Actually, this discussion was an epiphany for me. It helped me to realize, as I reflected and wrote about it, that my ideas were being broadened and deepened. Rather than feeling defensive and angry, I was feeling that this was the correct path, that my classroom must not just reflect my story, but must reflect, collectively, all the stories that would make up my classroom community. Change was under way and it was good, even though it was really uncomfortable.

The idea from the course that critical reflection is transformative continues to pervade my life. Since I was not yet a practicing teacher, I tried to apply my new thinking within the societal contexts in which I was operating. It became clear that the way in which I viewed the world was all about me, and not about those I marginalized. This painful understanding was so critical to being honest with myself and really exploring how I fit into the world then, and how I might fit into it in the future. In one of my later critical reflection and analysis papers, I began to see my transformation from an isolated, actionless person to an engaged critical thinker.

As the end of the course neared, it was time for one final "grand reflection." Frankly, I remember feeling exhausted at that point, but it was the good kind of exhausted, like after a rigorous jog or workout. As I wrote about the course, I saw it as the end of the beginning of my struggle toward greater awareness of the societal structures of race, gender, culture, and class and my place within these structures. At the same time, I recognized that I had changed, and that these changes would be ongoing, deeper, and more lasting as I moved into the future. No longer was I passive and uninformed; I was now active and engaged. I would be what Gatto (1994) calls an "agent of change." I had gained a personal understanding of my own story and valued it as a way to access, acknowledge, and integrate the stories of others into my classroom. In addition, I came away from the course with a greater understanding of how societal structures shape our words, actions, growth, and choices as teachers. This was a period of recognition for me, an opportunity to look deep inside myself and find ways of using my experiences to move closer to understanding the experiences of others. Five years later, this way of thinking is no longer an occasional point of view, but is now an active, everyday part of my life and how I relate to others, including my students, their parents, and my colleagues. I ended my final reflection paper for the course with an anecdote that I think is appropriate because it captures the essence of my transformation in Cultural Foundations:

> As I sat thinking of an appropriate way to end this paper, my mind wandered to an old apple tree in my backyard. Though this tree has stood dominant over this ground for generations, it has grown old and weak, suffering from disease, rot, and infestation. For a time, I worked hard to save it, not willing to surrender to the inevitable. But, alas, soon this tree will be cut down. And from this ending will come a beginning because, beneath the old tree, a new one has taken root. It is a different kind of tree, seeking its light with a multitude of branches. It will have a chance to flower once the tree that casts its long, controlling shadow is removed. Though our failed school institutions cannot be felled as easily as this old wood, a new paradigm for schooling waits like the sapling in my backyard. As teachers of the future, we are the stewards of this new growth with multicultural roots. And if we tend it properly, this new tree will grow out of those roots to watch over future generations. (Final Reflection Paper 5/4/99)

Today, the young sapling is indeed flourishing with myself and others as its humble tender.

In this next account, Brian J. Girard, who has been teaching for five years at Project Learn, an independent, cooperative school in Philadelphia, explores his experience of the course—its content and process—on his perception of himself and his role as a teacher who is also a "mediator of culture" (Grant, 1977). Brian's perspective on his gradual and powerful shifts in perspective and pedagogy shows that learning is not necessarily linear or immediate, but rather, that true learning happens in a spiral fashion, with incremental changes over a period of time. Brian shows the powerful impact that an interruptive experience like Cultural Foundations has had on his own sense of self, his role as a teacher, his pedagogy, and his overall perspective on schooling and education.

Multicultural Teacher Reflection as Lamarckian Evolution

Brian J. Girard: I enrolled at Arcadia University to pursue a master's degree with teacher certification in Secondary Social Studies. I quickly discovered that I was required to take a course called "Cultural Foundations of Education." I particularly dreaded this kind of course because I had spent four years in college attending multicultural training workshops and I felt I had all the sensitivity training I needed. And I don't mean to sound as if I thought this work was trivial. On the contrary, I had gone to all of those workshops with interest and enthusiasm. I knew that such a course was important; I just thought I didn't have that much more to learn in the multicultural awareness department. I knew about prejudice, institutional racism, cultural differences, class differences, White privilege, and so forth. I don't know that I would have gone so far as to call myself an "expert," but I felt rather confident about my knowledge and experience in the field. I feared a semester spent quietly squirming in my seat as yet another professor explained that prejudice was bad and diversity was good.

My preconception about Cultural Foundations was wrong on several levels. As I sit and reflect now, at a distance of four years, on the ways in which this course has continued to profoundly change me as a person and shape me as a teacher, I find it difficult to recall particular moments in class when I had a "eureka!" moment. Instead, I think the change was more gradual, occurring in me as if by Lamarckian evolution: with effort and intention. What I found was that although I was already committed to multiculturalism as a personal philosophical stance, I had not processed and struggled with the implications of such a view for my pedagogy. Cultural Foundations gave me the framework to examine a new part of my identity, that of a teacher—a White, upper-middle-class, male teacher—and subject it to rigorous evaluation, and even painful critique, through a multicultural lens.

This critical self-reflection began with the very first assignment; we had to complete a cultural autobiography. This was a powerful step toward placing each teacher at the center of the curriculum. It also let me know, and I suspect the function is similar for everyone who takes the course, that everyone has something valuable to contribute to the conversation about social inequality and multiculturalism. As Sharon stressed, everyone comes from a culture, not only students of color. No other multicultural training in which I had taken part included the step of honoring everyone who participated even as it rigorously challenged our positions and perspectives. The process gave everyone a voice in the conversation and also eliminated any notion that the need to learn about multicultural education didn't apply to every teacher. I certainly felt that my individual perspective was being honored and that Sharon wanted to know where everyone was coming from. There was a trend in my past "multicultural" experiences that White perspectives were not valued: We were only there to learn about other people, not to reflect on our own cultural roots and experiences (aside perhaps from evaluating our own prejudices) or to place ourselves explicitly in the discussion of multiculturalism, diversity, and oppression.

The cultural autobiography assignment also helped me to get all my cards out on the table, as it were. Using the writing process to create some distance between my experiences and my mind allowed me to reflect more easily. The act of critical self-reflection is difficult for anyone, but as we learned in the course, it is especially difficult for teachers because we bear an added weight. Namely, that when we find fault in our pedagogy, the potential for harm extends beyond the self and onto the students we teach. As Sharon continually pointed out, due to this heightened sensitivity when dealing with teachers around these issues, it is even more important that a safe space be established. Just as

Freire (1970) posits that the oppressor cannot free the oppressed, likewise the professor of a class on multicultural education cannot force her students to reflect and change. However, she can provide an environment that cultivates such self-reflection. Sharon did just that and, as a result, my teaching has taken on a considerably more political, critically reflective stance.

I remember quite distinctly the struggle some of my classmates went through in wrestling with the challenges a multicultural framework posed to their identity, their sense of self, and their pedagogy. In particular, many of my White classmates struggled to accept notions such as institutional racism and White privilege. They denied having a role within these issues. When a person has worked hard through school for most of her life, then chooses to continue her education at the graduate level, and is then told that in a certain respect she was "helped" by such nebulous factors as White privilege, it can be a hard pill to swallow. Even as people were pushed out of their comfort zones, that struggle was honored in Sharon's class, and I recall many lively and heated discussions around such topics. Perhaps not everyone in the class fully recognized such societal factors, but many more were able to see it because of the nature of the classroom discourse, which, while clearly shaped by Sharon's political beliefs and strong ideological stance on the need to actively counter social and institutional racism, sexism, homophobia, and the oppression of people with disabilities, still respected opposing views and allowed us as a group to work through them together. When such multicultural issues arose in other graduate classes that I have taken, there was often a brief argument between the professor and the student, who in the end typically felt silenced and railroaded. Cultural Foundations, on the other hand, had the benefit of dedicated time for such conversations and reflections which allowed students time to wrestle with difficult issues, feel challenged, and yet still be heard and understood. I realized that I still had more to learn in this area, that I could go deeper in my awareness about what it means to be a White man in this country in terms of how I benefit from my Whiteness, but even moreso, in terms of what I can do about that, which was the real thrust of the course. That attention to taking action toward a vision of social justice was a real gift of the course. As a teacher, it has helped me to begin to view myself as a social activist and then to cultivate that aspect of my identity over time.

In shifting from introspective analysis to contemplating my own pedagogy, Cultural Foundations introduced me to the notion of "teacher as a mediator of culture." We read and discussed in depth Grant's (1977) article "The Mediator of Culture: A Teacher Role Revisited," which challenged me to see myself in a different, more critical light. Rather than define a teacher as solely an instructor who passes along content-specific information and skill sets, Grant explores the notion of a teacher as a mediator of culture. As Grant states, a teacher is "a person who both transmits knowledge of the culture and *interprets* the knowledge being transmitted" (p. 103, emphasis added). This concept vastly expanded my self-image as a teacher, but not immediately, only after we worked it through in class. In my reaction paper to this article, I responded as follows:

I'm very interested in the notion of the teacher as a mediator
of culture, and I do believe it is an essential, and often
unconscious, task we carry out. Having said that, I take issue
with Grant's assertion that "this role . . . is the most important
for teachers to understand and properly carry out when
working in a pluralistic society" (p. 105). While being a more
sensitive, enlightened, and informed person around issues of
cultural difference certainly makes one a better teacher, it does
not supersede the primary function of teaching, which is to
prepare students with the basics of literacy and mathematics. I
realize I am over-simplifying matters, but would you rather
have a student who could read and multiply or one who was
deeply aware of social injustice perpetrated around the globe
on a daily basis, but had no skills to change it? Obviously, the
answer is that both are necessary, but neither trumps the other.

I can now see a real shortsightedness in my critique of Grant. As I
learned in the course, I was thinking too small. I wanted to hold on to my roles
as English teacher and history teacher, but multicultural education demands
more. I came to understand, by the end of the course, that my classroom was a
place in which I re-created our culture on a daily basis, and I could either
continue to do that with a blind eye toward the values and goals of
multiculturalism, thereby reproducing the very hegemony we learned about, or I
could take a closer look at my pedagogy and curriculum to find my strengths
and weaknesses and then make the appropriate changes and adjustments.
Furthermore, as important as it was for me to be aware of the way in which I
was interpreting the world and presenting it to my students, I came to view my
role as instructor as teaching my students how to effectively interpret the world
for themselves. Implicit within the term "interpretation" is the notion that there
are multiple ways to view a single set of facts. Helping students to both
understand other perspectives and create their own interpretations is, for me,
since Cultural Foundations, the very heart of multicultural education.

To improve upon my newfound role as a mediator of culture, I was
challenged to first turn to my curriculum to see how I was representing the
world to my students. In constructing my curriculum, was I guilty of
ethnocentrism in my selection of books? What cultures was I privileging and
what impact did that have on the worldview my students formed? After critically
reviewing my materials, I found that in my own curriculum there was the
ethnocentrism so many of the articles I had read for Cultural Foundations had
decried. For example, I taught a unit on Greek mythology and in response to the
coursework of Cultural Foundations, I changed the unit to a focus on
comparative myth, in which I centered the readings on universal mythical topics
ranging from "creation" to "tricksters."

I had initially chosen Greek mythology for two seemingly benign
reasons: I have always had a deep interest in Greek mythology and there

happened to be a set of Greek myth books in my classroom. I didn't see myself as imposing a European hegemonic curriculum on my students. On the contrary, I felt that I was simply sharing stories that I have a passion for and that I believe speak deeply to the human experience. Once I had an opportunity to self-evaluate and reflect on what I was teaching in relation to what I learned about the limited cultural scope of the canon, I realized that I needed to make some serious changes. I was, of course, moved to include stories whose heroes looked like more of my students, but more importantly, I was deeply moved by the tenet of multiple perspectives, and that a multicultural teacher provides his students with many ways of viewing and approaching the world. And while myths from around the world help students to see the beautiful depth and variety of cultures on this globe, they also tell a common story of our universal humanity, which shares themes of honor, love, justice, and friendship.

A more complex transformation occurred with the novel *To Kill a Mockingbird* (Lee) and the curriculum I developed to teach it. This is a book that I have always dearly loved, and it is one of my favorite to teach. In my reflections based on this course, however, I began to have some serious doubts about whether it was really a book I should use. Several aspects of the novel seemed to reinforce a worldview that I newly saw as problematic. Although the book brings to light the unjust world of racial inequality in the South prior to the civil rights movement, the hero, Atticus Finch, is an affluent White lawyer. The African Americans in the story are virtually unknown, with the exception of Calpurnia, the Finch's housekeeper. Furthermore, the "n" word is used on several occasions in the book, and that hurtful word is problematic, to say the least. I wondered if there were not other books that covered similar terrain, but which avoided one-dimensional African American characters and racial epithets. In fact, I knew there were other options like *Roll of Thunder, Hear My Cry* (Taylor).

I didn't give up on *To Kill a Mockingbird*. As part of the resource gathering assignment for Cultural Foundations, I had found a series from PBS called *Culture Shock* that explored shocking artistic movements in their historical context, including jazz. One of the topics of the series was *The Adventures of Huckleberry Finn* by Mark Twain. The series looked at how a group of Cherry Hill, New Jersey High School teachers developed a curriculum to deal with this piece of classic American literature that contains many of the same problems that I had with *To Kill a Mockingbird* (i.e., stereotypical portrayal of African American characters and use of the "n" word). The series helped me to reposition the perspective from which I approached the book. Rather than treat it as just a story, I also began using it as a historical artifact to deconstruct and interpret together as a class. I had always explored with my students what the book revealed about the South during the Great Depression. To deepen the encounter with *To Kill a Mockingbird*, I took another step back and asked why the book would be written the way it was in 1964, the year of its publication? How might a modern-day Harper Lee write it differently? Given the timing and historical context, what effect did the book's publication have on the nation? Cultural Foundations gave me the framework to conduct this sort of critical reflection upon my own curriculum, allowing me to adapt my personal beliefs of multiculturalism into a new personal multicultural pedagogy.

However, as Sharon continually pointed out to us during the course, curricular reform is the easiest step along the path to becoming a multicultural teacher. More important are the interpersonal and pedagogical shifts that need to occur in order for teaching to be antiracist, multicultural, student-centered, and culturally responsive, all stances that Sharon framed as ethical choices that teachers must consider at all stages of teaching. My own definition of what it means to be a multicultural teacher aligns closely with Nieto's definition in her book, our course text, *Affirming Diversity* (2000), namely education that is antiracist, social justice–oriented, and, as Sharon puts it, "constructively critical" of the world. To this definition I would now add, after taking the course, the following elements, drawn from my final reflection paper from the Cultural Foundations course.

- *There is no formula*
  This sentence can be completed with any number of different phrases, but they all relate to the mercurial nature of teaching. There is no formula for a perfect lesson plan, a teacher preparation program, or the way to engage with students. This theme was repeated throughout our readings and is validated in my own teaching experience. All teachers are individuals, as are students. That may seem to be a trite assertion, but examine our educational system to find the one-size-fits-all curriculum that abounds . . .
- *Balance is a tricky thing*
  Teaching must remain flexible and dynamic because there is a line to balance along in dealing with issues of multiculturalism. The easiest example to provide would be letting what we know about Native American learning preferences inform our teaching without making assumptions about every Native American individual's learning style.
- *Teaching is a political act*
  As Nieto (2000) states so succinctly, "Every educational decision made by a teacher or by an entire school system, reflects the political ideology and world view of the decision maker" (p. 316). I think many people become teachers because they want to make the world a better place, but then they end up simply helping to replicate the world we have. Multicultural education values different perspectives and action wedded to thought. It is important for such action to come from the students and not exclusively from the teacher. In other words, the teacher is a resource and a catalyst for student action, but not the agenda setter.

As I mentioned earlier, the notion of perspective-taking as a central tenet of multicultural education has come, since taking the course, to permeate my curriculum. I center my teaching on providing alternative views of the world through literature and history. Before taking Cultural Foundations, I believed teaching was political, but in a much more narrow way. I saw it as an opportunity to share my own worldview with my students, but I have had to retract myself and open the class up to a wider range of perspectives, and the hardest part about doing so means being willing to be wrong as the teacher as well as having to reflect on my own social and cultural biases and make changes in them in a daily, ongoing way.

I made a surprising discovery about Cultural Foundations as I worked on this reflection. While we learned to critique the "hidden curriculum" of school dogma and canon, the course had a "hidden curriculum" of its own. But in this particular case, I view this hidden curriculum as a benefit. In his description of teacher as a mediator of culture, Grant suggests that "how you teach may often be more important than what you teach" (1977, p. 109). In that regard, I think the teaching style that Sharon brought to the class was the most important element of the Cultural Foundations class, insofar as she modeled for every teacher how to be a *multicultural* teacher—one who affirms and includes a wide range of perspectives while actively challenging students to become more critical thinkers. Building from that, the material, which was provocative and challenging, seemed to make sense and have appeal to people who would have been even more resistant to it. As mentioned previously, Sharon created a safe space in our classroom in which people felt comfortable extending themselves without fear of attack or criticism. Particularly when dealing with issues of people's "isms," students need a classroom characterized by a humanistic teaching style that is organic, flexible, and understanding of individual needs and differences. Sharon has described the organization and structure of the class already, so I will only speak to my own experience with her style.

The most important aspect to Sharon's teaching style is her ability to be present as herself. There is no mask or filter of Sharon the Professor, Dispenser of Knowledge, Keeper of Grades, or Handler of the Pen of Corrections. While she brings her immense expertise, intelligence, and wisdom to the class, Sharon remains Sharon. Her authenticity and presence from the first day of class allowed me to trust her, which in turn allowed me to open up in both my writing and in-class discussions. She asked us to write our cultural autobiography, but she also shared her own cultural autobiography. She clearly understood that we were individuals with busy lives beyond the classroom, and she honored that with flexibility and understanding even as she pushed and challenged us to see in which ways we represent and reproduce hegemony.

Prior to the course, I had a vision of my teacher-self being like Robin Williams in *Dead Poet's Society*; I would float into my classroom, entertaining and educating my students with the pearls of my accumulated wisdom. Through Sharon's example, I came to realize that such a notion of teaching is selfish and limiting. Teaching from on high builds an invisible wall between a teacher and his students, which makes the work of creating a multicultural classroom impossible. I have done my best in my subsequent years of teaching to become more myself when I teach, as I continually question and examine myself and my ways.

Finally, as I mentioned at the beginning of this reflection, at the start of the course I thought I knew most of what I needed to know regarding multiculturalism. Cultural Foundations helped me to see that there are not static, simple answers to being a multicultural teacher. There is no formula. There are no hard and fast answers. There is only a process of achieving ever-deeper levels of self-awareness and a critical perspective on schools and classrooms that I can adopt. Cultural Foundations set me on a trajectory of asking ever-harder questions about myself as a person and as a teacher. I have many more questions now than I did four years ago, and I am taking leave of teaching to pursue a Ph.D. in education so that I can attempt to find answers to some of these questions. As I do so, I know that I will take with me the promise that a critical multicultural vision brings with it for empowered teaching and learning.

MOVING INTO CRITICAL PEDAGOGY: LEARNING FROM AND WITH OUR STUDENTS

Both Reed's and Brian's reflections portray, in rich detail, how they continue to make meaning of the shifts they experienced both during and after the course; shifts in their sense of self, identity, perspectives on issues of social and institutional marginalization and oppression, equity, diversity, and multicultural pedagogy. Each author helps us to understand the complexity of learning about these issues in a teacher education context and the unique and deeply personal ways that students make sense of and make use of this kind of multicultural learning experience. Their reflections help us to remember how individualized each student's learning is and, particularly, that White students can learn to critically reflect on themselves, society, and educational practices—to change, grow, learn, and, most importantly, to unlearn—when they are provided with a context that allows for thoughtful reflection and honest struggle and which gives them the room to make sense of their own identities by bringing them into the course in ways that simultaneously honor their individuality and challenge their traditional ways of thinking about the world.

Central to both Reed's and Brian's reflections is the idea that certain conditions made it possible for them to make profound shifts in their perspectives, shifts that have ultimately influenced their ideologies and their practices as teachers. While the structural and pedagogical conditions necessary were discussed at the beginning of this chapter, I believe that an overall condition necessary in order for such learning to take place must be that the instructors of such courses are fully committed to our own processes of critical self-reflection and an ongoing interrogation of our pedagogy so that we can be role models of viewing critical self-reflection as an ethic of teaching. Taking this stance on our teaching translates into more student-centered teaching and a more systematic and proactive approach to engaging students in intensive explorations of issues central to multicultural teaching. On this subject, Maxine Greene (1995) asserts that teacher educators must make a commitment to engage in ongoing self-reflection as a part of our pedagogy. She writes,

> I think how much beginnings have to do with consciousness and the awareness of possibility that has so much to do with teaching other human beings. And I think that if I and other teachers truly want to provoke our students to break through the limits of the conventional and the taken for granted, we ourselves have to experience breaks with what has been established in our own lives. (p. 109)

Greene's sentiments stand as a reminder to teacher educators that the nature of learning is a dialectical struggle that is never complete, and that we must continuously challenge ourselves to engage in and model reflective practice. In this way, teaching must be conceptualized and presented as an active process of learning; a dialectical process of learning about oneself, one's students, and the shifts and changes that happen as a result of the intersection of the two (Rosenberg, 1997). Learning for the teacher educator, then, is as much about learning as it is about unlearning, about relearning in relation to one's students. But this recursive process of learning, unlearning, and relearning cannot happen without a commitment to engage in rigorous self-reflection in relation to oneself and one's practice. Thus, in order for teacher educators to be as engaged as we try to be engaging, and to be true role models of reflective practice and a willingness to change, we must become reflective practitioners ourselves. In this way, teacher educators can provide learning environments that teach our students to be reflective practitioners by example.

As Malcolm X said decades ago, "We can't teach what we don't know and we can't lead where we won't go" (Howard, 1999, p. 4). For teacher educators this suggests that if we are to urge our students to be "introspective ethnographers" in their classrooms (Hidalgo, 1993; Sanday, 1976), we ourselves must lead the way. Based on the premise that teacher educators must practice what we teach (Martin, 1995), we must model what reflective practice looks like, how it happens, and what strategies can be employed to achieve it. However, being reflective practitioners should not simply be thought of as a measure that would enhance the quality of our teaching, but, rather, as an ethic of teaching that teacher educators must adopt. Without critical interrogation (hooks, 1993) of ourselves and of our own pedagogy, our advice to our students to engage in reflective practice is hollow. Further, in order to create the conditions necessary for our students to engage in learning that engenders changes in their views of and approaches to teaching, teacher educators must revise our own pedagogical philosophies and approaches in ongoing ways and we must share the messiness, inspiration, and vulnerability of our processes with students.

My stance on teaching in my course, and in teacher education more generally, is that teacher educators must acknowledge and understand differences in our students and utilize these differences as resources with which we structure our classes so that we attend to each individual student's particular ways of learning. As Rosenberg (1997) states,

> bell hooks's invitation to us as teachers to participate in an "engaged pedagogy" presents us with an enormous challenge, especially around issues of race and racism. Since there is no prescription for engaged pedagogy, we all must negotiate our own knowledge, authority, and experience around these issues with ourselves as well as our students, taking care to recognize the contextual nature of this work. (p. 87)

For those of us teaching against the normative pedagogic grain, recognizing the contextual nature of our work means that we must view teaching as a relational, collaborative, and democratic process of understanding how to work with our students in order to create and develop critical learning. For those of us teaching predominantly White students in courses that focus on issues of diversity, multiculturalism, inequality, oppression, and intercultural communication, our pedagogy focuses on issues that are, for most of our students, difficult to discuss and even taboo and scary (Tatum, 1992/1996). Even more so in these types of courses, in which the nature of learning is deeply personal and often causes students to experience feelings of discomfort, shame, anger, and/or self-consciousness, I believe that teaching and learning must be reciprocal, symmetrical, and respectful of the experiences and perspectives that students bring to the classroom. This way of teaching allows for students to feel safe enough to take the kinds of risks that facilitate critical movement and, ultimately, paradigm shifts. Such paradigm shifts, I believe, are the hope for a new generation of teachers who are aware of and able to acknowledge the relationship between their biases, belief systems, and their pedagogy and who are willing and able to engage in reflective practice in which they unlearn as much as they learn, continually over time. This kind of pedagogy holds promise for teachers who teach not in spite of their students' differences, but in relation to them, and who see multicultural education and critical pedagogy not as a burden, but as an ethic of teaching.

NOTES

1. While there are a variety of approaches that call themselves multicultural, many are superficial and based on a "cultural tourism" model that lacks a substantive critique of social and institutional oppression (Erickson, 2004; Sleeter, 1996). The approaches represented in this chapter go beyond the mere insertion of multicultural themes into curriculum in an additive way and are therefore referred to as critical multicultural education.
2. For a discussion of critical autobiography see Erickson, 2004.

REFERENCES

Allport, G. W. (1958). *The nature of prejudice.* New York: Double Day Anchor Books.

Banks, J. A. (1991). *Teaching strategies for ethnic studies.* Boston: Allyn & Bacon.

Brookhart, S. M., and D. J. Freeman. (1992). Characteristics of entering teacher candidates. *Review of Educational Research, 62* (1), 37–60.

Brown, C. A., and H. Borko. (1992). Becoming a mathematics teacher. In D. A. Grouws (Ed.), *Handbook of research on mathematics teaching and learning* (pp. 209–239). New York: Macmillan.

Cochran-Smith, M. (2000). Blind vision: Unlearning racism in teacher education. *Harvard Educational Review, 70* (2), 157–190.

Delpit, L. (1995). *Other people's children: Cultural conflict in the classroom.* New York: New Press.

Erickson, F. (2004). Culture in society and in educational practices. In J. A. Banks and C. A. M. Banks (Eds.), *Multicultural education: Issues and perspectives* (pp. 31–60). Hoboken: Jossey Bass.

Freire, P. (1970). *Pedagogy of the oppressed.* New York: Continuum.

Gatto, J. T. (January 30, 1994). A different kind of teacher. Keynote address at Gate Conference, Omega Institute, Rhinebeck, NY.

Giroux, H. A. (1988). *Teachers as intellectuals: Toward a critical pedagogy of learning.* New York: Bergin & Garvey.

Giroux, H. A. (1994). Insurgent multiculturalism and the promise of pedagogy. In D. T. Goldberg (Ed.), *Multiculturalism: A critical reader* (pp. 325–343). Cambridge: Blackwell.

Goldberg, D. T. (Ed.). (1994). *Multiculturalism: A critical reader* (pp. 1–44, 325–343). Cambridge: Blackwell.

Grant, C. A. (1977). The mediator of culture: A teacher role revisited. *Journal of Research and Development in Education, 11* (1), 102–116.

Greene, M. (1995). *Releasing the imagination: Essays on education, the arts, and social change.* San Francisco: Jossey-Bass.

Haft, S. (Producer), and P. Weir (Director). (1989). *Dead Poet's Society* [Motion picture]. United States: Touchstone.

Hidalgo, N. M. (1993). Multicultural teacher introspection. In T. Perry and J. W. Fraser, (Eds.), *Freedom's plow: Teaching in the multicultural classroom* (pp. 99–106). New York and London: Routledge.

hooks, b. (1993). Transforming pedagogy and multiculturalism. In. T. Perry and J. W. Fraser (Eds.), *Freedom's plow: Teaching in the multicultural classroom* (pp. 91–97). New York and London: Routledge.

Howard, G. R. (1999). *We can't teach what we don't know: White teachers, multiracial schools.* New York: Teachers College Press.

Ladson-Billings, G. (1994). *The dreamkeepers: Successful teachers of African-American children.* San Francisco: Jossey-Bass.

Ladson-Billings, G. (1995). Multicultural teacher education: Research, practice, and policy. In J. A. Banks and C. A. M. Banks (Eds.), *Handbook of research on multicultural education* (pp. 747–759). New York: Macmillan.

Lee, H. (1960). *To kill a mockingbird.* Philadelphia: Lippincott.

Martin, R. J. (1995). Deconstructing myth, reconstructing reality: Transcending the crisis in teacher education. In R. J. Martin (Ed.), *Practicing what we teach: Confronting diversity in teacher education* (pp. 65–78). New York: SUNY Press.

McCarthy, C. (1993). After the canon: Knowledge and ideological representation in the multicultural discourse on curriculum reform. In C. McCarthy and W. Crichlow (Eds.), *Race, identity, and representation in education* (pp. 289–305). New York and London: Routledge.

McLaren, P. (1994). White terror and oppositional agency: Towards a critical multiculturalism. In D. T. Goldberg (Ed.), *Multiculturalism: A critical reader* (pp. 45–74). Cambridge: Blackwell.

McIntosh, P. (1990). White Privilege: Unpacking the invisible knapsack. *Independent School, 9* (2), 31–36.

Nakkula, M. J. and S. M. Ravitch. (1998). *Matters of interpretation: Reciprocal transformation in therapeutic and developmental relationships with youth.* San Francisco: Jossey-Bass.

National Commission on Teaching and America's Future Report (2003). Washington, DC: National Commission on Teaching and America's Future.

Nieto, S. (2000, 2004). *Affirming diversity: The sociopolitical context of multicultural education.* New York: Longman Press.

Ogbu, J. U. (1995). Understanding cultural diversity and learning. In J. A. Banks and C. A. M. Banks (Eds.), *Handbook of research on multicultural education* (pp. 312–334). New York: Macmillan.

Olson, R. A. (1998). White privilege in schools. In E. Lee, D. Menkart, and M. Okazawa-Rey (Eds.), *Beyond heroes and holidays: A practical guide to K–12 antiracist, multicultural education and staff development* (pp. 81–82). Washington, DC: Teaching for Change.

Perry, T., and J. W. Fraser. (Eds.). (1993). *Freedom's plow: Teaching in the multicultural classroom.* New York and London: Routledge.

Ravitch, S. (2000). *Reading ourselves between the lines: White teachers reading, writing, and talking about diversity, inequality, and pedagogy.* Unpublished diss., University of Pennsylvania.

Remillard, J. T. (2000). Prerequisites for learning to teach mathematics for all students. In W. G. Secada (Ed.), *Changing the faces of mathematics: Perspectives on multiculturalism and gender equity* (pp. 210–226). Reston, VA: NCTM.

Rosenberg, P. M. (1997). Underground discourses: Exploring whiteness in teacher education. In M. Fine, L. Weis, L. C. Powell, and L. M. Wong (Eds.), *Off White: Readings on race, power, and society* (pp. 79–89). New York and London: Routledge.

Sanday, P. (1976). Cultural and Structural Pluralism in the U.S. In *Anthropology and the public interest* (pp. 83–101). New York: Academic Press.

Schultz, K. (1997). Crossing boundaries in research and teacher education: Reflections of a White researcher in urban schools and communities. *Qualitative Inquiry* 3(4), 491–512. Thousand Oaks, CA: Sage.

Sleeter, C. E. (1993). How White Teachers Construct Race. In C. McCarthy and W. Crichlow (Eds.), *Race, identity and representation in education* (pp. 73–89). New York and London: Routledge.

Sleeter, C. E. (1995a). Reflections on my use of multicultural and critical pedagogy when students are White. In C. E. Sleeter and P. L. McLaren (Eds.), *Multicultural education, critical pedagogy, and the politics of difference* (pp. 415–438). New York: SUNY Press.

Sleeter, C. E. (1995b). An analysis of the critiques of multicultural education. In J. A. Banks and C. A. M. Banks (Eds.), *Handbook of research on multicultural education* (pp. 81–94). New York: Macmillan.

Sleeter, C. E. (1996). *Multicultural education as social activism.* New York: SUNY Press.

Sleeter, C. E. (1997). Foreword. In A. McIntyre, *Making meaning of whiteness: Exploring racial identity with White teachers.* New York: Merrill/Macmillan.

Soto, L. D., and T. Richardson. (1995). Theoretical perspectives and multicultural applications. In R. J. Martin (Ed.), *Practicing what we teach: Confronting diversity in teacher education* (pp. 203–218). New York: SUNY Press.

Tatum, B. D. (1992/1996). Talking about race, learning about racism: The application of racial identity development theory in the classroom. In T. Beauboeuf-Lafontant and D. Smith Augustine (Eds.), *Facing Racism in Education* (pp. 321–348). Cambridge: Harvard Educational Review.

Taylor, M. D. (1976). *Roll of thunder, hear my cry.* New York: Puffin Books.

Turner, T. (1993). Anthropology and multiculturalism: What is anthropology that multiculturalists should be mindful of it? *Cultural Anthropology, 8* (4), 411–429.

Twain, M. (1922). *The adventures of Huckleberry Finn.* New York: Harper Books.

Wehmiller, P. (1992). When the walls come tumbling down. *Harvard Educational Review, 62* (3), 373–383.

CHAPTER TEN

What Lies Beneath
Critical Dialogue for Culturally Relevant Pedagogy

Ayala Younger
Pajaro Valley Unified School District

Bill Rosenthal
Hunter College

The consciousness of self is not the closing of a door to communication.
Philosophic thought teaches us, on the contrary, that it is its guarantee.
(Fanon, 1963, p. 247)

OVERVIEW

In fall 1999, Ayala Younger, then a senior at Muhlenberg College, took an independent study in multicultural education with me, Bill Rosenthal, a teacher educator, as her advisor. Our "course work" quickly moved into sensitive and often-silenced issues of race and class in education. Over the years, this discussion has matured from a student-mentor to a colleague-colleague relationship in which the conversations continue to challenge and advance our thinking.

This chapter will focus on how and why our interchange of ideas promotes self-questioning, pushing us toward a raw, critical self-consciousness. We have particularly devoted ourselves to the "identity work" of increasing consciousness of ourselves as teachers and learners. From the birth of this discussion, we have been concerned with—consumed by—the intersections and interactions between this identity work and culturally relevant pedagogy as practiced by White Anglo, suburban, middle-class teachers responsible for the education of Black urban children from working-class backgrounds. Close readings of scholars such as Lisa Delpit (1988, 1995), Michèle Foster (1995), Gary Howard (1999), Gloria Ladson-Billings (1995a, 1995b), Sonia Nieto (1999), Vivian Paley (1979), and Christine Sleeter (1993), together with individual and conversational reflection upon our own cultural awareness, eventually converged on the process of "self-questioning." A hypothesis we have developed is that *essential* to teaching students culturally different from oneself is the courage to question—profoundly, relentlessly, and dialogically—one's own beliefs and practices.

We invite you, our reader, to listen in as we reenact our dynamic discussion over the past few years. Upon rereading our past e-mail conversation, debating our older ideas, and rethinking our thinking, we embarked on an entirely new dialogue. The conversation below is a metacognitive approach to our journeys together, our own questioning, and our reflections on the beginning of our dialoguing and our thoughts for future conversational exchanges. Be kind, please; bear in mind that we are not seasoned scholars in the field, merely a couple of upper-middle-class, White, suburban-raised teachers muddling our way through the community gardens and vacant lots of contemporary urban education. Our goal is to support your exploration of your understandings of race and class in education, especially any identity work undertaken as part of your growth as a theorist and practitioner of culturally relevant pedagogy. Although a great many words have already been written toward this goal, we have worked hard to make a fresh contribution, however small, to this body of work.

THE DIALOGUE

Ayala: Hi! Well, it was actually very fascinating to reread our old e-mail conversations. I feel like some of the ideas I wrote about are now invalid, some need to be refined, and some are still valid. I can see where I have grown as a professional, and where I need to continue to question myself.

(Mr.) Bill: It's now been over three years since we started this dialogue. We were both in Allentown, you as a senior at Muhlenberg, I in my second and last year in the Department of Education there. Now, as we speak, I've just started my third year at Hunter. You've come and gone even further—first to Philadelphia for a wild, courageous year teaching at a new charter school, then back home for a year of contemplation and renewal, and now, in late 2002, to the shores of the Pacific to begin a graduate program at Stanford.

Ayala: I remember the beginning of the beginning, in September 1999, when I approached you to begin an independent study inquiry into multicultural teaching during the last year of my undergraduate studies at Muhlenberg College. Who would have thought that such a simple request would become an ongoing search for answers to relevant and charged questions? What I foresaw as a simple semester project grew into a series of conversations and presentations through which we continue, to this day, to reanalyze our ideas. From our initial conversations emerged the theme of self-analysis. In a sense, self-reflection and self-questioning act as vehicles for effective teaching of students of differing socioeconomic backgrounds. By challenging the biases we each held, reading the works of other educators who also struggled with similar issues, and challenging our thinking about these questions, we developed a few theories.

(Mr.) Bill: Our theorizing took me by surprise. I was expecting you, as a neophyte in the field, only to learn the established canon of culturally relevant pedagogy. For myself, if I had any expectations at all, these were limited to a ringing endorsement of some of my most-cherished existing beliefs, along with some insights on how to do better at "selling" culturally relevant pedagogy to Muhlenberg's upper-middle-class, White Anglo, suburbanite teacher candidates. Despite incessantly exhorting my students to question *their* beliefs, I was not in the market for another medium of self-analysis for myself. It's now clear that I underestimated the power of critical dialogue.

Ayala: Nor was I expecting to engage in ongoing dialogue. I had chosen an independent study as an innocent attempt to learn more about the issues in education and to share my concerns, frustrations, and hopes about those issues with someone who would back me up in that struggle. I did not think I would be pushed so far in my thinking and personal grappling with these issues. Yet, here I am, years later, still doing just that.

(Mr.) Bill: Me, too. What's odd is that I didn't begin issue-grappling about my own practice until I moved from Muhlenberg to Hunter—and you from Allentown to Philadelphia—in late 2000. Curious, since once we put a hundred miles between us, our conversations went from continual to sporadic. One of those inexplicable outcomes of genuine, uncoerced human learning, I suppose.

I'm getting way ahead of the chronology here. When we embarked on your independent study, all I was thinking about was supporting you in your struggle. Do you remember how we struggled at the beginning to get focused? From the get-go, you made it clear that your interests lay not down the well-traveled road of studying multicultural curriculum—what to teach about various cultures—but, instead, the thornier issue of how a teacher can effectively teach children whose backgrounds are different from her own. You raised two related yet distinct questions that are often conflated in accounts of culturally relevant teaching. As my aging brain recalls, one prong of your curiosity involved teaching a culturally diverse class of children ("diverse" meaning "varied," as it should, not the sloppy use of the word to refer to minority children). Your other question was somewhat starker: How does a White teacher teach children culturally different from herself?

Ayala: I knew we would not actually find "the answer" to my questions, but rather would only begin to tackle the complexity of these issues. Our initial conversations in 1999 were truly just that—the beginnings of a recurring series of identity issues as they relate to urban education. I know we have continued to wrestle with these issues as both teachers and as students. Our conversations in 1999 only made it clear to me that the process of boldly facing the gaps in teacher and student backgrounds was critical, multifaceted, and necessary for urban school reform. Through our independent study dialogues I learned to be honest with myself about my fears, concerns, beliefs, biases, hopes, and so forth. I think I began to trust my voice, to develop the courage to face who I was and who I felt I wanted to be.

(Mr.) Bill: It is fascinating to hear, over three years later, more about what the inner Ayala was experiencing (without being fully aware?) as the twentieth century ran down. At the time, I didn't have a clue that what you were doing inside you with what we were doing between us was diving deep down to your identity!

Ayala: I cannot say the process of critically "facing oneself" (with all my biases, fears, hopes, etc.) is an easy undertaking. In fact, it is frightening. With a consciousness of self comes added doubts, challenges, and ideas to reevaluate. In a sense our dialogue threw me off balance.

(Mr.) Bill: Which reminds me of a little Piagetian process called disequilibration. Being thrown off balance is necessary for learning, if the man is to be believed.

Ayala: However, it also allowed me to recenter and reorient myself. I can now push myself further in my thinking about thorny issues. More importantly, I feel I am better armed with the skills and courage to push others to question themselves about their conscious and subconscious convictions. Isn't that what learning is all about—to continuously be both teacher and learner?

(Mr.) Bill: For sure. Isn't it what *teaching* is all about, too? I know some teachers—you're a prime example—who have the courage to model learning for their students through being learners in their classrooms, especially from their students. It seems at best inconsistent and ineffective, and at worst hypocritical, to ask or demand that students "question themselves about their . . . convictions" unless we do so ourselves. Like using semicolons and factoring binomials, questioning one's own convictions doesn't seem to happen naturally; rather, it's a skill that needs to be taught.

Your inclusion of our *subconscious* convictions raises the stakes immeasurably. No wonder you characterize facing oneself as frightening! Our dialogue has raised my conscious awareness about what lies beneath in my pedagogical subconscious. It's enabled me to become far more cognizant of some harmful underlying beliefs at work in my teaching of pre-service teachers culturally different from myself. Not that that's that forevermore, of course. I'm 99.9 percent confident that there are more such tacit theories of which I'm gloriously clueless at this point. Telling you so makes me feel both frightened and excited.

Ayala: We agreed to pursue our question about the role of self-questioning in effective multicultural teaching practices through the final semester of my undergraduate career in spring 2000. Without hesitation, and with encouragement and support from you, I presented these ideas at several conferences to share our insights with colleagues in the field of education. First, a presentation in April 2000 at the Centennial Conference Student Research

Colloquium at Dickinson College, whereby we realized we had much work and thinking to do on the subject.

Graduation the next month did not end our conversations. As I began my first job teaching in Philadelphia, our e-mail exchanges were critical to my growth and confidence as a novice educator. I was suddenly *in* the very environment we had read about during our meetings together. The opportunities to put our theories into practice were readily available to me. However, without our e-mail exchanges, I would not have had the courage to try to implement great changes. Certainly, I would not have had the patience to continue to be reflective on my own attitudes, progress, and approaches as a teacher of urban youth. When you asked for permission to present our thoughts and experiences to colleagues at the Penn Ethnography Forum in March 2001, I was suddenly aware of the relevance our idea sharing held not just for myself, but for other educators as well.

(Mr.) Bill: Preparation for the ethnography forum was so very important. We had both become so consumed in our day-to-day responsibilities that the e-mail exchanges and occasional phone calls had slowed to a trickle. Writing the paper for the forum got us moving again, both to recapitulate what we'd already done and to restart the dialogue. Now, in writing this chapter, I find the same process reoccurring. Perhaps we're destined to proceed in fits and starts, with brief intervals of intense communication motivated by a deadline alternating with lengthy latency periods. That's not how I'd like it to be, though.

Ayala: Maybe those fits of latency and intensity are necessary for sustainability. I find that after I leave something and then later return to it, my perceptions and insights are deeper and cleaner. I feel those latent periods give me time to breathe, to rejuvenate, so I can reenter our conversations with the energy and courage needed to critically analyze where I am, where I have come from, and where I wish to go in my reflective thinking.

During those latent periods, I was also making some life transitions, which in turn fed the fires of concern regarding my identity as it relates to urban education. In each of these new experiences, I came to understand moreso the importance of our conversing. We have taken the first steps toward urban education reform; we have admitted we are part of the "problem," part of the larger (and more privileged) society, and therefore responsible on some levels for the effective implementation of needed educational reforms.

(Mr.) Bill: As a child of the 1960s, I'm reminded of the guilt-trip-inducing commandment, "If you're not part of the solution, you're part of the problem." It seems to be so very difficult for teachers—no less so for teacher educators—to stop blaming everyone under the sun for the difficulty of reforming urban education, and instead to acknowledge and address our own responsibility—to become "aware of one's complicity in that which one critiques" (Lather, 1991,

p. 10). It took me only about a decade and a half of teaching to get started getting complicit. You're so far ahead of me it's not even funny.

About a decade ago, during a really boring meeting at Michigan State, I got to thinking about how reflexively uncomfortable most of us seem to be with the "self-reflection" so prominent in so many teacher education programs. The barriers that we put up against looking and listening inward appeared so high and well constructed that (I thought) they couldn't be connected only to practices and even beliefs. There must be some threat to who we are—to our identities.

Until you and our dialogue came along, though, this hypothesis just made teaching harder for me. Now I sensed that my cajoling White, Anglo, middle-class, monolingual teacher candidates to be self-reflective about their Whiteness, their middle-classness, their suburbanness was perturbing their identities, but I had no idea what to do with the counterreactions. Things weren't much better in this regard at Muhlenberg. It was only after our conversations implanted themselves deep inside me that I was able to do more than just threaten people's senses of self and leave it at that.

Ayala: Agreed. Just threatening someone's sense of self doesn't bring us to the brink of reform action. I think reflection needs to be accompanied by a sense that while our identity is shaken, our character remains intact. Most people in education are good-hearted people. We all want to do what is best and to help others.

(Mr.) Bill: Teachers almost invariably act according to what they believe is in the best interests of their students. This I must remember when I am a party to practices of which I disapprove.

Ayala: Therefore, while what we represent (in my case, "white, privileged, middle-class majority") is part of the problem, I have come to understand that I personally am doing what I feel I can to overcome that. I cannot be burdened by guilt or blame, or that would stop me in my efforts to bring about positive change. Self-reflection is not intended to make people so uneasy they lose faith in their good efforts. Instead, it is meant to be an ongoing process whereby we acknowledge what the structure of society creates, where the flaws, weaknesses, strengths, and areas of hope lie. Through the process of self-reflection and critical, supportive dialoguing, we hopefully develop the willingness not only to press our own thinking, but also the structure and people of the system. While it begins small, with an individual or two, it should also be given room to grow larger. In doing so, perhaps change is brought about through a ripple effect, emanating from the inside outward.

(Mr.) Bill: I engage in self-reflection with these qualities. So do you. My ripples meet your ripples meet other people's ripples. Our ripples join and reinforce and accelerate each other. The personal becomes political.

Ayala: The recurring theme for both of us was what we termed a "self-consciousness about our identity." We struggle with the discomforts and challenges of being White amidst minority students—this brings us to questions about cultural differences, socioeconomic differences, and biases/perceptions about who we are and whom we feel we are evolving into.

(Mr.) Bill: I love the term "self-consciousness." When you first used it, years ago, something didn't feel quite right to me. My preconceived sense of the term is that self-consciousness is undesirable, related to awkwardness, doubt, a lack of self-esteem. Gradually you were able to teach me to think of self-consciousness more literally, more plainly, more positively, and more pragmatically—as a consciousness of self.

Ayala: The themes of our dialoguing raised this admission of responsibility; essentially it brought our consciousness of this to the forefronts of our thinking. On many levels these steps have been of the utmost relevance to my development as an educator and researcher of urban education issues. I am no longer in this crusade solely for self-gratification or to alleviate some guilty feelings, but rather because I am now acutely conscious of the role and responsibility I have in the state of our urban education system today. Reform is no longer just about me; it is about us, all of us.

(Mr.) Bill: Other people's children, indeed! In *The Brothers Karamazov*, Dostoyevsky said something to the effect that "all are responsible for all." Getting past being a teacher for one's own gratification is—because someone loves children, is infatuated with a subject, or believes he's no good at anything else (as was the case with me)—just so important, and we barely touch it in teacher education. I want this work of ours to flower further into fresh, exciting theories and practices for turning pre-service teachers' attention away from themselves and onto their children. (Maybe for this to happen, we'll have to make some progress in turning teacher educators' attention away from themselves and onto their pre-service teachers.)

Ayala: I could not have reached the shifts in my thinking and a clearer consciousness of myself had there not existed throughout our conversations this rawness—and very obvious honesty—that is both critical and supportive. In our earlier conversations, we dealt with my own experiences, confusions, questions. Your responses were encouraging and reassuring, yet also continuously urged me to delve deeper into the topics raised. You withheld somewhat from sharing your own opinions, problems, burning questions.

(Mr.) Bill: I never before realized that I was withholding from you! Certainly my conversational shyness was not intentional. Now I recall that after you left Muhlenberg and started teaching in Philly, I continued relating to you as teacher to student—worse yet, not as a teacher who is actively trying to be a learner himself.

Ayala: Gradually, our conversations turned toward you as well, where you were raising questions and sharing experiences which now link us together in certain areas.

(Mr.) Bill: This transition seems to have occurred all of a sudden, sometime in spring 2001. It's very clearly documented in our e-mails. Here is the moment:

> (Ayala) I find I am becoming increasingly louder, more aggressive, sassier, and also taking on an attitude. It seems to be a survival strategy for me. If I wasn't tough enough to adapt to them in some ways, they would have eaten me alive by now. These seem to be observations of many other teachers, especially those with particularly difficult classes, like my own.

> (Mr. Bill) You know . . . I'VE recently become much more assertive and in-your-face with MY students . . . .

Just like that, Ayala! For the first time, almost out of the blue, the veil comes off my own teaching practice vis-à-vis culturally relevant pedagogy. The "you know" with which my comment starts was one of sudden realization. I went on to write a lengthy remark that includes the first question I ever posed to you about my teaching:

> So HERE'S a researchable question about MY practice that I would like to pursue with you, **Ayala:** How do I encourage self-questioning so as not to make my students throw up walls around themselves? Even better to start with: What about my ways of promoting self-questioning might be MAKING my students feel they have to defend rather than question themselves? I want a very direct and completely frank answer from you on this one!!

Although you did answer directly, frankly, and helpfully, this thread of our conversation got left behind. What mattered far more was, as you've said, that the dialogue became an authentically reciprocal one in which our experiences, questions, and concerns were intertwined. We continued along the path of our assertiveness as teachers:

Ayala: Yes, I am much more direct with my kids. I don't beat around the bush or try to put things politely—it doesn't work. I just flat out say it—and say it with a bit of attitude or they ignore my direction. It's a delicate balance between maintaining professionalism, while dying to throw back at them a whirlwind of insults, just as they constantly do to each other.

(Mr.) Bill: You know, you've helped me realize why I've been flat-out saying it more than ever. One reason is that Dr. Carbone [the chairperson of Muhlenberg's Education Department] taught me that to do otherwise can be misleading, even dishonest. Although I've been conditioned by critical-progressive pedagogy to detest "I want you to . . ." commands to students, when I really do want students to do something, it's quasi lying to suggest otherwise. The other reason for my shift toward being more directive harks back to our old friend, culturally relevant pedagogy. The relevance here was to the culture of New York City—in your words, loud, sassy, full of attitude, flat-out say it. My breakthrough was giving "what for" to an academically malfeasant not-so-nice Jewish woman from Long Island—who lived in the next town from where I was raised. Perhaps the proximity to my own cultural heritage was what enabled me to break out of the Mr. Nurturing Nice Guy role and assert some discipline toward this student.

     I now know that at first, I was able to "get tough" only with White Anglo women (there are almost no men in my Hunter classes). Ordering women of color around wasn't something this White boy could do, even as their teacher. Sometime later, a realization hit me upside the inside of my head with the force of a Category 5 hurricane: On the whole, the African American women in my classes were getting significantly lower grades than the other groups, including Latinas and Afro-Caribbean women. This lightning bolt struck me soon after you had written about your increased directiveness with Black students. There was something buried way deep in my identity as a teacher that was working against what I wanted to accomplish. Absent our conversation, it might never have percolated up to my consciousness.

Ayala: I, too, am certainly able to be more honest with myself and all my shortcomings and strengths—other than the sneaking suspicion that our dialoguing has made me more honest with myself, perhaps more critical of our education system, and freer to express that to not only you, but to other colleagues as well. But then again, can we ever really know how far-reaching the effects of events and interactions in our lives are?

(Mr.) Bill: Amen. Could you please try to convince the "scientifically based research" crowd of the absolute truth of what you're saying?

Ayala: I see a lack in the school I am at now of truly reflective and supportive dialoguing among teachers. While the school is small, and staff are fairly supportive of each other, there still seems to be a somewhat reserved approach to talking about ourselves as teachers and our growth as educators. Partly, that is because so much is expected to be accomplished and covered in one day's time that we teachers lack the space in time to devote ourselves to real reflection.

Many of the workshops are partly venting sessions and partly feeding us lesson ideas—both of which are necessary and great, but lacking somehow.

(Mr.) Bill: As one of the leaders in a young school-university partnership, I am dealing with similar issues. After almost three years, we're beginning to perceive some successes in being less reserved and more open. But there's nothing yet resembling the raw honesty of the critical dialogue you and I conducted. Perhaps in time.

Ayala: Especially as a new teacher, I feel disconnected from my practice in a sense. I am in the Beginning Teacher Support Program, which pairs me up with a mentor teacher and involves lots of paperwork in an attempt to get me to reflect on my practice. However, the dialogue there is forced and almost seems overburdening among all the other pieces of being a teacher I am responsible for on a daily basis. We are overworked and I am tired. Quite frankly, I feel trapped. In a sense I fear I am losing sight of me, but meanwhile am simultaneously discovering and redefining me. I guess I am not describing it well. I do not mean to sound disillusioned or negative about the whole system, but I also need to just write . . . . and you seem like a willing audience.

(Mr.) Bill: I'm ennobled and enriched by your confidence in me. You have me thinking that critical dialogue can't be forced into a program or a course—certainly not into a bureaucracy! Ayala, even with everything else that's on our plates, I think that we should make a concerted effort to restart our critical dialogue in earnest. Now that I've gotten myself involved in tutoring hyperkinetic African American fifth graders on Saturday mornings, God knows I need it back!

Ayala: This dialogue seems to me to be quite significant in terms of a book on how these courses challenge students and teachers. We see very clearly here my evolution from a thoughtful, but somewhat selfish thinker, to a person who now understands that to gain more from the conversations, there needs to be an equitable push to further our thinking; whereby we both reflect, question, and seek answers to the challenges and doubts we each candidly discuss. I mean to say, you acted as a model of how to convert my thinking from that of a student to that of a learner—a distinction I believe you understand well. In essence, the dialogue itself promoted self-questioning and exploration, but rereading what we wrote in the course of composing our chapter also has deepened my sense of self-awareness. We have come full circle, and are still ready to go round again.

REFERENCES

Delpit, L. (1988). The silenced dialogue: Power and pedagogy in educating other people's children. *Harvard Educational Review, 58* (3), 280–298.

Delpit, L. (1995). *Other people's children: White teachers, students of color, and other cultural conflicts in the classroom.* New York: New Press.

Dostoyevsky, F. (1999). *The brothers Karamazov*, trans. C. Garnett. New York: Signet Classics.

Fanon, F. (1963). *The wretched of the earth*, trans. C. Farrington. New York: Grove Press.

Foster, M. (1995). African-American teachers and culturally relevant pedagogy. In J. A. Banks and C. A. McGee Banks (Eds.), *Handbook of research on multicultural education* (pp. 570–581). New York: Macmillan.

Howard, G. R. (1999). *We can't teach what we don't know: White teachers, multiracial schools*. New York: Teachers College Press.

Ladson-Billings, G. (1995a). But that's just good teaching! The case for culturally relevant pedagogy. *Theory into Practice, 34* (3), 159–165.

Ladson-Billings, G. (1995b). Toward a theory of culturally relevant teaching. *American Educational Research Journal, 32* (3), 465–491.

Lather, P. (1991). *Getting smart: Feminist research and pedagogy with/in the postmodern*. New York: Routledge.

Nieto, S. (1999). *The light in their eyes: Creating multicultural learning communities*. New York: Teachers College Press.

Paley, V. G. (1979). *White teacher*. Cambridge, MA: Harvard University Press.

Sleeter, C. E. (1993). How white teachers construct race. In C. McCarthy and W. Crichlow (Eds.), *Race, identity, and representation in education* (pp. 157–171). New York and London: Routledge.

EPILOGUE

Where Do We Go from Here?

Norah Peters-Davis and Jeffrey Shultz

Arcadia University

Given that individual and group identity plays such a major role in what happens in pluralism and diversity courses, it would be difficult for us to provide the reader with a "how-to" conclusion. In this epilogue, we choose instead to explore the commonalities that emerge from the writings of the faculty and students who contributed to this volume so that others can use their insights to reflect on what is happening in their own classrooms and on their campuses.

From the moment that we began soliciting manuscripts for this book, we found recurring themes. This was surprising to us. We assumed that others were struggling, but not necessarily struggling with so many similar issues to the ones that we confront in our course. However, in spite of the many different types of institutions represented in this volume, certain themes appeared over and over again. For one, it was obvious that many of us were dealing with these issues in isolation, assuming it was our private struggle, our particular institution, our own students. What is reassuring, and at the same time daunting, is that it is everyone's struggle, everyone's institution, everyone's students.

As we state in the preface, this book was born in the midst of conflict. Out of conflict can sometimes come change. This is what these chapters have shown us: that in spite of the enormous difficulties and strains associated with teaching diversity courses, there are also meaningful opportunities for change and growth in many areas. We begin this epilogue with the opportunities born from challenge.

THE OPPORTUNITIES

The most salient opportunity sounds like a cliché—the possibility of making a difference in the lives of our students. What we find striking about this, however, is that what we hear in the student voices is not necessarily what one imagines when thinking about "making a difference." The "politically correct" interpretation of this phrase is that students will "appreciate difference," "celebrate diversity," "make a better world." This is not necessarily what we read here. What we read here is the real first step in transformation—the ability to explore and ultimately to understand one's self. In these chapters, students discuss the importance of understanding their own identities, developing a sense of self, learning to take risks. As Dana Szwajkowski writes in Chapter 7: "This class challenged my carefully pieced together identity. At heart, I felt that there was something wrong with me. . . . I finally began to understand the unrest that I had been feeling for so long. . . . Like a deep wound reopened, it was often painful . . . The work in Pluralism was painful, but for me, it was necessary pain" (p. 100). To quote Emily Hayes in Chapter 8, "I left class that day with a renewed sense of self. This was the beginning of a change in me. I began to approach my differences in a different manner, viewed others and myself in a different light, and felt myself becoming more open-minded; and the learning and growth that resulted were incredible" (p. 119). For students, then, these courses serve as a mirror within which they can explore who they are and continue to work on their identity development.

Many faculty members who teach these courses engage in identity work as well. They use these explorations of self as pedagogical strategies to help students deal with and integrate course concepts. For the most part, these courses focus on concepts related to race, class, gender, and/or sexual orientation rather than the "group-a-week" model (what our colleague Doreen Loury refers to as "drive-by pluralism"), which was more prevalent in the past. Rather, these concepts are used to help students make sense of the causes and consequences of inequality and group conflict. Through the emphasis on creating safe environments and establishing dialogues, students reflect on their own understandings of the world and ways in which their identities have been shaped by institutions and societal forces.

Faculty can also benefit from this opportunity for self-reflection and identity work, not just in the wider sense of making a difference but in their own lives as well. The faculty team that we are a part of had been teaching Pluralism for a number of years before we confronted the ways in which differences in our individual identities affected our relationships with each other, with course material, and with students. We feel that the course has become much more effective as we have focused on our own identity development and the multiple layers of identity each one of us inhabits. Once faculty members begin to focus on their own role in the dialogue, the opportunity for continued growth presents itself with every class. Gary Perry, who writes of his vulnerability early in Chapter 2 later reflects: "In a word, navigating and negotiating the academic landscape requires that I reconstruct my oppressed selves. . . . Finally, understanding that being an oppressed person does not mean you are paralyzed has allowed me to search for and engage in my human agency" (p. 29).

One of the most important ways in which these identity changes and transformations can take place is by not always focusing on the "other." For majority faculty members, work related to Whiteness and White privilege provides a place to start.[1] In some cases, students and faculty from under-represented groups do not sense that their White counterparts are either willing or able to address these issues, as discussed in Ana María García and Angela Gillem's chapter. However, Sharon Ravitch's chapter highlights the growth and identity work that can be accomplished by White male students. As she writes: "Reed's and Brian's reflections on their learning processes challenge typical notions of White men as ignorant and resistant to learning about their own racism, ethnocentrism, and unearned privilege" (p. 123). The possibility for change and growth is not limited to the potentially more mature graduate student. Branden Coté, an undergraduate student, writes in Chapter 3, "The experiences that African American students shared about the many forms of racism and discrimination they have encountered provided a real wake-up call for many of us. True understanding comes from experience—and our efforts to connect as much as possible with these experiences" (p. 47). His focus is on his own need to connect and understand, not on trying to imagine what life is like for someone who is different from him. What is clear is that all sorts of students: male, female, Black, White, straight, or gay, are able to reflect on identity issues as long as they are in a class in which the instructor encourages such exploration and also serves as a model for how to do so.

This ability to reflect on one's own identity and engage in the kind of work that is necessary for real transformation is many times the result of the sorts of dialogues that these chapters have shown do occur in some of these classrooms. As Brian Girard, one of the graduate students in Chapter 9, states "Just as Freire (1970) posits that the oppressor cannot free the oppressed, likewise the professor of a class on multicultural education cannot force her students to reflect and change. However, she can provide an environment that cultivates such self-reflection" (p. 137). In the last section of this epilogue, we summarize many of the pedagogical strategies that faculty have embraced to create a climate that encourages self-reflection. Dialogues, as a way toward intercultural communication and reflection, are one of the opportunities for reflection that result from these strategies and form a bridge between what the faculty member is trying to accomplish and understanding on the part of students. Examples of these dialogues are seen in Chapters 3, 5, and 8. The last chapter, "What Lies Beneath," illustrates how one such dialogue unfolded and the resultant self-reflection and awareness experienced by both the faculty member and the student.

Other opportunities exist for faculty in these classes: the ability to teach about one's passion and, for those for whom this is important, to engage in teaching that is, by its nature, political. As so clearly articulated in Chapter 2, "But I am also motivated by hope, by the belief that social change is possible, that this work, teaching these kinds of courses, is crucial to building the kind of society I want to live in, and that there are, *there must be*, effective ways to do it. My hope is that by documenting the experiences of those in the trenches; by making visible their challenges, obstacles, and successes; and by analyzing their ideas and understandings about the work of teaching diversity, we can contribute to creating an environment where this mission can flourish" (p. 30). When students begin to make the connections to self as we have highlighted throughout this section, faculty members can be inspired to continue to navigate this difficult terrain. An excitement is generated. It is the excitement that is felt by a teacher any time a student understands a difficult concept or begins to make sense of the overall importance of the course work. When one is teaching about issues that students have not "neutralized," that they feel to be a part of their own value system and lives, then the students' awareness and learning generate tremendous excitement and energy. This is the opportunity that presents a counterpoint to the challenges that follow.

THE CHALLENGES

When Dana Szwajkowski writes, in Chapter 7, "I was angry with the professors. Here they were, coolly telling me to tear open the wounds I had made tolerable, while they (the three White professors) returned to their comfortable White lives, leaving me to clean up the mess alone" (p. 100), we are two of the White professors to whom she is referring. Could any statement more clearly describe our dilemma, not to mention the layers of complexity with which we are confronted when we teach this course? We, who have done a great deal of hard work in preparing to teach this course, have still evoked anger and frustration from the students whom we believe we are reaching, are bonding with, and sharing with. To us, this statement was one of the most powerful comments we have heard about this course, and it points to the necessity for anyone embarking on this journey to think deeply about his or her identity and its connection to societal privilege and power—or his or her own identity as it relates to oppression, fear, anxiety.

In many ways, reading through the chapters of this book, it seems as if the authors focus primarily on the challenges of teaching about diversity. It is hard to deny that the overriding themes throughout these accounts refer to the challenges that are faced by both faculty and students related to their personal identities, group affiliations, interactions in the classroom, and lives, more generally, outside the classroom.

Regardless of the instructor's race, class, gender, or sexual orientation, there are likely to be pain and emotional hazards when one teaches about diversity. Their positions of privilege allow faculty members from majority groups to choose to ignore this pain, focusing instead on issues of diversity as merely the subject matter of the course. In this way, they can intellectualize the issues about which they are teaching and keep at arm's length the emotional aspects engendered by these topics. Faculty members from underrepresented minority groups, on the other hand, do not have this luxury: They are teaching about their lives and the pain, anger, and frustration that emerge are inescapable, as is clearly illustrated in Ana María García and Angela Gillem's chapter (Chapter 7).

For students of color and GLBT students, the pain is present when they feel the faculty do not support them. They are particularly angry at having to be spokespeople, at being used as teaching tools, as Lillian West describes in Chapter 7. And GLBT students may suffer in silence. We find that in Pluralism, while White students may not say what's on their mind in terms of race (as they can "see" students of color in the room), they do not check themselves when discussing sexual orientation. Neither situation allows for learning. In the first, students are not working through their own racism—in the second, they are unaware of their homophobic and heterosexist behaviors. One of the best examples we have seen of this is when we have students participate in improvisations in our Pluralism course. When White students need to portray students of color they are often so "careful" that the audience would never be able to determine the race of any of the players. The students neutralize color. Yet, when straight students are portraying someone who is gay, particularly a gay male character, they rarely hold back on the flamboyant stereotypes.

Gary Perry, in Chapter 2, notes: "My vulnerability . . . stems from a variety of issues: (1) my stigmatized identities; (2) my marginalized presence within the academy; (3) the negative perceptions that my students, fellow colleagues, and faculty/administrators have about me; and (4) my nontraditional ideologies and critical worldviews" (p. 27). This quote points to some very central issues: the complications arising from the intersections of different social identities for both faculty and students; and, the social hierarchies that inevitably highlight power differentials both inside and outside the classroom. The fundamental issue at the heart of diversity courses, the privilege of some and the oppression of others, is mirrored in the lives and acted out in the relationships of the players in the classroom. Just as conflict arises from inequities in society, conflict can arise in the classroom. This can also lead to a situation in which faculty and students of color shut down, while White faculty and students gloss over the issues that matter most. The opportunities described earlier in this epilogue are then lost. For White faculty, White students, and White campuses, the pain is, in many ways, optional. Peggy McIntosh's (1988) invisible knapsack need not be unpacked. For faculty and students from underrepresented groups, the pain is there, it is palpable. It is part of the fabric of these courses, embedded in the teaching and the learning, the interaction in the classroom, just as it is part of life. The result of this mismatch, a point that we'll return to at the end of this section, is that these courses and the learning engendered within them fall short of the mark. They make no real difference in the lives of students. As our colleague Ana María García (1999) has written, they become examples of "as-if" multiculturalism.

The flipside of the opportunity to teach about one's passion, to teach what must be understood as political, is that the work may become marginalized and be used against graduate students and nontenured faculty in matters such as hiring, reappointment, tenure, and promotion decisions. Especially given the current political climate, the assault on Affirmative Action, and the charges of political correctness surrounding diversity work, the campus and the wider community can present an enormous challenge. Helen Moore, in Chapter 2, delineates what must happen on a campus for multicultural education to be successful. However, as she states, the reality is that "[a]s we teach multicultural elements that encourage educational transformations, instructors collide against a curriculum in which students lack systematic linkages to multicultural scholarship before or after this specific course requirement. Instead, it is experienced by both students and instructors as an add-on that often clashes with the worldviews of students themselves and those of their other university instructors" (p. 21). Overall, then, there is no question that there are challenges that arise when teaching these courses. However, the effort expended to do so is worth it if both students and faculty confront the complex concepts involved. In the next section, we discuss some pedagogical strategies that may be helpful in this process.

EMERGING PEDAGOGICAL PRACTICES

So how does one navigate the challenges and seize the opportunities of teaching these courses? There are no magic bullets. One size does not fit all. What is reflected in our thoughts about the opportunities is that this work is best done in a setting that emphasizes dialogue and identity development. What has come through over and over again is that individual and group identity are at the heart of this teaching. As a result, the choice of specific pedagogical strategies depends upon the particular identities of the instructor and the students. In applying these strategies to other settings, a number of issues must be considered. These include the instructor's identity, the demographic and sociopolitical nature of the particular campus, and, most importantly, the demographic composition of the class itself, the political climate outside of the campus, and the nature of the course (is it a general education requirement, is it a requirement for a particular major or is it an elective, is it offered for undergraduate or graduate credit, etc.?).

Several of the contributors in this volume have listed specific activities or strategies they have used successfully in their diversity courses. They range from the inclusion of films, speakers, and novels that raise issues of diversity to structuring the enrollments so that there is a mix of students within the classroom. Sometimes these tools do not work as anticipated—for example, Megan Reynolds, an undergraduate teaching assistant at Johnson State College, provides an example in Chapter 4 related to the reactions of White students to two speakers brought to campus during the same academic year. As she writes, when comparing the visit of Sara Willie, a well-known Black studies scholar to that of Deb Cohan, a doctoral student at Brandeis who used the film *American History X* in her presentation: "[T]he analysis Cohan offered posed little threat to the audience, who did not identify at all with the behaviors of these overt racists . . . . Possibly Willie's talk came across as more 'threatening' to her White listeners' sense of themselves as nonracist, tolerant, even progressive— here was a Black college professor presenting a 'radical' and relational analysis underscored by her personal experiences that didn't let Whites (liberal or otherwise) off the hook" (p. 65). Those of us who teach these courses need to be aware of the consequences of the pedagogical strategies we use to get our points across. Students don't always respond in ways that fit with the goals of our instruction. Given the potentially explosive nature of some of the material we present, as instructors, we need to be particularly sensitive to what students take away from our classes.

We walk a fine line when teaching these courses. We get buy-in from White students when we don't threaten or alienate them. And yet without being made to question their assumptions and made to feel uneasy, there is no real identity work being done, no real transformation. We lose the opportunities discussed above for change. We must not let our students, or ourselves, off the hook too easily.

It has long been our sense that the best work in diversity courses takes place in classrooms with a diverse group of students. The demographics of the classroom are crucial. For many of our campuses, we often end up with just one or two students from underrepresented groups within a course who then, by our actions or by their own sense, become the spokespersons for their group. Or they shut down and simply try and survive the semester. As Ana-María Wahl writes in Chapter 3:

> The importance of a "good mix" of African American and White students invites more open dialogue for several reasons as well. The racial and ethnic composition of our class worked against the tendency to treat students of color as "ambassadors" for their group. If there are only one or two minority students, European American students tend to forget that these individuals are, in fact, individuals and not spokespeople for their race. In many classes, White students mistakenly assume that the opinions of a particular minority student represent the opinion of all minority students. In our class, African American students perhaps spoke more freely because they did not have to worry as much that they would be seen as spokespersons for their group." (pp. 47–48)

A class made up primarily of White students on a predominantly White campus presents another challenge. As Ana María García and Angela Gillem discuss in Chapter 7, in teaching Pluralism, we struggled with the issue of assigning students to the small sections of the course. In the year about which they write, the decision was made to assign all students from underrepresented groups into one of two sections to insure that these sections had a critical mass of minority students (one ended up with eight students of color, the other with seven). By default, the other four sections of the course were made up entirely of White students. At one point during the semester, some of the White students noticed the difference among the groups. They wrote a petition asking the faculty to reconsider their decision. Some of these students were outraged that they were "segregated." They said that they could not learn about diversity if they didn't have students of color in their class. Contrast that to the words of Lillian West, an African American student in one of the mixed group sections: "Small group was like a haven. . . . That is where we talked about issues between the races and in the races. That is where I was Lillian West first and then the intelligent, beautiful, chocolate, big girl from around the way. Even though we talked about things that disturbed me, I felt that I could just be me" (p. 98).

Susan Warner and Millicent Mickle, in Chapter 5, present an alternative—if diversity does not exist on your campus, go find it at another institution. Of course, their pairing did not elicit exactly the learning experience that they had hoped for initially. Since students did not know each other at all, it was almost impossible to create the level of trust that must exist within a setting of diverse voices. And yet, this is a strategy that holds promise and could use more development. One might think of using distance-learning techniques to join courses across campuses and then arrange for several face-to-face meetings throughout the semester.

This issue of trust is more complex than we imagined. We were struck by Emily Hayes's story in Chapter 8. Oppression doesn't always accompany difference and there are categories of difference that are often overlooked in diversity courses. Taking a stance that argues that everyone is different trivializes and glosses over the real consequences of difference in our society. Yet Emily's struggle with trust, not as a student of color or as an individual who identified as GLBT, stemmed from her identity as someone who had suffered a brain injury while attending a high-status academic institution. This serves as a poignant reminder of the unnoticed differences that students bring to the classroom. They cannot be dismissed and, indeed, must be uncovered, if we are to establish trust with and among our students.

WHERE DO WE GO FROM HERE?

Given the current political climate, the changing demographics on our campuses and the globalized world in which we reside, the need for courses on diversity continues and grows with each academic year. And yet, as these narratives illustrate over and over again, this is not an easy path to navigate. There is no question that there are rewards, both personal and professional, that result from teaching these courses. Strategies exist that help create a classroom climate where students can engage with these complex and difficult issues. If this encounter is to be successful, faculty members need to be prepared to tackle the emotional and intellectual responses engendered by this subject matter.

Given the difficulties described above, questions remain: How can we encourage more faculty to take on the challenge of teaching courses on diversity? How can the academy become a place where the sort of identity work that needs to be done by faculty in these courses can occur? As Ana María García and Angela Gillem, the colleagues who first challenged us, write: "As faculty of color, we have done the work of identity and racial/ethnic representation in our personal lives and continue to do so within the pluralism courses. This is quite different from many of our White colleagues who have not needed to integrate their Whiteness into their definition of self on both a personal and professional level" (p. 89). This is the ultimate challenge of multicultural education: to create a space where all persons, whether they are from the majority or the minority, understand their own identity, their relationships to others who are different from them, and the real implications of diversity for our society.

NOTES

1. Throughout this epilogue will we draw the distinction between faculty and students who represent privileged positions and those who represent oppressed positions. In some cases, we will refer to these privileged identities as "majority" or "White" or "straight." For those identities that represent oppressed positions in our society, we will use references such as "of color."

REFERENCES

Freire, P. (2002). *Pedagogy of the oppressed* (30th anniversary ed.). New York: Continuum.

García, A. M. (1999). Multiculturalism: An "as if" phenomenon. *International Journal of Qualitative Studies in Education, 12* (3).

McIntosh, P. (1988). *White privilege and male privilege: A personal account of coming to see correspondences through work in women's studies* (Working Paper 149). Wellesley, MA: Wellesley College Center for Research on Women.

INDEX